THE
END OF EDEN

"In an extraordinary tour de force, Graham Phillips pinpoints a major mystery with important implications for our understanding of the remote past and the origins of ancient religion. Painstakingly researched and soberly presented—but never less than eminently readable—this book provides an answer so explosive that it should instantly ensure itself a place among the great revelations of history."

Lynn Picknett and Clive Prince, authors of
The Templar Revelation and The Sion Revelation

"This is a very exciting and important book, which suggests a highly plausible reason why organized cruelty seems to have come into the world at a surprisingly late date. I believe Graham Phillips's ideas are going to cause widespread controversy."

Colin Wilson, author of The Outsider and
Atlantis and the Kingdom of the Neanderthals:
100,000 Years of Lost History

THE
END OF EDEN

The Comet That Changed Civilization

GRAHAM PHILLIPS

Bear & Company
Rochester, Vermont

Bear & Company
One Park Street
Rochester, Vermont 05767
www.BearandCompanyBooks.com

Bear & Company is a division of Inner Traditions International

Library of Congress Cataloging-in-Publication Data

Phillips, Graham.
    The end of Eden : the comet that changed civilization / Graham Phillips.
        p. cm.
    Summary: "Presents compelling evidence that civilizations worldwide became warlike and monotheistic after Earth passed through the tail of a comet in 1500 BC"—Provided by publisher.
    Includes bibliographical references and index.
    ISBN-13: 978-1-59143-069-8
    ISBN-10: 1-59143-069-0
    1. Comets—1486 B.C. 2. Archaeoastronomy. 3. Megalithic monuments. 4. Religion, Prehistoric. 5. Warfare, Prehistoric. 6. Civilization, Ancient. I. Title.

    QB724.P55 2007
    904'.5—dc22

                                          2007007963

Printed and bound in the United States by Lake Book Manufacturing

10 9 8 7 6 5 4 3 2 1

Text design and layout by Virginia Scott Bowman
This book was typeset in Sabon and Stone Sans with Minion Condensed and Stone Sans as display typefaces

To send correspondence to the author of this book, mail a first-class letter to the author c/o Inner Traditions • Bear & Company, One Park Street, Rochester, VT 05767, and we will forward the communication.

In loving memory
of Marion Sunderland

Contents

Acknowledgments

The author would like to thank the following people for their invaluable help: Professor Joseph Carter, Michael Dyer, and Dr. Philip Payne, without whose help this book would not have been possible, and Louise Simkiss for her invaluable research. And all at Inner Traditions International: Jeanie Levitan, Anne Dillon, Jon Graham, Kelly Bowen, Patricia Rydle, Rob Meadows, and Cynthia Ryan. I would also like to offer a very special thanks to Debbie Cartwright for her continued and invaluable encouragement, and Yvan Cartwright for his computer support and compiling the index.

For more information about Graham Phillips, his books, and his research, please visit his Web site at www.grahamphillips.net.

AUTHOR'S NOTE CONCERNING
THE DATING OF HISTORICAL EVENTS

Our modern Western calendar begins the first year at what is thought to have been the birth of Christ, and is referred to by the Latin term *anno domini,* meaning "in the year of our Lord." It is abbreviated by the letters AD, although this prefix is usually omitted. The years before the time of Christ's estimated birth work backward and are suffixed with the abbreviation BC, meaning "before Christ." Unlike AD dates, the higher the number of the BC date, the further it is back in time. Because the initials AD and BC are a Christian dating system, many modern scholars use the alternative abbreviations CE, short for "common era," instead of AD, and BCE, short for "before common era," instead of BC. Because the layperson is generally more familiar with the terms AD and BC, however, these are the abbreviations that are used in this book.

1

Stonehenge and the Megalithic Culture

STONEHENGE, IN SOUTHERN ENGLAND, is not only one of the world's most famous ancient monuments; it is also one of the most enigmatic. Just why it was built is one of history's most intriguing mysteries. An even greater mystery, however, is: What happened to the people who built it?

The Stonehenge builders are known as the megalithic people, a prehistoric culture that existed in Britain, Ireland, and part of northern France between approximately fifty-five hundred and thirty-five hundred years ago. We have no idea what they called themselves, as they left no written records; the name *megalithic* used today is derived from the word *megalith,* meaning a large, shaped stone, and refers to the monuments these people left behind. These monuments include single standing stones, rows of such stones, and stone circles, of which Stonehenge is just one of many. The megalithic people also built earthworks of considerable size, such as chambered mounds, artificial hills, and many examples of a circular ditch and embankment known as a henge. It is from such an earthwork surrounding Stonehenge that the monument gets its name. As the megalithic people had no form of writing, the purpose of these monuments remains a mystery. What can be said for certain, however, is that they were a remarkable people; they built their monuments with nothing more than Stone Age tools. Stonehenge alone is an astonishing feat of prehistoric engineering.

Stonehenge originally comprised well over a hundred stones, up to 22 feet high and weighing up to 45 tons. They were cut from solid rock,

1

shaped, and then neatly trimmed with simple stone axes and picks made from antlers. These huge stones were then dragged from where they were quarried for mile after mile without the help of draft animals, such as horses or oxen, by a people who had not invented the wheel. Then, in some way that is not fully understood, the builders planted and hauled the stones into upright positions and, more astonishing still, without cranes or machines of any kind, they managed to raise and position thirty 6-ton blocks on top of 13-foot-high stones to form a continuous ring of adjoining arches almost 350 feet around. And all this is only a small part of the full story of the construction of Stonehenge.

Stonehenge is the most famous megalithic monument, but it is just one of hundreds of such stone circles these people erected—and it is far from the biggest. Twenty miles to the north of Stonehenge in the village of Avebury, there is a stone circle so large that it encompasses much of the village. Stonehenge's outer circle of stones is around 110 feet in diameter, but the Avebury stone circle measures well over 1,000 feet across. The monument originally consisted of almost two hundred stones, many as large as those at Stonehenge, and its outer henge earthwork is more than 20 feet high and has a circumference of three quarters of a mile. The megalithic people built artificial mounds around Stonehenge, and some of these impressive hillocks are over 10 feet high and as much as 50 feet across, but close to Avebury there is a megalithic mound that dwarfs them all. Known as Silbury Hill, it is a staggering 130 feet high and covers an area of five and a half acres. It is estimated that moving the half-million tons of rubble to build this mound alone would have taken as much as eighteen million man-hours. The term *man-hours,* however, is almost certainly misleading. It has also been estimated that for Silbury Hill to have been completed in the fifteen years archaeologists believe it took to build, a large percentage of the population of south-central England would need to have worked on the project: this would clearly have necessitated women, and perhaps even children, working on it too.

Stonehenge and Avebury are just two of hundreds of such megalithic complexes that were constructed all over Britain, Ireland, and northern

France, which continued to be built and used for a period spanning two thousand years. The monuments of the megalithic people may well have served some religious purpose, as did the great cathedrals of the European Middle Ages, or some may have been constructed to honor the dead, as were the pyramids of ancient Egypt, or perhaps they were built for some other reason entirely. Whatever their true purpose, the megalithic monuments were astonishing achievements. Taking into consideration that the estimated population of the entire British Isles at the time was less than a million, and bearing in mind the simple Stone Age tools they employed, monuments such as Stonehenge and Avebury were as spectacular accomplishments as anything from medieval Christendom or ancient Egypt.

These megalithic monuments were constructed not only throughout mainland England, Scotland, and Wales but also on the coastal islands, over the Irish Sea in Ireland, and even across the English Channel in northern France. Although the communities of people who built them were separated by hundreds of miles, the similarity of their constructions over many centuries is clear evidence that they had, and continued to have, a common culture. Moreover, they were arguably a unified civilization. Although they did not build cities, but rather continued to live in simple farming communities, their monumental construction projects, occurring simultaneously throughout what are today five separate countries, indicate social cohesion, an efficient communication network, central administration, and considerable organizational skills: all the features of a civilization. And if the megalithic people were a civilization, then they were one of the world's first. Their oldest surviving structures date from around fifty-five hundred years ago, and they predate the pyramids of Egypt by almost a millennium.

There are many mysteries regarding the megalithic people. What, for instance, was the purpose of Silbury Hill? It was once thought to have been a tomb, but excavations have revealed no internal burial chamber or evidence of even a single body inside. And why were some of the massive stones for Stonehenge quarried 135 miles away in south Wales when there was equally suitable stone very much nearer by? And

Key locations in megalithic Britain

why are the standing stones of megalithic monuments so often aligned to the significant seasonal positions of the sun, moon, and stars? One of the most baffling mysteries concerns what held this civilization together. Pedestrian communications must have been painfully slow, and as far as we know there was no army or law enforcement of any kind. Yet somehow, time and again, vast multitudes of people from miles apart were mobilized into a unified workforce. It has been estimated from the size and number of certain megalithic construction projects, which were on occasion simultaneously initiated that for year after year, well over half the entire population of Britain had to have been directly involved in the work. What drove them to carry out such long-term and backbreaking endeavors? Furthermore, what impelled the rest of the population to continue to feed them?

The megalithic people must have been united by a single devotion to whatever religion or belief system they embraced. They left no written evidence as to what this was, but it had to have been intrinsically nonviolent. One thing is certain: they were a remarkably peaceful culture. Archaeology has unearthed no evidence whatsoever of organized warfare or tribal feuding, such as the existence of defensive structures or forts, and no human remains have been discovered bearing evidence of wounds inflicted in battle; indeed, the only weapons the megalithic people are known to have manufactured were suitable merely for hunting.

The greatest mystery of all, however, is what ultimately became of them. For two thousand years the megalithic culture endured; then, suddenly, around 1500 BC, virtually overnight in archaeological terms, it ceased to exist. The megalithic monuments were abandoned, no new ones were erected; instead the once peaceful people began to build fortifications and started to manufacture weapons of war. DNA tests on the bones unearthed from graves of this period show no evidence of foreign invasion, nor do excavated animal or plant remains hold evidence of climate change, to account for the sudden onset of civil strife. For some completely unknown reason, this peaceful two-thousand-year-old civilization seems to have ended by tearing itself apart. The fate of the megalithic culture thus remains a mystery.

This book is an investigation into the demise of the megalithic people. The search for answers takes us far beyond the shores of the British Isles and leads to truly alarming discoveries. It now seems that the horrific cataclysm that befell these gentle people also terminated peaceful civilizations throughout the world. Moreover, it changed the course of world history to such an extent that it still has repercussions today. Most disturbing of all, what destroyed the megalithic civilization may be about to destroy our own.

To grasp just how puzzling the abrupt end of megalithic civilization actually was, we need to understand something of the culture itself: its peaceful nature, its longevity, and the extent of its extraordinary achievements. First we should examine the monuments they left behind, and consider the enormity of the task involved in constructing them with nothing more than Stone Age tools and ancient ingenuity. We begin with the most famous megalithic monument, Stonehenge.

Standing on the open lowland of Salisbury Plain in south-central England, around seventy miles southwest of the outskirts of London, Stonehenge is now one of Britain's most popular tourist sites. What few visitors to the site realize, however, is that the stone circle is in fact merely a part of a much larger megalithic complex. This consisted of a series not only of stone structures but also of earthworks and timber constructions that were built, rebuilt, and modified over a period of more than two thousand years.[1]

At the heart of this ancient megalithic complex is the stone circle that sightseers flock to see today. Although it still inspires awe, Stonehenge is a shadow of its former self. Many of the stones have fallen, while for centuries others were broken up by local people and taken away to be used for building materials to construct houses in nearby towns. It is only in modern times that the monument has been protected and partly repaired.

The Stonehenge stone circle is in fact a series of stone circles. The outer ring, called the Sarsen Circle after the hard-grained sarsen sandstone from which it was built, originally comprised thirty upright stones, or monoliths, supporting thirty horizontal stones, or lintels, in a continuous circle of arches 110 feet in diameter. Only seventeen uprights and half a dozen lintels still stand. It is astonishing that anything has survived at all, considering that these stones were originally set in place over four thousand years ago. The standing stones of the Sarsen Circle rise 13 feet above the ground, are an average of 6½ feet wide and 3 feet thick, and weigh up to 25 tons, while the 10-foot-long lintels on top of them weigh around 6 tons each.

Just inside the Sarsen Circle there was another ring of stones known as the Bluestone Circle, the term *bluestone* referring to the type of igneous rock from which it is constructed, with a further oval arrangement of such stones, called the Bluestone Oval, inside that. Altogether there were originally around eighty bluestones, averaging around 6 feet high, 3 feet wide, and 1½ feet thick, each weighing around 4 tons. Only a few survive. Standing between the Bluestone Circle and the Bluestone Oval were the enormous trilithons (named after the Greek word for "three stones"), a series of double freestanding upright sarsen stones connected by individual lintels. There were originally five separate trilithons, spaced equidistantly in a horseshoe shape aptly called the Trilithon Horseshoe, of which three survive intact; the other two have one of their uprights standing, while their lintels and second standing stone now lie on the ground. The trilithon uprights are Stonehenge's largest stones, up to 24 feet tall and weighing as much as 45 tons. Finally, within the Trilithon Horseshoe, just in front of the central trilithon, there is the Altar Stone, so called because some scholars believe that it was once the focal point for whatever ceremonies were performed here. It is a flat horizontal stone, fashioned from green micaceous sandstone 16 feet long; 3 feet, 6 inches wide; 1 foot, 9 inches high; and weighing approximately 6 tons. (Some scholars suggest that the Altar Stone originally stood upright as a single large monolith.) This, then, is the Stonehenge familiar around the world from photographs and from television and movie images. However, this is only a part of Stonehenge.

In the immediate area around the outer Sarsen Circle, archaeologists have discovered that the ancient builders dug three rings of concentric holes encircling the monument. The inner ring, consisting of twenty-nine holes, referred to by archaeologists as the Z holes, was around 6 feet from the Sarsen Circle, and a second ring of thirty holes, called the Y holes, were some 15 feet farther out. Almost 100 feet farther out still there was a third ring of fifty-six holes known as the Aubrey Holes, after the seventeenth-century scholar John Aubrey, who first recorded them. These pits, each an average of 3 feet deep and 3 feet wide, are something of an enigma. Archaeologists have found no telltale evidence that they were dug to contain stones or even timbers; excavations have revealed that the earth which now fills them accumulated over years by natural weathering, so it is clear they were simply meant to be holes. Even more mysterious is that in the Z and Y holes, archaeologists discovered that a small piece of bluestone had been deliberately buried at the bottom of each pit.

Just outside the Aubrey Holes, and encompassing the main Stonehenge monument, is a circular embankment around 350 feet in diameter with a ditch outside it. This is the henge construction after which Stonehenge is named. Now eroded and covered with grass, the embankment is estimated to have originally been 6 feet high and the ditch 6 feet deep, the bank having been built from fragments of the chalk bedrock hacked out of what became the ditch.

The stones of the stone circle are not the only monoliths at Stonehenge. Approximately in line with the Aubrey Holes, just inside the embankment to the north and south of the henge, there were circular ditches around 3 feet deep and around 35 feet in diameter, and at the center of each ditch a small single upright sarsen stone was erected, both around four feet high. Two similar stones were also erected just inside the embankment, to the northwest and southeast of the henge, although these did not have a ditch dug around them. Together, these four stones are known as the Station Stones, of which only two survive, and one has fallen. Two, or possibly three, much larger sarsen stones stood at what is thought to have been the main entrance to Stonehenge, to the northeast of the site where a 40-foot gap was left in the encircling embankment. Only one of these stones survives, and it now lies flat on the ground.

Fashioned from sarsen stone, 20 feet long, 7 feet wide, and 5 feet thick, it is almost completely buried in the ground.

For many years the stone was believed to have been an altar used for sacrifices, which has led to the inappropriate name by which it is still known: the Slaughter Stone. However, by excavating the ground around it, archaeologists now know that the Slaughter Stone originally stood upright and was one of a pair of freestanding monoliths that flanked the entrance to the site. Finally, there is another large sarsen monolith that stands in front of the entrance, some 80 feet outside the embankment. Like the Station Stones, it is surrounded by a ditch of around the same dimensions. Some 20 feet long and 7 feet wide, this stone is unique at Stonehenge in that it does not appear to have been artificially shaped; rather, it seems to have been a natural formation that was dragged here to be inserted upright. Now leaning at an angle with 16 feet showing above the ground, it is known as the Heel Stone. Originally called the Friar's Heel, it got its unusual name because of a local legend that a friar or monk once confronted the devil, who was said to reside at Stonehenge. The devil responded by hurling the huge stone at the friar but just missed him, scraping the man's heel as he ran away.[2]

So this is Stonehenge. Let's now consider the enormous task of building it. Stonehenge may not seem that impressive when compared to some of the accomplishments of other early civilizations, such as the temples and pyramids of Egypt. But we need to be aware that the megalithic culture was unique among ancient civilizations in that it had no cities, not infrastructure, no beasts of burden, and no form of writing. Moreover, for much of its existence the megalithic civilization remained in the Stone Age, with little more than flint axes and knives for cutting, and tools made from deer antlers and cattle bones for digging and even shaping stones.[3] The contemporary civilization in ancient Egypt, by comparison, had all these things and more. The Egyptians had cities that were linked both by roads and the easily navigable waters of the Nile; they had an army to maintain order and implement national cohesion; they had horse-drawn transport and employed caravans of pack animals; they had writing in the form of hieroglyphics; and they employed metal-based technology, smelting such metals as gold, silver, copper, and tin and crafting bronze weapons and tools.

The nearest place to Stonehenge that the type of sarsen stone used to construct much of the monument can be found is the Marlborough Downs, a hilly area around twenty miles to the north. And here archaeologists have found the precise locations where these stones were obtained. Imagine the work involved in quarrying and then neatly trimming such stones as those used for the Sarsen Circle with nothing more than flint or bone tools. Remember, the uprights average 6½ feet wide and 3 feet thick and are some 18 feet high, with about a further quarter of their height below the ground. Then imagine hauling these 25-ton stones across Salisbury Plain. Archaeologists believe that stones were loaded onto heavy wooden platforms to which ropes were attached, and then hauled along on wooden rollers, or possibly on rails greased with animal fat or vegetable oil. It has been estimated that it took five hundred people to pull each stone in this way, with another one hundred employed to continually move and lay the rollers or tracks.

The twenty-mile journey must have been excruciatingly slow. When eventually they reached their destination, the stones were dropped into predug holes and had to be hoisted into an upright position with ropes and timber levers. But all this is child's play compared to the problems involved in getting the lintel blocks on top of these standing stones. The megalithic people did not have the benefit of the kind of pulley blocks that allowed the Egyptians and other ancient civilization to hoist massive stones 13 feet into the air. It is thought that the Stonehenge builders levered them up a few inches at a time, and then slid cross timbers under them, one by one, to form a tower. It is an astonishing feat, involving considerable manpower and ingenuity, to heave the 10-foot-long, 6-ton stones into their final positions.[4] The Trilithon Horseshoe was an even greater undertaking. These stones, some as long as 30 feet, weigh up to 45 tons.

Then there's the construction of the henge earthwork that encircles Stonehenge. Just below the turf is solid chalk that had to be hacked out from the 6-foot-deep, 10-foot-wide ditch before being piled up to form the bank. In the ditch and within the rubble of the embankment, archaeologists have found the remains of the tools the megalithic people used to dig out the chalk: nothing more than picks made from the antlers of red deer and shovels made from the shoulder blades of cattle. Once again, an astonishing, backbreaking endeavor, considering that the circumference of this earthwork is nearly 1,100 feet.[5]

Impressive stuff! But Stonehenge was only the central feature in a much larger complex of megalithic constructions spreading for over two miles in every direction. Outside the main entrance to Stonehenge, along the alignment of the Slaughter Stone and the Heel Stone, the megalithic people constructed what is known as the Avenue. It is now much eroded and is visible only from the air, but it was originally a causeway flanked by parallel banks some 3 feet high and 70 feet apart. The Avenue goes northeast for around a quarter of a mile, then turns east before continuing in an arc to run southeast to reach the river Avon.

This two-mile-long causeway is thought to have formed a processional road to link the river Avon to Stonehenge. Participants in whatever ceremonies took place at Stonehenge may well have arrived from elsewhere by way of the river. Excavations have uncovered the remains of the two main types of boats used by the megalithic people: dugout canoes made from hollowed-out tree trunks and much larger frame-hulled boats. The latter type of boat, known as a curragh, was made from shaped tree branches lashed together to form a framework that was covered with animal skins or hides sewn together.

To make it watertight, the seams were filled with animal fat. Some of these boats, which were rowed by teams of oarsmen, were of considerable size, as much as 40 feet long, and could have held at least twenty people.[6] Having alighted from such vessels, the participants may then have made their way along the Avenue, entered Stonehenge between the two giant monoliths flanking the gap in the embankment, passed through the Sarsen Circle, and finally entered the Trilithon Horseshoe, which was open toward the main entrance.

We can guess the function of the Avenue, but some half-mile north of Stonehenge there is another huge earthwork, the purpose of which remains a complete mystery. It is a long rectangular bank that runs for one and a half miles in a roughly east–west direction. Over 300 feet wide and more than 6 feet high, it was, like the circular embankment at Stonehenge, built from chalk hacked from the bedrock. Today it is known as the Cursus, because it was once (erroneously) thought to have formed the central area of a Roman racetrack of that name. However, it is now known to have been built three thousand years before the Romans arrived and well before horses were even domesticated, let alone used for racing. What purpose the Cursus served is an enigma. It would have been useless as a defensive structure, as there was no barrier, artificial or natural, at either end, and it is far too wide to have been of any strategic use. Whatever it was, it must have been extremely important to the megalithic people; it boggles the mind to think how much time and grueling effort went into building it.[7]

Two miles to the northeast of Stonehenge there is an even more impressive megalithic earthwork, known as Durrington Walls. This was a circular henge construction like that surrounding Stonehenge, but much larger. Its ditch was almost 20 feet deep and over 50 feet wide, while the bank rose 10 feet above the ditch. The Stonehenge embankment is around 350 feet in diameter, but Durrington Walls is almost four times wider, around 1,600 feet across, a circumference of almost a mile. Like Stonehenge, Durrington Walls had its own external causeway, leading from a gap in the embankment that seems to have formed the main entrance and running southeast to the river Avon. Although it is around the same width as the Avenue at Stonehenge, it was only some 500 feet long. Nonetheless, it was probably more impressive in its day, as it seems to have been paved with compacted chalk.[8]

The magnitude of the construction of Durrington Walls dwarfs the building of the Stonehenge embankment, together with the Avenue and the Cursus combined. It would have been a colossal undertaking. One archaeologist who worked on recent excavations at the site concluded that most of the population of southern England must have been involved in its construction. Those who were not directly involved in the building work must have supported those who were.[9] Once again, its purpose remains a mystery. There is no archeological evidence that the megalithic people built a stockade around the top of the embankment, such as telltale postholes, so it could not have served any defensive purpose. Besides, it was much too big to have been defended by the limited manpower and types of weaponry of the time. There were, however, wooden structures erected inside—and these are just as puzzling.

There appear to have been no stone monoliths erected within the Durrington Walls enclosure, but modern geophysical surveys reveal that two circular wooden structures once stood within the embankment. Geophysics enables archaeologists to see what lies below the ground without digging: sophisticated electronic equipment, such as ground-penetrating radar, produces a three-dimensional computer-generated image of what lies buried, and can also detect and map areas of soil excavated and refilled in the remote past. Such surveys showed that one of the wooden structures stood near the main entrance to the southeast: the findings revealed a series of five concentric rings of holes, with an outer diameter of 125 feet, while subsequent excavations found that these had been used to hold wooded posts. The second structure, to the north, was 90 feet in diameter and had only two rings of postholes, but this one also had what appears to have been an avenue of wooden posts leading up to it. Only the postholes remain, so it is impossible to know if the timbers of either of these structures supported a roof. The consensus is that they didn't. There is no evidence that they were permanently inhabited, so they may well have been open-air constructions, like a stone circle but made of wood.[10] In fact, just such a timber circle stood very near by.

Sixty yards to the south of Durrington Walls, there was another megalithic monument. What survives is a circular ditch and bank earthwork around 280 feet in diameter, and within it archaeologists have discovered the remains of postholes that once held timbers: 168 in all, arranged in six concentric rings. Some of the holes were more than 6 feet deep and 3 feet wide, meaning that a post would have risen to over 25 feet above the ground. It is estimated that such huge posts, made from 3-foot-diameter tree trunks, weighed around 5 tons. The layout and size of such timbers has led archaeologists to doubt that the monument was a roofed structure; they think instead that it was an open-air arrangement of huge wooden posts, which has been aptly named Woodhenge. Visitors to the site can get some idea of the original timber circle, as the positions of the postholes are now marked with concrete posts.[11]

There are three other types of megalithic monuments that are found all around Stonehenge: long barrows, round barrows, and tumuli. In fact, they dominate the landscape. The first and largest, the so-called long barrows, were rectangular-shaped earthen mounds, averaging 100 feet long, 40 feet wide, and 6 feet high, surrounded by a vertical stone wall. At the heart of these barrows were small stone-lined chambers in which the bodies of the dead, presumably people of special importance, were laid to rest. These date from the earlier megalithic period; later burials were housed in round barrows. Round barrows were similar constructions to the long barrows except, as their name suggests, they were circular mounds up to 10 feet high and 50 feet across. Another name for the round barrow is *tumulus,* the plural being *tumuli,* but this is a somewhat confusing term. Some of these tumuli have been found to contain skeletal remains, while others contained cremation urns, but some never appear to have been used for burials at all. They were simply small, artificial hillocks, and their purpose remains a mystery. On a map, you usually see both round burial barrows and these small artificial hills marked as tumuli, but for convenience' sake it is easiest to use the word *tumulus* to refer specifically to a round barrow that was not used for burial. Individual tumuli are found scattered around Stonehenge in every direction, but the barrows tend to fall in groups, or cemeteries, usually strung out along natural ridges. The largest of these barrow cemeteries are found at Normanton Down, half a mile south of Stonehenge; the Winterbourne Stoke barrow group, a mile and a quarter to the west of Stonehenge; and the King Barrows, on a prominent ridge about a mile to the northeast of Stonehenge.[12]

We now have some idea of just how much time, effort, and sheer devotion went into creating Stonehenge and the monuments of the surrounding megalithic complex: extraordinary achievements for a Stone

Age civilization without cities, beasts of burden, sophisticated tools, or any form of writing. As there was no infrastructure to bind the megalithic people together, no communication network other than by foot, and no armies to make them obey, whatever it was that drove them to work together en masse to build such creations must have been a deeply entrenched, heartfelt, and shared belief. However, the work and coordination involved to erect the complex of megalithic structures around Stonehenge is nothing compared to what must have been involved in creating the contemporary megalithic complex around the village of Avebury, twenty miles to the north.

2

A Unified Society

LIKE STONEHENGE, THE AVEBURY STONE CIRCLE was part of a wider megalithic complex, although on an even more ambitious scale. The first person to alert historians to the existence of the Avebury monument was John Aubrey, the seventeenth-century scholar after whom the Aubrey Holes at Stonehenge are named. Aubrey was an antiquarian, someone who collected historical curios; he also documented and speculated on sites of historical interest, sometimes even conducting excavations at such sites. In fact, antiquarianism was a seventeenth- and eighteenth-century precursor to the scientific discipline of archaeology that emerged in the nineteenth century.

Aubrey was already familiar with Stonehenge, which he regarded as an astonishing piece of ancient engineering. When he first visited Avebury in 1649, however, he was so astounded by its size that he wrote in his journal, "[It] does as much exceed in greatness the so renowned Stonehenge, as a cathedral doeth a parish church."[1] Sadly, Avebury has since suffered much damage. Avebury village grew rapidly in the eighteenth century, and the villagers broke apart many of the stones to construct new houses and farm buildings. Thanks to plans and sketches made by Aubrey, though, we know what the monument looked like in his time, and with the help of geophysics, twentieth-century archaeologists have also been able to plot the locations of other stones that had been destroyed even before Aubrey's day.

Although much larger than Stonehenge, the Avebury stone circle was a less complex construction. There was an outer circle with two smaller circles inside, but the monoliths were more widely spaced, and none of them were joined by lintels. Nor were they cut to the same precision, being more irregular in shape. Like many of those at Stonehenge, the monoliths at Avebury were sarsen stones brought from the Marlborough Downs, although in this case they had to be dragged for only two miles. The outer ring, over 1,000 feet in diameter and covering an area of some 28 acres, originally consisted of around one hundred stones, of which only twenty-seven remain. They vary in height and shape, but they would still have taken enormous effort to erect. Ranging from between 9 to over 20 feet high, many weigh as much as 40 tons; only the uprights of the Trilithon Horseshoe are anything like this heavy at Stonehenge.

The two inner circles were not concentric, as were the inner circles at Stonehenge, but instead were two separate rings of approximately the same size within the north and south areas of the main circle. The southern ring was approximately 340 feet in diameter and had twenty-nine stones, of which five remain; a single large monolith, over 18 feet high, once stood in the center, along with an alignment of smaller stones, until they were destroyed in the eighteenth century. The northern circle was 320 feet in diameter and consisted of twenty-seven stones, of which four remain, and at the center of this circle there stood an arrangement of three huge stones known as the Cove. Two of these Cove stones survive, the larger of which is around 16 feet high and 18 feet wide and is estimated to weigh a staggering 100 tons.

Surrounding the outer circle, there is a henge earthwork similar to that at Stonehenge but on a much larger scale. Cut from the chalk bedrock, the ditch was originally 30 feet deep and 60 feet wide, and the bank was 20 feet high and 40 feet wide. Almost 1,400 feet in diameter, the embankment enclosed an area of nearly thirty acres. As with the ditch and embankment at Stonehenge, the megalithic people created this massive earthwork with crude stone tools, bone shovels, and antler picks. In this case, however, they dug out an estimated 4 million cubic feet of rock to make the ditch and piled up 200,000 tons of it to create the bank. This would have required an even greater effort than the building of Durrington Walls, yet, once again, the structure seems to have served no defensive purpose. Not only did it lack any form of stockade, but also the ditch was on the inside of the embankment, a ludicrous arrangement for a protective rampart. What makes it even less likely to have served any military function is that there were no fewer than four 60-foot gaps in the embankment. These equally spaced entrances, to roughly the north, south, east, and west, would have been quite impractical to defend simultaneously.

Stonehenge had a single Avenue, but Avebury had two, each around 50 feet wide: one, now called the West Kennett Avenue, led for almost a mile and a half in a southeasterly direction from the southern entrance, and the other, known as the Beckhampton Avenue, led west from the western entrance before curving to the southwest, and was about a mile long. Unlike the Stonehenge Avenue, these were flanked not by embankments but by rows of around one hundred standing stones, spaced some 80 feet apart and varying in size between 4 and 13 feet high. The monoliths of much of the first half of the West Kennett Avenue survive upright and intact, but many of the rest are now buried under fields or were damaged by road workings. The Beckhampton Avenue, however, has suffered far worse.

Only one stone now remains standing, the others having being broken up and used for building materials over the years. This avenue seems to have ended at an arrangement of three huge stones similar in size and layout to the Cove in the north circle at Avebury. Only one of these stones survives, along with another close by, which is the only surviving monolith from the avenue itself. (Today these two stones are marked on the map as the Long Stones, but local people refer to them as Adam and Eve.) The West Kennett Avenue ended at a smaller stone circle near what is now the village of West Kennett, after which the avenue gets its name: known as the Sanctuary, it stood on a small hill overlooking the river Kennett just to the south. Although it was small only in relation to Avebury, its circumference was still large enough to encompass the entire Sarsen Circle at Stonehenge. Originally it was two concentric rings of upright stones, but nothing survives today; the original positions of the stones have been marked with concrete blocks.[2]

As at Stonehenge, numerous megalithic barrows dominate the landscape around Avebury, the most significant group being near the Sanctuary. Among these is one of the largest long barrows to be found anywhere in Britain. Known as the West Kennett Long Barrow, it is well over 300 feet long and almost 8 feet high; much of its surrounding wall is in place, as are two huge portal stones and a 6-foot-wide, 8-foot-high sarsen slab that once sealed the entrance. Inside, there survives a series of stone-lined burial chambers that run for 30 feet into the dark interior, and here archaeologists found forty-six separate skeletons. It seems that this tomb alone had been in constant use for more than a thousand years.[3]

There are also many megalithic tumuli and artificial mounds around Avebury, the largest by far being Silbury Hill. Silbury Hill stands about a mile south of Avebury, halfway between the Beckhampton and West Kennett Avenues, which was probably intentional; its location indicates that it may well have been the focus of ceremonial activities for the entire Avebury complex. Silbury Hill is the tallest prehistoric artificial mound in Europe. In fact, it is one of the largest anywhere in the world. Standing some 130 feet high and 550 feet in diameter, it has a flat-topped summit around 100 feet wide. Archaeological excavations have revealed that it was built from alternate layers of cut chalk and gravel—almost 9 million cubic feet of the stuff. Its purpose, however, remains a mystery, as it never appears to have contained a single burial; at the heart of this huge undertaking, all that was found was a core of sarsen boulders. As with other megalithic earthworks, antlers and cattle bones were found among the rubble, showing that it was built with the simplest of Stone Age tools.[4]

The megalithic people not only had a preoccupation with building artificial hills; they also reshaped existing hills, which often took the form of what are called causewayed enclosures. The largest example in the British Isles is found at Windmill Hill, a mile to the northwest of Avebury, where three concentric ditches and internal embankments, some 6 feet high and deep, were dug around the hilltop, the outermost having a diameter of 1,200 feet and enclosing an area of almost twenty-one acres.

These circular earthworks could not have served any defensive purpose, as they were built in segments with numerous gaps in the banks up to 20 feet wide; here the ditches were crossed by raised causeways, after which such monuments get their name. Although excavations at Windmill Hill have revealed much pottery and many discarded animal bones, thought to be evidence of ritual feasting, there is no indication of permanent occupation. This, coupled with the fact that there is no natural water supply at the site, suggests that the construction was never meant to be lived in, making this causewayed enclosure yet another example of the many baffling monuments of the megalithic age.[5]

When John Aubrey likened Avebury to a cathedral, comparing it to Stonehenge as a parish church, he may well have chosen an appropriate analogy. The two complexes seem to have been interconnected, and Avebury was probably the more important. The Avebury outer ring is by far the largest stone circle in the British Isles and, along with Silbury Hill, may therefore have been the center stage for megalithic ritual activity in south-central Britain. Avebury was clearly linked with Stonehenge, as the sarsen stones for both were quarried at exactly the same site on the Marlborough Downs, just two miles to the east of Avebury. Furthermore, it seems that both the Avebury and Stonehenge complexes developed concurrently: they appear to have been simultaneously built and modified over a period of around two thousand years, between approximately 3500 and 1500 BC, a period spanning the entire megalithic age.

Before proceeding further, it is important to say something about the dating of the Stonehenge, Avebury, and other prehistoric structures. The megalithic people left no written records, so how do we know when these monuments were built? The word *prehistoric* means literally "before historical records," and there are a number of ways by which archaeologists can date prehistoric sites, remains, and events: chief among them are dendrochronology, thermoluminescence, and radiocarbon dating.

Dendrochronology is the dating of past events through the study of tree-ring patterns. During the spring and summer of each year, a tree grows, and during the winter, it falls partially dormant. This creates a series of concentric rings in the tree's trunk and branches, each indicating a separate year of growth; in years when conditions are better for growth, the rings are wider, and vice versa. Because weather varies from year to year, consecutive growth rings are like fingerprints of the past, unique to a particular location and period, and archaeologists have compiled charts of such ring patterns going back many centuries. When timbers from an old building are found, they are often datable because dendrochronology can determine the year the tree for the wood was felled.[6] Because of Britain's damp climate, few timbers are preserved from the megalithic age. Pottery, however, has survived from this time, and this can be dated by the scientific technique of thermoluminescence dating.

Pottery is made by shaping clay and then baking it hard by firing. During firing, molecular changes occur, and thermoluminescence dating enables scientists to determine just how long ago a piece of pottery was fired.[7] Thermoluminescence dating has proved helpful in determining the age of various megalithic settlements and also burial mounds where pottery has been found among grave goods. However, the most useful procedure in dating megalithic monoliths and earthworks has been radiocarbon dating, or carbon dating for short.

During their lifetimes, living organisms, both animal and vegetable, absorb a form, or isotope, of the element carbon known as carbon 14. Once the organism has died, the carbon 14 gradually decays until, some sixty thousand years later, it disappears altogether. By a chemical analysis of the amount of carbon 14 still present in a dead organism, scientists can determine how long ago it died. Only organic matter can be carbon dated, which obviously excludes stone, so how do scientists date such structures as Stonehenge? The answer is indirectly, by dating megalithic tools, many of which were made from antlers and cattle bones, which, of course, are organic remains. It is fair to assume that such animals died only shortly before their bones and antlers were adapted for tools. Often the broken remains of these tools are found lining the bottom of the pits into which monoliths were sunk, and the carbon dating of these remains provides a likely date for the erection of the stones.

The age of megalithic earthworks, such as embankments and

artificial mounds, can also be determined by carbon dating the broken implements excavated from the soil and rubble they were built from. Because the amount of carbon 14 in the atmosphere varies over time, carbon dating is accurate only to within around one hundred years, or fifty years either side of a central date. When samples are cross-referenced with dates obtained from other finds, such as pottery, however, fairly reliable dating can often be established.[8]

Although there is still some disagreement regarding the precise period when certain megalithic activities were initiated, such as instances when stones were repositioned or when earthworks were later modified, these dating procedures have given archaeologists a fairly good idea of when the monuments of the Stonehenge and Avebury complexes were erected. Here, then, are the approximate dates when these megalithic activities were undertaken:

3500 BC   The first long barrows are constructed around what would later be Stonehenge, as is the West Kennett Long Barrow near Avebury.

3300 BC   The causewayed enclosure at Windmill Hill is constructed to the northeast of what would later be the Avebury stone circle.

3100 BC   The Cursus earthwork is built to the north of what would later be Stonehenge.

3000 BC   The Stonehenge outer ditch and embankment are constructed, and the circular pits known as the Aubrey Holes are dug.

2800 BC   The Avebury north and south inner stone circles are erected.

2750 BC   Silbury Hill is built to the south of Avebury.

2600 BC   The bluestones are erected in two concentric crescents in the center of Stonehenge. (This is known from the excavations of the holes in which they were originally set, known as the Q and R Holes.) The Altar stone is also erected at this time.

The huge circular ditch and embankment is constructed at Durrington Walls to the northeast of Stonehenge.

The main outer stone circle is erected at Avebury, and the surrounding ditch and embankment are constructed.

2400 BC   The West Kennett and Beckhampton Avenues are constructed at Avebury.

2300 BC   At Stonehenge the Station Stones, the Heel Stone, and the portal stones (which included the Slaughter Stone) are erected, and the Avenue is constructed.

2100 BC   At Stonehenge, the Sarsen Circle and the Trilithon Horseshoe are erected.

The Sanctuary stone circle is erected at the end of the West Kennett Avenue at Avebury.

2000 BC   The Woodhenge monument is constructed.

1550 BC   At Stonehenge, the bluestones are repositioned to form the Bluestone Circle and the Bluestone Oval, and the Z and Y Holes are dug.

We can see that the megalithic complexes of Stonehenge and Avebury were built, improved, and modified over a period spanning two thousand years, and so were clearly constructed by a people who held common beliefs—whatever they may have been—throughout this time. But Stonehenge and Avebury were only a part of what seem to have been an interlinked series of megalithic sites stretching across much of southern Britain.

The Sanctuary stone circle at the end of the West Kennett Avenue seems to have been something of a terminal for ancient visitors to the Avebury complex. Immediately to the east of it was the Ridgeway, an eighty-five-mile prehistoric track leading to other megalithic sites to the northeast. For example, sixteen miles away in the Uffington Hills, in what is now the county of Oxfordshire, there was another complex of contemporary prehistoric monuments. This included Wayland's Smithy, one of Britain's oldest and best-preserved long barrows, and Dragon Hill, a natural chalk hillock that was artificially fashioned into a conical shape with a flattened summit, similar to Silbury Hill.[9] The Sanctuary also overlooked the Kennett River, immediately to the south, which would have connected Avebury to megalithic communities along the Kennett Valley to the east, such as at Newbury, twenty-five miles away.

There were certainly close ties between Avebury and Stonehenge twenty miles to the south, as the sarsen stones used at both were obtained from the very same location in the Marlborough Downs that rise directly above the Sanctuary. It is the other type of stone used to build Stonehenge, however, the so-called bluestone, that reveals something of the true extent of the interrelationship among megalithic sites. These are now known to have come from 135 miles away.

Bluestone is the common name for a form of dolerite rock that appears blue when wet. Geologists had long realized that the stones used to build the Bluestone Circle and the Bluestone Oval at Stonehenge were a particular type of dolerite known as plagioclase feldspar, specifically found in the Preseli Mountains of south Wales. Only recently, however, has the precise location where they were quarried been discovered. In 2005, the British archaeologist Professor Tim Darvill, of Bournemouth University, discovered the site at Carn Menyn in the Welsh county of Pembrokeshire, 135 miles to the west of Stonehenge.[10] We have already seen the considerable time and effort it would have taken to move the sarsen stones twenty miles from the Marlborough Downs to Stonehenge. The challenge of moving the eighty 4-ton bluestones as much as 135 miles must have been gargantuan, particularly since some of the journey required hauling the stones through mountains. In fact, the distance of 135 miles is as the crow flies; the actual journey would have been more like 250 miles.

It has been suggested that parts of the journey were made easier by transporting the stones on rafts along various rivers, but even so it still meant that at least half of the journey would have been overland. Just why the Stonehenge builders decided to use stones from so far away as the Preseli Mountains when they had a supply of sarsen stone much closer to home is yet another mystery. Nevertheless, the fact that they were quarried here reveals much about the cultural relationship among megalithic communities in southern Britain.[11]

To start with, whatever beliefs lay behind the building of Stonehenge, religious or something else entirely, they must have been shared by the people of the Preseli Mountains. Here there was a concentration of megalithic monuments rivaling in number, if not size, those on Salisbury Plain. As well as earthworks, burial mounds, and rows of standing stones, there were at least three stone circles of around 60 feet in diameter and a monument in the form of an oval-shaped arrangement of bluestones very similar to the Bluestone Oval at Stonehenge.[12] The similarity of these constructions to those around Stonehenge and Avebury show that the inhabitants of this area shared an identical culture with the inhabitants of south-central England. Moreover, they had to have cooperated closely with one another. The Stonehenge builders not only obtained their bluestones from the heart of the megalithic complex around Carn Menyn, but they also cut them from the same quarries that the Preseli Mountains people used for their own structures. At the very least, they had to have had permission, if not actual help, from the local inhabitants to excavate here. Remember, the Stonehenge builders had no such thing as an army to protect them while they carried out the work.

On a wider front, the Stonehenge builders also must have had close relations with the peoples who inhabited the regions of south Wales and south-central England between the Preseli Mountains and Stonehenge. During the years it must have taken to move the stones, the workers would have been terribly exposed to any hostile peoples along the route; they could not possibly have accomplished the task without local cooperation across more than two hundred miles of southern Britain. This reveals just how interrelated megalithic communities throughout this entire area had to have been—an exceptional historical situation. At most other times in ancient British history, the country was fragmented into dozens of separate tribes that were often openly hostile to one another. We know from Roman records that when the Romans conquered Britain, in the first century AD, the country was divided into dozens of tribes that fought more with each other than they did against the invaders. At this time the route between the Preseli Mountains and Stonehenge would have passed through at least four separate tribal zones.

The Romans managed to unite the country, but only because they had the best army the ancient world had ever seen. Once they left, in the fifth century, Britain immediately broke apart into its earlier tribal kingdoms, enabling the Anglo-Saxons, from what is now southern Denmark and northern Germany, to invade all of what is now England. The Anglo-Saxons themselves quickly separated into numerous kingdoms, and it was not until AD 927 that they were effectively united into the single kingdom of England by the army of the Saxon king Athelstan. Even then, Wales remained outside Saxon control and continued to be divided into separate squabbling kingdoms.

It took the even more powerful conquers, the Normans from France, to finally unite southern Britain under a single leadership, in the twelfth century AD. When we consider the moving of the bluestones along a route of around 250 miles from south Wales and across west-central England to Salisbury Plain, it is reasonable to assume that the megalithic peoples of this part of Britain shared a greater affinity with one another than would their successors for the following twenty-five hundred years. Indeed, further evidence for this comes from a recent discovery made near Stonehenge.

In April 2003, during road improvements at Boscombe Down, three and a half miles to the southeast of Stonehenge, workmen accidentally uncovered a megalithic burial site containing the remains of seven people: three children, a teenager, and three men, whom the press nicknamed the "band of brothers."[13] Carbon dating of the bones determined that these individuals died around forty-three hundred years ago, about the same time that the Avenue was being built at Stonehenge, but examination of the teeth revealed that they were not native to the area. As enamel forms on children's teeth, it absorbs chemicals from the rock over which the local water supply flows. By testing the tooth enamel, scientists can determine with remarkable precision exactly where a person grew up.

In the case of the band of brothers, it was discovered that they grew up in south Wales and seem to have lived in the very area of the Preseli Mountains where the bluestones were quarried.[14] From this and other evidence, archaeologists have concluded that families from 135 miles away in south Wales were willing and able to settle near Stonehenge three centuries after the bluestones were brought here. All this suggests close ties between communities widely spaced along a broad swath of south-central Britain, and over a considerable period of time. However, when we consider the actual work necessary to accomplish some of the megalithic projects at and around Stonehenge and Avebury, we can only conclude that these people were unified into a single society.

Archaeologists have initiated a number of simulations to determine the number of people that would have been required to work on various megalithic projects, such as cutting and shaping monoliths, digging ditches in solid chalk, and building artificial mounds. For the construction of earthworks, for instance, it is thought that workers were organized into gangs of three: one to dig with an antler pick, one to shovel with a cattle-bone spade, and one to carry away the rubble in baskets. Additionally, each worker had to be fed, sheltered, and clothed, and others would be needed to carry out the usual daily activities normally required of them. It is estimated that each worker would have required the backing of three others. In other words, for all those directly involved in the work, three times as many would have been indirectly involved.[15]

It was once assumed that it would have taken many decades for some of the megalithic projects to have been completed, but more recent surveys suggest that even the grandest undertakings were completed in a remarkably short period of time, averaging around fifteen years. When this time scale is coupled with the probable makeup of the labor force and the backup necessary to enable it to continue working, archaeologists are able to estimate how many people would have been needed to construct various megalithic monuments. For example, they figure that Silbury Hill would have taken 18 million man-hours to build, which means that for it to have been completed in fifteen years, about twenty-five hundred people would have been working on the project full time. This may not seem that many by today's standards, but it was a huge number considering that even the largest megalithic villages had populations of only around three hundred. If just half the population of each village was tied up in the project, at least sixteen megalithic communities spread out around Salisbury Plain would need to have cooperated, and continued to cooperate for a decade and a half.

The main building project at Stonehenge, in about 2100 BC, was the erection of the Sarsen Circle and the Trilithon Horseshoe, and this would have involved even more people. The cutting and shaping of the stones is estimated to have taken 20 million man-hours, and the hauling and erection of the stones a further 17.5 million man-hours. To complete all this in fifteen years would necessitate around 5,250 people working full time on the project. Both these projects combined, however, were dwarfed by the simultaneous activities surrounding both Avebury and Stonehenge in 2600 BC.

At this time, moving the Stonehenge bluestones from south Wales alone would have involved thousands of individuals. Each 4-ton stone would have required at team of at least 150 people to both haul it and move the rollers or lay the rails; and this is only over level ground, let alone up and down steep inclines or over rough terrain. So this number can probably be doubled. It is highly unlikely that they moved each of the eighty stones one at a time: to do it in fifteen years would have taken a team of at least two thousand workers, plus six thousand in support, or eight thousand people in all.

At the same time, the main building project at Avebury was also taking place: the construction of the henge and the erection of the main stone circle. It would have taken an estimated 1.6 million man-hours to dig the ditch and build the embankment, and a further 6 million man-hours to cut, move, and erect the stones. Together, this would require eleven hundred people working full time for fifteen years. Simultaneously, Durrington Walls was also being built, which was almost as large a project as the Avebury ditch and embankment, so we can estimate another five hundred people permanently engaged here.

Altogether, this is a total of almost ten thousand people tied up in megalithic construction projects at a time when the entire population of south-central England was only about thirty thousand. The relative percentage of the population that would have had to have been mobilized for these projects to have been completed is astonishing. One in three: this is a higher percentage of the population than is estimated for the ancient Egyptians to build the pyramids of Giza. For such megalithic projects to be accomplished would have necessitated a central authority, a well-organized social structure, efficient coordination, and the cooperation of the population spread over an area spanning south-central Britain.[16]

There can be little doubt that the megalithic peoples of what are now the English counties of Wiltshire, Oxfordshire, Berkshire, and Hampshire, together with those in the mountainous area of south Wales, functioned as a single society; and they did so sharing a sophisticated culture for some two thousand years. This is remarkable considering there was no army to force anyone to cooperate, and only the most primitive infrastructure to bind them together. What is even more remarkable is that this unified society appears to have stretched to every corner of the British Isles and beyond.

3
Living in Harmony

THE RELATIONSHIP SHARED BY the megalithic communities of south-central England and south Wales also seems to have included the inhabitants of the far southwest of England. Here, 180 miles from Stonehenge, is the Land's End peninsula in the county of Cornwall, and it was from the local rocks of this area that many of the stone axes found around Avebury and Stonehenge were made. This was once believed to have been due to simple trading, but it is now considered more likely that Cornish workers were themselves directly involved in the construction of these monuments; they certainly built similar megalithic monuments of their own.[1]

The megalithic monuments of the English southwest are generally smaller than those we have examined so far. The prevalent local rock is granite, which is considerably harder than the bluestone or sarsen stone used in south-central Britain. It would therefore have taken much more work to quarry and shape; consequently, the monoliths of this area tend to be scaled down. Stone circles, of which many still survive in Cornwall, were usually composed of stones averaging around 4 feet high, although single freestanding monoliths could be considerably larger. For example, the Boskawen-Un stone circle near the Cornish village of Catchall is around 80 feet in diameter and has nineteen stones between 3 and 5 feet high, at the center of which is a single monolith 8 feet tall. Cornwall's best-preserved stone circle is near the village of Boleigh. Known as the Merry Maidens, it comprises nineteen stones standing up to 4½ feet high, which form a perfect circle 77 feet in diameter, and in fields just to the northeast of the circle are two freestanding monoliths 13 and 15 feet tall.

Throughout Cornwall, we find a myriad of other megalithic remains: solitary standing stones known as menhirs, from an old Celtic word meaning "long stone," of which around one hundred survive; there are also tumuli, earthworks, and burial barrows, as well as numerous dolmens. Coming from another Celtic word meaning "table," the term *dolmen* refers to three or more upright stones surmounted by a flat horizontal capstone. A typical example is Lanyon Quoit, which stands alone on open moorland in the heart of the Land's End peninsula. On top of three 7-foot-high uprights, there is a 9-by-17-foot capstone weighing over 13 tons.

The most significant concentration of megalithic monuments in Cornwall is found on the windswept uplands of Bodmin Moor. At the heart of this complex are the so-called Hurlers, an arrangement of three separate 110-foot-diameter stone circles along the same axis, originally made up of some twenty-five stones each, of which around half remain. It seems likely that the Hurlers was a major center of megalithic activity in Cornwall, as the stones are somewhat taller than usual for this area, some measuring over 6 feet high. There is also a proliferation of burial mounds around the site, the most notable being the Rillaton Barrow, where excavations unearthed a skeleton dating from the late megalithic period together with a contemporary gold beaker. The Hurlers complex may even have been the "cathedral" of megalithic Cornwall, holding a similar status to Avebury in south-central England. Unlike Avebury, though, there are no stone avenues at the Hurlers.

However, some twenty-five miles to the northeast, in the adjacent county of Devonshire, there is a stone circle with three such avenues. Standing among the craggy hills of Dartmoor, the Shovel Down megalithic complex consists of an arrangement of three concentric stone circles, the outer being around 30 feet in diameter, with a Y-shaped arrangement of stone rows around 500 feet long, one terminating at a single 10-foot monolith. In many ways the complex is like a miniature Avebury, with the avenue being only 4 feet wide and the stones 3 feet high. In another part of southwest England, however, there is another stone circle in many ways identical to that at Avebury.[2]

Just outside the village of Stanton Drew in the County of Somerset is the second-largest stone circle in the British Isles. Made from local limestone and breccia rock, which are easier to quarry, cut, and shape than the granite of Cornwall, many of the stones are comparable in size to those at Avebury. The circle was 370 feet in diameter and consisted of thirty stones, of which twenty-seven remain; it was also surrounded by a henge almost 450 feet in diameter. As with Avebury, there were two avenues of standing stones, some of which survive: one of these stone rows is 100 feet long and leads to the nearby River Chew, and the other, 180 feet long, leads to a second, smaller, 100-foot-diameter stone circle of eight stones to the northeast.

To the southwest of the main circle, around 800 feet away on the same axis as the second circle, there is an arrangement of three much larger stones similar to the Cove at Avebury. The Stanton Drew complex even had its own version of Silbury Hill. A mile and three quarters to the north, there is an artificial mound called the Tump that was built on top of a natural hill called Maes Knoll. Now much eroded and surrounded by the remains of a later Iron Age fort, it is still almost 200 feet in diameter and stands around 30 feet high.[3]

The megalithic people of southwest west England clearly enjoyed a common culture with their contemporaries in the south-central part of the country, building the same kind of monuments for a period of around two thousand years. But it does not stop here; the same was happening throughout British Isles. For instance, 150 miles to the north of Cornwall, in the Welsh county of Clwyd, we find the remains of stone circles, menhirs, dolmens, and tumuli, and the second-largest prehistoric artificial hill in Britain.[4] Known as Gop Cairn, it was built around the same time as Silbury Hill at Avebury. Although it was con- siderably smaller—only 45 feet high, as opposed to Silbury Hill's 130 feet—it may well have taken even greater effort and required far more people to construct. Gop Cairn stands on the summit of a natural hill almost 800 feet high, and the limestone blocks from which it was built had to be quarried in the valley below and carried all the way up this steep-sided mount.

For the local inhabitants to have mustered such manpower, it must have been a particularly important megalithic monument for the area. Indeed, as with the mass construction projects of south-central England, there is evidence that the labor force was supplemented from communities elsewhere in the country: stone axes from Cornwall, for example, have been found by archaeologists excavating around Gop Cairn. Like Silbury Hill, Gop Cairn was probably the focal point of ceremonial activity in north Wales, as it was surrounded by a concentration of other megalithic monuments, in particular burial barrows, the most notable being the mound of Bryn yr Ellyllon near the modern town of Mold. Here, in a central stone-lined burial chamber, along with the skeleton of a man, there was found a four-thousand-year-old collar and shoulder adornment made from solid gold, which became known as the Mold Cape.[5]

In some areas of the British Isles we find even more impressive versions of individual megalithic monuments than those around Avebury or Stonehenge. A further 135 miles to the northeast of Clwyd, near the town of Bridlington in the English county of Yorkshire, there is a megalithic complex known as the Gypsey Race, where the earthworks dominating the landscape are very similar to those surrounding Stonehenge. These include not only long barrows, henge monuments, and tumuli, but no fewer than four cursus embankments just like the mysterious earthwork near Stonehenge. Although around the same height and width as the Stonehenge Cursus, together they add up to more than five and a half miles in length; the Stonehenge Cursus is only a mile and a half long. At the center of this intricate megalithic complex stands the tallest monolith in Britain. Called the Rudston Monolith, this huge grit-stone menhir is over 25 feet tall.[6]

A further four hundred miles to the north, off the northern coast of Scotland, lie the Orkney Isles, and on Mainland, the largest of these islands, there is one of the most impressive megalithic complexes in Britain. Here stands the Ring of Brodgar, the third-largest stone circle in the British Isles. Measuring almost 350 feet in diameter, it consisted of sixty stones ranging between 7 and 15 feet tall, of which twenty-seven remain.

Like Avebury and Stonehenge, it is surrounded by a circular ditch 10 feet deep and 30 feet wide, outside of which there was an outer embankment built from the rubble excavated from the ditch. The Ring of Brodgar was connected to a second stone circle to the southeast by a stone causeway similar to that found at Durrington Walls near Stonehenge. This, however, was much longer—three quarters of a mile in all—and crossed over a narrow land bridge separating two lakes. This second circle, known as the Stones of Stenness, is just over 100 feet in diameter and is surrounded by a circular ditch 7 feet deep and 23 feet wide, with an accompanying outer embankment.

The circle originally consisted of twelve stones averaging around 15 feet high, of which, sadly, only four survive. And just outside this stone circle to the northwest there stands a further single 18-foot-high monolith called the Watch Stone. (The stones of the Brodgar and Stenness circles are straighter, more slender, and cut to a greater precision than those at Avebury and Stonehenge, having been made from a local form of sandstone that was much easier to work than the harder sarsen stone of the Marlborough Downs.) Like Stanton Drew in Somerset, the Mainland complex even had its own equivalent of Silbury Hill. Three quarters of a mile to the east of the Stenness circle is Maeshowe, an artificial mound some 25 feet high and 120 feet in diameter. Like Silbury, it is surrounded by a small ditch and bank; however, unlike Silbury, it was also used for burials.[7]

The megalithic people no doubt traveled back and forth across the twenty miles of sea separating Mainland, Orkney, from the northern tip of Scotland in the larger kind of boats they used to navigate rivers, such as the skin-hulled curraghs. Such boats also carried megalithic civilization over the Irish Sea to Ireland. Here, across seventy miles of open water from north Wales, we find exactly the same kind of megalithic monuments as in Britain, such as menhirs, dolmens, barrows, earthworks, and artificial hills, and of course the trademark of megalithic culture, the stone circles.

The main concentration of Ireland's megalithic remains can be found on the east coast of the central part of the country. Here, most of the monoliths are made from hard granite, and so tend to be around the same size as their counterparts in Cornwall. Typical is the stone circle at Broadleas in County Kildare, which is approximately 100 feet across and consists of thirty-nine stones averaging between 4 and 5 feet high. As in Cornwall, the solitary monoliths can be much larger; at Punchestown in County Kildare, for example, there is a standing stone 23 feet high. Some Irish stone circles are surrounded by henge earthworks, such as the Castleruddery Stone Circle in County Wicklow, although, once again, the granite bedrock made such constructions smaller than those in south-central England or the Orkney Isles. The 120-foot-diameter embankment at Castleruddery is 4 feet high, as opposed to Stonehenge's 6-foot bank or the 7-foot bank surrounding the Stones of Stenness. So similar, in fact, are the Irish megalithic complexes to their British counterparts that Ireland even had its own wood circles; in the 1960s archaeologists excavating at Knowth in County Meath discovered the remains of a wooden henge exactly like the Woodhenge monument near Stonehenge.[8]

There are hundreds of megalithic burial barrows in east-central Ireland, one of the oldest being Newgrange in County Meath. This 44-foot-high, grass-covered artificial hillock, around 250 feet in diameter and covering an area of more than an acre, is one of the largest megalithic burial mounds to be found anywhere. Like many of the long barrows of Britain, it was surrounded by a supporting wall, but on a much larger scale. It consisted of ninety-seven huge oblong granite stones laid horizontally and topped by a wall of white quartz. From the entrance, behind a line of twelve 10-foot-high standing stones, a 60-foot-long stone-lined passage leads to a cross-shaped chamber with a corbeled roof 20 feet high. Astonishingly, this chamber has remained not only intact, but also essentially waterproof, for over five thousand years.[9]

It was not only in Britain and Ireland that the megalithic culture flourished, but also across the English Channel in northwest France. Here, in the province of Brittany, there are some really vast monuments

Key locations in megalithic Ireland

of the period. Among the typical stone circles, menhirs, dolmens, henge and cursus earthworks, artificial hills, and burial barrows, there are some of the largest megalithic monuments of all. The tallest menhir in the British Isles is the Rudston Monolith, which is 25 feet high. Although it now lies fallen on the ground, a menhir in the Breton district of Locmariaker originally stood an astonishing 70 feet high. In fact, it is by far the tallest monolith from the entire megalithic age, and just how it was erected is an utter mystery. Brittany can also boast the largest number of standing stones for any single megalithic site. Near the village of Carnac, in southern Brittany, is a complex of dolmens, menhirs, stone circles, and stone rows totaling more than three thousand monoliths in all. At the heart of the complex are the remains of at least five stone circles connected by alignments of as many as thirteen rows of standing stones over 300 feet wide, which run for more than two miles through the countryside.[10]

All the megalithic monuments we have examined so far are only a sample of those that existed in Britain, Ireland, and northern France. There were many more complexes of such structures, interspersed with individual monuments such as solitary menhirs, dolmens, tumuli, and smaller isolated stone circles. They were the same kind of monuments that, for a culture without an infrastructure, beasts of burden, or sophisticated communications, were spread throughout a vast area. If we take Stonehenge as a point of reference, these are the sort of distances involved. The Land's End peninsula of Cornwall is 180 miles to the southwest; the Preseli Mountains are 135 miles to the west; Clwyd is 160 miles to the northwest; and the Gypsey Race of Yorkshire is 210 miles to the northeast. The Mainland complex of the Orkneys is 550 miles to the north and across 20 miles of storm-ridden sea; the megalithic monuments of east-central Ireland are 200 miles to the northwest and across a further 70 miles of sea; and the Carnac complex of Brittany is 300 miles to the south, and across yet another 50 miles of open water.

Some of the oldest megalithic monuments are found in Brittany, and so it seems that the megalithic culture was established here before spreading north into Britain and Ireland. The first of the megalithic constructions were the chambered burial barrows, which date from around 3500 BC and were pretty much the only significant monuments to be built for the next couple of centuries. The earliest of these are found in Brittany. Shortly after, the long barrows, such as the West Kennett Long Barrow and Wayland's Smithy, were built in south-central England.

They were followed in sequence by barrows progressively farther north and west, culminating with those at the tip of Scotland, such as a chambered tomb known as the Unstan Cairn at the Mainland complex on the Orkney Isles, and in Ireland with monuments such as Newgrange. It was once thought that from this point in history individual megalithic communities throughout France, Britain, and Ireland continued in relative isolation. If this theory were correct, however, each settlement, or local group of settlements, would either have developed along different lines or, at the very least, remained the same. But they didn't: the megalithic complexes throughout the area appear to have developed and been modified in parallel.

Around 3100 BC, when the Cursus was constructed at Stonehenge, other identical earthworks were built elsewhere in Britain, such as the linear earthworks at the Gypsey Race complex in Yorkshire. About a hundred years later, when the henge monument was constructed at Stonehenge, other henge monuments appeared throughout the megalithic world—as far north as the Mainland complex on the Orkneys and as far west as Castleruddery in Ireland. Then, around 2750 BC, the mysterious artificial hills were simultaneously constructed throughout the British Isles. For instance, at the same time as Silbury Hill was being built at Avebury, the Maes Knoll Tump was built at Stanton Drew, Gop Cairn was built in north Wales, and Maeshowe was built in the Orkneys. Although some individual stone circles date from earlier times, there was a synchronous mass building of these monuments around 2600 BC. At precisely the time that the first stone circle was erected inside the embankment at Stonehenge and the main circle was erected at Avebury, in Cornwall the Merry Maidens, in Scotland the Ring of Brodgar, and in Ireland the stone circle at Castleruddery were erected—and these are just a handful among hundreds.

There are many more examples of new types of monuments, similar building trends, or identical modifications to existing structures that occurred concurrently at megalithic complexes scattered all over Britain, Ireland, and northern France. Here are just a few. The addition of stone avenues to stone circles occurred simultaneously around 2400 BC; the

West Kennett and Beckhampton Avenues at Avebury, for instance, were built at the same time as the stone rows were added to the Stanton Drew stone circle in Somerset and to the Shovel Down stone circle in Devonshire. About 2000 BC, when Woodhenge was erected near Stonehenge, an almost identical monument was built at Knowth in Ireland; and the huge freestanding monoliths, such as the Rudston Monolith in Yorkshire, the Punchestown Menhir in County Kildare, and the Locmariaker Menhir in Brittany, all went up around the same time.

We have already estimated the vast number of people that would have had to be repeatedly mobilized for the periodic mass construction projects in south-central England. We can now see that this was only a small part of the overall picture. Other similar building projects were initiated concurrently throughout the country, and also in Scotland, Wales, Ireland, and Brittany. Again and again, a large portion of the megalithic population—perhaps as much as a third—was motivated into action and coordinated to complete these projects. There can be no doubt whatsoever that the entire megalithic culture was united for a period of two thousand years, something unique in the history of the area in which it flourished.

At the end of the Dark Ages, the Anglo-Saxons managed to unite only what is now England, and that lasted for a mere two centuries. The earlier Romans had done slightly better by ruling both England and Wales for three and a half centuries. Even at the height of the British Empire—in the nineteenth and early twentieth centuries, after England, Scotland, Wales, and Ireland were amalgamated into the United Kingdom—southern Ireland secured its independence after little more than a century. Somehow, without leaving any evidence of armies, infrastructure, or sophisticated communications, the megalithic civilization lasted longer than the Anglo-Saxons, the Roman Empire, and the British Empire combined. For the megalithic people to have repeatedly been mobilized en masse to work on their vast construction projects, surely someone or some group had to have been coordinating things. In other words, there had to have been some kind of central authority; but here lies yet another mystery.

In civilizations throughout the world and throughout history, central authority required a capital city or, at the very least, some kind of command center. Yet from the evidence they left behind for archaeologists to examine, there appears to have been no principal megalithic citadel, just individual settlements of roughly equivalent size. Indeed, few of these settlements even had the impressive monuments built within them. Some of the largest megalithic structures, such as Stonehenge, Avebury, Mainland, and Stanton Drew, were well outside the communities where their builders lived. It would appear, then, that living places had no political, ideological, or even religious significance.

Stranger still, although certain individuals seem to have enjoyed a higher status in society than others, as evidenced by their more elaborate tombs, there is no evidence that the megalithic civilization ever had an overall king or central government of any kind. Whatever it was that bound the megalithic people together and motivated so many of them to willingly share the long and arduous endeavors necessary to build their monuments, and to have done so repeatedly over a period of two thousand years, it does not appear to have been an expression of political power such as the impetus behind the building of the pyramids of Egypt or the Coliseum in Rome. Of course, military or political power is not the only kind of authority that can bind people together; there is also religion. So was it a common religious belief that cemented the fabric of megalithic culture?

The megalithic people may well have shared a religion, but a central religious authority seldom guarantees the kind of long-term harmony that the culture appears to have enjoyed. Indeed, a dominant religion can often be divisive. For centuries Christianity may have dominated Europe, but Europe has also been repeatedly divided by the bloodiest wars in history, many of these caused by the intolerance of the various factions of this same religion. For most of their history the nations of Islam have been similarly divided, while it was the inability of the Hindu kingdoms of India to live peacefully with one another that allowed the British to take over the entire county between 1757 and 1947.

But if it was not the power of the sword, politics, or even religion that kept the megalithic civilization together, what might it have been? If clues to this enigma do survive, they are in the form of the monuments the megalithic people left behind. Perhaps, as some believe, the megalithic monuments served some practical purpose. Maybe they were something else entirely. Whatever it was that so inspired the megalithic civilization for so long, after two millennia it all came to an abrupt end. Could its sudden demise have anything to do with the nature of the culture itself? Before we examine the tumultuous end of megalithic civilization, we should consider the riddle of why they erected such mysterious structures.

4
Enigma

IN THE POPULAR IMAGINATION, megalithic stone circles are often associated with the druids. The druids were the priests of the ancient Celts, and modern druids still perform their widely publicized ceremony at Stonehenge on the morning of the midsummer solstice, the longest day of the year, around June 21. Presumably, one might think, to solve the mystery of the megalithic monuments, we simply have to ask the druids. But the modern druids have no direct connection with the original Celtic druids, and the original druids did not arrive in Britain or France until the seventh century BC, almost a millennium after the megalithic culture came to an end. In fact, the Celts were not even indigenous to northwest Europe.

Today the name Celt is usually applied to Gaelic-speaking people such as the inhabitants of Ireland and Scotland, as it was in such outlying areas that Celtic culture endured the longest. Celtic culture, however, once extended throughout much of Europe. The Celts originated around what is now Austria and Hungary, from where they ultimately spread to dominate much of northwestern Europe through the use of iron. In the eighth century BC, most of Europe was still in the Bronze Age, meaning that the metal used for tools and weapons was bronze. Sometime around 750 BC, the Celts learned how to smelt iron, a much harder metal, and so entered the Iron Age. Anyone wielding iron rather than bronze weapons had a distinct advantage, and as such the Celts became the most powerful people anywhere in central or northern Europe.

Around 700 BC, a series of disastrous crop failures caused by prolonged and bitter winters brought famine to the Celts' homeland, forcing them to migrate to the north and west. The indigenous populations of these areas attempted to defend their native soil against the invaders, but with their inferior bronze weapons, they stood little chance. Within around half a century, the Celts came to occupy a large part of northwestern Europe, including France, Britain, and Ireland, and this era of Celtic supremacy lasted until the Romans conquered France in the mid-first century BC and Britain a century later. The Celts had no form of writing of their own, and it is therefore from the Romans that we know about the Celtic priesthood, the druids. Writers such as Julius Caesar tell us that their shrines were natural places, such as hallowed springs and lakes, and their temples were situated in groves of sacred oak trees. So how did the druids come to be associated with artificial stone monuments such as Stonehenge?[1]

Although some Roman writers, mystified by the stone circles in Britain and France, speculated that they had been built by the Celtic priests, the first writer in more recent times to connect the megalithic monuments with the druids was John Aubrey, the antiquarian who wrote about Stonehenge and Avebury in the seventeenth century. Aubrey had no direct evidence for such an assumption; he simply drew his conclusions from the brief references in old Roman works suggesting such a connection.[2] Nevertheless, Aubrey's speculations led to a scholarly fascination with the druids, so much so that in 1717 an Irishman named John Toland founded a new order of druids, calling it the Ancient druid Order, reconstructing rituals from what he could learn from Roman sources, and it was not long before these new druids began performing their ceremonies at Stonehenge. The man most responsible for popularizing the supposed link between the druids and megalithic sites was the eighteenth-century English antiquarian William Stukeley. His books, such as *Stonehenge: A Temple Restored to the British druids of 1740*, were best sellers of the time.[3]

Thanks to modern archaeology, we now know that the Celts did not arrive in what had once been the megalithic homeland until at least 850 years after the last megalithic monument had been built. This is a time span as long as that separating us today from the reign of the English king Richard the Lionheart, the period in which Hollywood has portrayed the story of Robin Hood. As for the first written accounts of life in this area, it was the Romans who brought writing to Britain and northwestern France, and that was fifteen hundred years after mega-lithic civilization ended. That is as long a period as that which separates us from the collapse of the Roman Empire itself. So there is not only no one who can tell us why the megalithic monuments were built; there is no ancient writing to consult on the matter either. It all comes down to guesswork, and in recent years many theories have been proposed.[4]

One of the most popular speculations concerning the megalithic people is that their stone circles were an ancient form of calendar. Many stone circles have single or small groups of other monoliths standing just outside the main ring. Over the years archaeologists have noticed how some of these stones, when viewed from the center of the circle, align with the rising and setting sun on specific days of the year. A good example is the Heel Stone at Stonehenge, which, although standing 80 feet outside the surrounding henge, was visible through the entrance gap in the embankment.

If you stand in the middle of Stonehenge on Midsummer morning, the sun is seen to rise directly over this monolith. It is reasoned that by observing such events the megalithic people would know exactly what day in the solar year it was; and as the year progressed, other specific dates could be determined by the sun rising between or above the stones of the circle itself.

This would have been extremely useful for knowing when to plant and harvest crops, anticipate the migration of animals, or perhaps cal-culate the days when seasonal rituals should be performed. Some stone circles, it has been suggested, even functioned as clocks. The single cen-tral monolith at the Boskawen-Un stone circle in Cornwall, for example, was erected at an angle, just like the gnomon (arm) of a sundial. Some scholars, noting that stones at various stone circles were oriented to the positions of certain stars at particular times of the year, have even sug-gested that stone circles were ancient observatories, perhaps necessary for astrological purposes. Others, however, put down such astronomical alignments to pure chance. With so many stars in the sky, they argue, you will always find stones that align with one or more of them.[5]

At one time the calendar and observatory theories even led to suggestions as to why the megalithic civilization ended so abruptly: climate change brought cloudier skies. With the stars and sun obscured for so much of the time, the megalithic monuments became essentially useless and were therefore abandoned. It is now known, however, that there was no such climate change at the time. The main argument against the stone circles ever being used as calendars or observatories is a simple and convincing one. If stone circles really were oriented to the positions of heavenly bodies, why would stone circles such as Avebury, Stanton Drew, and the Ring of Brodgar need to be so big? Regardless of whatever astronomical alignments might exist, the ancient calendar and observatory theories fail to account for so many other features of the megalithic complexes: the henge structures, stone avenues, artificial hills, and cursus embankments, to name just a few.

Over the last century a number of other, more fanciful theories have been proposed to explain the enigma of the megalithic monuments. One idea that gained considerable following in the 1950s was that the monuments were built by aliens. At the time, it was a mystery how prehistoric people could have moved and erected massive stones such as exist at Avebury and Stonehenge. But once archaeologists discovered how such monuments could have been built with the Stone Age technology of the time, the alien theory was discredited. Nonetheless, in the 1960s a new slant on the alien hypothesis followed the immensely popular books of writers such as Erich Von Daniken.[6] Von Daniken and others suggested that there was evidence—for example, in ancient temple carvings— showing that extraterrestrials had visited early civilizations. A number of authors, inspired by these "ancient astronaut" ideas, suggested that the megalithic people built their stone circles and accompanying monuments to represent alien technology, likening them to the so-called cargo cults of the twentieth century.

Certain tribes living in remote areas, such as the rain forests of South

America, were cut off from modern civilization until the mid-twentieth century. Consequently, they watched in amazement when foreign visitors used radios to talk to one another, fired guns that brought down game, and drove along in trucks and Jeeps. Having no understanding of technology, they decided that they could make such mysterious devices for themselves by simply copying their physical form. They made representations of walkie-talkies out of wickerwork with sticks for antennas, cut wood into the shape of rifles, and even made full-size models of road vehicles out of stone and clay. Of course, these devices didn't work, and so the tribal priests decided that the seemingly miraculous gadgets needed to be imbued with the power of the Westerners' gods. They came to the conclusion that the aircraft that brought the wondrous cargo to the foreigners were either the gods themselves or the exotic birds on which they flew.

To venerate these gods in the hope of securing their favor, the tribesman went to extraordinary lengths to make full-size models of airplanes in clearings in the forest, and even cut runways and built huge wooden huts in the form of aircraft hangars in the hope that the gods would land for them. The building of such mock-ups of modern technology by previously isolated groups occurred independently around the world, not only in South America but also on the Pacific Islands and in Southeast Asia, and the groups that adopted such practices came to be known as cargo cults.[7]

In the 1960s, various authors proposed that the megalithic culture had been nothing less than an ancient cargo cult. At the time, the subject of UFOs was taken quite seriously; the U.S. Air Force even had a department called Project Blue Book to investigate reports of flying saucers. One British author, John Michell, in his book *The Flying Saucer Vision,* published in 1967, drew attention to the remarkable similarity between the kind of disk-shaped UFOs that were being reported and the appearance of Stonehenge. Stonehenge's outer embankment, he suggested, could delineate the flying saucer's disk, the main stone circle was the central cockpit, and the rings of holes, such as the Aubrey Holes, could be the portholes.[8] Others followed suit, and it soon became a popular notion that all stone circles represented UFOs. It was also suggested that that stone circles' accompanying avenues represented runways, and the huge earthworks such as the cursus monuments represented UFO hangars. It was proposed that, similarly to the cargo cults of the twentieth century, the megalithic people had tried to emulate the technology of the aliens that were visiting Earth. Some even went so far as to propose that the megalithic civilization came to an abrupt end because the aliens who inspired it, and presumably also kept the peace, finally left Earth.

As fascinating as such theories were, they depended on the reality of UFOs and on the possibility that such craft really had visited Earth in the distant past. Both notions were, of course, ridiculed by archaeologists. What, they asked, would an advanced spacefaring civilization need with runways and hangars, and where is the physical evidence that such alien structure ever existed at all? The subject of whether or not UFOs are real, or whether ancient civilizations were visited by aliens, will no doubt be argued about for years to come. Whatever the truth concerning this subject, it does seem highly unlikely that the megalithic monuments were inspired by extraterrestrials.

To begin with, the fact that Stonehenge resembles the popular image of a UFO, and that its avenue resembles a runway or the surrounding earthworks hangars, has to be pure coincidence. It is now known that the Stonehenge megalithic complex was built over an immense period of time. The Cursus was constructed around 3100 BC; the henge and Aubrey Holes a hundred years later; the stone circle four centuries later, around 2600 BC; and the Avenue three hundred years after that. If Stonehenge was meant to resemble a flying saucer, it took centuries of periodic construction work to finally get around to it. Indeed, it is the great length of time over which the megalithic monuments were built that works against the cargo cult theory.

The twentieth-century cargo cults lasted only for a few months, or a year or two at most. Once the isolated tribes realized that their mock-ups weren't going to work, they gave up on them. The megalithic people, on the other hand, continued to build their monuments for two thousand years. If they were a cargo cult, they were a particularly stupid one, and all the evidence suggests that the megalithic people were far from stupid. Their ability to coordinate massive workforces and the ingenuity shown in moving and erecting gigantic stones testify to this.

Another unorthodox theory concerning the megalithic monuments that did at one time appeal to some archaeologists is the notion of ley lines. Ley lines are said to be alignments of megalithic sites that stretch for miles across the landscape. Avebury, for example, is said to have been connected to Stonehenge, twenty miles away, by a straight line of other megalithic monuments such as solitary monoliths, individual tumuli, and linear earthworks. The concept of such alignment was first proposed by an Englishman named Alfred Watkins in the 1920s. While traveling the countryside around his home in the county of Hereford-shire, he concluded that many of the megalithic monuments he came across in the area actually lined up. He examined maps of other regions of Britain to see if the same thing occurred elsewhere and decided that it did. Watkins coined the term *ley lines* for these supposed alignments because of the frequency in which the suffix "ley" appeared in place names along them, such as Crossley, Endley, and Longley. In 1925 he published his book *The Old Straight Track,* in which he reasoned that ley lines were ancient pathways or trade routes marked out by monuments in the distant past.[9]

Although one or two archaeologists did take Watkins seriously, most were scornful of his ideas. Why, they asked, if such ancient trackways existed, were they marked out by such huge monuments as henge circles, massive earthworks, and artificial hills, when simple stone markers would have sufficed? More damaging to Watkins's theory was that many of his proposed ley lines passed directly through obstacles such as mountains and marshes, and even across river estuaries, rather than around them, which would surely have been the case if they were really trackways.

Such scholarly criticism meant that Watkins's theories were virtually forgotten for decades. But then, in the 1960s, New Age authors conceived the idea that Watkins's ley lines were not trackways at all but conduits of mystical "earth energy." Chief among them was writer

John Michell, the same man who had likened Stonehenge to a UFO. In his book *The View over Atlantis,* published in 1969, Michell suggested that the ley lines were similar to the dragon lines of China.[10] The ancient Chinese believed in geomancy, the idea that streams of life-giving energy flowed through the earth, and that by building shrines and temples at certain places along these lines, this energy could be tapped. It could be used, for example, for inducing spiritual harmony and mystical experiences, aiding in healing, and generally bringing good fortune to the community as a whole. Along these dragon lines, so called because in China the dragon was a symbol for the universal life force, there were not only religious buildings but also the tombs of those hoping for greater power in the afterlife.

The New Age authors proposed that, just as the Chinese had built temples, shrines, and tombs along dragon lines, the megalithic people had erected stone circles, earthworks, and barrows along similar lines of earth energy in Europe. Ley lines delineating life-force channels, rather than being trackways, it was argued, also accounted for why they ran in straight lines over natural obstacles such as mountains and estuaries. The new ley line theory went something like this: The megalithic people discovered the existence of these lines of earth energy by dowsing, or some similar practice, and marked out their course by small monuments, such as tumuli, dolmens, and single monoliths, and built larger structures, such as stone circles and earthworks, where they crossed. One extension of the New Age ley line theory is that the megalithic civilization came to an abrupt end because, like some kind of mystic oil reserve, the earth energy they were using ultimately ran out.

For the last few decades, enthusiasts have plotted the supposed course of ley lines, of which there are said to exist hundreds all over Britain, Ireland, and France, and today there are books, pamphlets, magazines, and Web sites devoted to the subject of "ley hunting," as it is called. Needless to say, few archaeologists have taken such notions any more seriously than they took Watkins's original theory of ancient trackways. After all, they object, there is no scientific evidence whatsoever that such earth energies exist, only the word of dowsers, psychics, and mystics who claim to feel or channel it. Whether such earth energies exist is actually beside the point, however. The important thing is this: Did the megalithic people believe in them? The ancient Chinese certainly did. A more serious objection, though, concerns whether such megalithic alignments exist at all.

To prove that the megalithic people really did erect their structures along deliberately planned straight lines, you need to show that the number of monuments along a proposed ley line is more than would be expected by chance. Skeptics have pointed out that even the most famous ley lines, such as the so-called Saint Michael Line, said to run from the Saint Michael's Mount at the Land's End peninsula of Cornwall for over 350 miles to England's eastern coast, not only are delineated by megalithic monuments but also include later Celtic remains such as holy wells, the sites of Roman temples, and even medieval structures such as churches. Take away these later sites, they maintain, and you are left with no more megalithic monuments along these supposed ley lines than would be expected by chance alone.

Ley hunters counter such objections by drawing attention to the fact that when one culture is supplanted by another, its sacred sites often continue to be venerated by those who follow. The Romans, for instance, made a point of building their temples on sites sacred to earlier Celtic gods; the Catholic Church followed suit. In Britain, for instance, sites that were considered sacred to earlier pagan gods were reconsecrated to equivalent Christian saints, and churches were built on them.

The tallest megalithic stone in Britain, Rudston Monolith in Yorkshire, stands in a churchyard. Another example often cited is a megalithic mound called Old Sarum, around nine miles south of Stonehenge. This was later used by the Celts as a fortified camp, the Romans and Anglo-Saxons both built defensive earthworks around it, and in the Middle Ages it became the site of a cathedral. As such, it is argued, the sites of later cultures along ley lines were originally megalithic sites that were subsequently used by the Celts, Romans, Anglo-Saxons, and Christians.

The problem, however, is determining if a particular church, holy well, or Roman temple really was constructed on the site of an original megalithic monument. Although obvious examples such as the Rudston Monolith and the Old Sarum mound can be cited, without extensive archaeology it is impossible to know whether the majority of the post-megalithic sites that delineate ley lines really were megalithic in origin. Eventually, in the mid-1970s, archaeologists used computers to prove to their satisfaction that, even when including post-megalithic sacred sites, ley lines comprised nothing more than random alignments.

Using the same parameters as enthusiasts had used to plot ley lines (the number of points along a straight line of a certain length that was deemed to be above chance—say, five or six over twenty miles), the number of sites of various areas were fed into a computer program that was instructed to produce alignments of these points by chance alone. Evidently, the computers came up with far more alignments than the ley hunters had discovered for themselves.

Although archaeologists held that they had statistically disproved the existence of ley lines, many New Age devotees refused to abandon the notion. In fact, ley hunting got its third wind in 1978, after the publication of *Needles of Stone* by British author Tom Graves.[11] Graves revived the theory linking ley lines with Chinese dragon lines by drawing parallels between geomancy and acupuncture. Graves proposed that the megalithic people inserted monoliths into the ground to channel earth energy to selected locations, in much the way that acupuncturists direct what they believe to be the human life force to specific parts of the body by inserting needles into the skin. As such, earth energy could be diverted and rechanneled through the landscape to chosen places such as temples and settlements. It followed, therefore, that ley lines did not necessarily need to follow a straight course. Accordingly, the fact that alignments had been statistically disproved was irrelevant: ley lines could meander in whatever pattern the ancients desired.

Once again, whether such geomantic energy really exists, or whether acupuncture is a genuine phenomenon, is beside the point. It could have been what the megalithic people believed. The problem with the idea that ley lines could zigzag in any direction, however, makes it impossible to prove their existence statistically. Moreover, apart from the conviction of dowsers and psychics, what solid evidence is there that megalithic people ever did conceive the notion of earth energy currents?

So far, both archaeology and the alternative theories have failed to explain convincingly the purpose behind the megalithic monuments. Perhaps we shall never know why these structures were built. There is, though, the possibility that their secrets were preserved in folklore. After their culture collapsed, the megalithic people's descendants could have retained some knowledge of their earlier culture in the form of legend. When the Celts arrived in northwest Europe around 700 BC, the descendants of megalithic people still inhabited the area, and from them the newcomers might have heard such legends and incorporated them into their own mythology. Something similar has happened many times throughout history. For example, after the Romans incorporated Germanic mercenaries into their army during the later empire, they adopted much of their mythology, and when the Romans became Christians in the fourth century AD, Christianity absorbed much of this earlier pagan mythology. Even today, many pagan elements exist in Christianity.

Immediately before Emperor Constantine the Great made Christianity the state religion of the Roman Empire in AD 325, the chief Roman deity had been the sun god Sol Invictus, and the new Roman Christianity retained many of the traditions associated with this god but attached them to Jesus. The Bible does not reveal when during the year Jesus was born, and so the Roman Catholic Church made the formal mass to celebrate Christ's birth (Christ Mass—Christmas) coincide with the pagan ceremony to mark the birth of the Roman sun god on December 25. Like the Jews, the early Christians celebrated their weekly holy day on a Saturday, but the Roman Church changed it to what had been the sacred day of the sun god, Sun Day, which is why it is called Sunday even now.

One of the chief deities of the Germanic peoples of northern Europe was the moon and fertility goddess Eostre. A ceremony to celebrate her annual resurrection, symbolizing the rebirth of summer, was held each year on the first full moon after the pagan New Year's Day on the spring equinox around March 21. The Roman Church decided to incorporate this day into its own religious calendar and made it the annual festival to celebrate the rebirth—the Resurrection—of Christ. The date of the festival was calculated in exactly the same way as the pagans had calculated their original festival, the only difference being that it was held on the first Sunday after the first full moon following the equinox. In fact, the very name of this event, Easter, comes directly from the name of the goddess associated with the earlier pagan ceremony, Eostre.

Even some of the customs associated with these festivals that survive today have pre-Christian origins. The Christmas tree comes from the Germanic tradition of celebrating midwinter by bringing a conifer tree, sacred to the sun god, indoors; mistletoe comes from a similar Celtic tradition; and Easter eggs come from another Germanic rite, of hatching sacred dove eggs to represent the rebirth of Eostre. These are just a few examples among many, so it is quite possible that when the Celts spread into northwest Europe, they incorporated indigenous mythology into their own. Legendary accounts concerning the megalithic monuments could have become assimilated into Celtic legend and thereafter passed down in the form of local folklore. Indeed, there are some excellent examples where just such a scenario must have occurred.[12]

Astonishingly, after so long, local folklore does appear to have preserved at least some secrets from the megalithic age. A local legend attached to Rillaton Barrow, on Bodmin Moor near the Hurlers in Cornwall, told of a mysterious holy man who would appear from the ancient burial mound to help travelers lost on the moor by offering them a drink from a golden chalice. The legend is known to have existed in the seventeenth century, yet it was not until 1837 that the mound was excavated and a gold cup was found that had lain buried with the tomb's occupant for over thirty-five hundred years.[13] Another, similar legend was attached to the burial mound of Bryn yr Ellyllon in north Wales. A folktale recorded as early as the Middle Ages told of a man in golden armor who would appear on the mound when the Welsh were threatened by invasion.

It was not until 1833 that the male skeleton buried with the four-thousand-year-old golden collar and shoulder adornment known as the Mold Cape was discovered here.[14] Along with the Rillaton Cup, the Mold Cape is now on display at the British Museum; although it probably formed part of priestly or ceremonial attire, it does look remarkably like armor. There can be little doubt that the knowledge of what these burial sites contained was handed down from generation to generation until it became a folktale. Could similar folklore preserve secrets of other megalithic monuments, perhaps even the reason they were erected?

Such a legend certainly seems to have developed concerning the Heel Stone at Stonehenge. The stone gets its unusual name because for centuries it was called the Friar's Heel, from the legend holding that this huge stone was hurled by the devil at a local friar, hitting him on the heel. In the original pronunciation, however, the stone's name was Freya Seal, which was simply old Celtic for "day of the sun." It seems that the stone was originally named after its association with the midsummer sunrise and then corrupted over time into English as Friar's Heel, and at some point the story of the devil and the friar was concocted to account for this seemingly incongruous name.

At megalithic sites throughout Britain, Ireland, and France there are remarkably similar folktales concerning people being turned to stone. The Merry Maidens stone circle in Cornwall is named after local folklore that tells how the megaliths were girls turned to stone for the sin of dancing on a Sunday, while the nearby freestanding monoliths are known as the Pipers, as they are said to have been men who played the music while the maidens danced. A similar Cornish legend concerns the so-called Dancing Stones, another megalithic stone circle near the town of St. Just, and yet another at a stone circle at Boskednan called the Nine Maidens. Other Cornish stone circle folktales concern men being petrified, such as the Hurlers triple stone circle on Bodmin Moor, which is said to be men turned to stone for profaning the Lord's Day by playing a ball game known as hurling.

All across Britain we find similar legends attached to stone circles, such as the Stanton Drew stone circle, which is said to be a wedding party turned to stone for merrymaking on a Sunday; and Stonehenge, once known as the Giants' Dance, as the monoliths were said to be giant men turned to stone. In Ireland, too, almost identical folklore survives. For instance, a stone circle at Athgreany in County Wicklow is known as the Pipers Stones, after a local legend that tells of a group of merry-makers dancing to a piper's tune on a Sunday when God turned them to stone; and the Broadleas stone circle in County Kildare is known locally at the Dancing Maidens. Even the massive stone rows at Carnac, in Brittany, are said to have been a Roman legion turned to stone when they danced to celebrate their victory over the local Celts.[15]

Like the Heel Stone at Stonehenge, these astonishingly similar legends might be due to mistranslations of the Celtic language. The legends of megalithic standing stones being petrified maidens almost certainly derived from a confusion of two Celtic words. The old Celtic word for a monolith was *menhir,* which simply means "long stone"; the very similar word *meinir,* which is still preserved in modern Welsh, means "maiden." Later English speakers probably confused the two words and assumed the stones were called maidens, and the subsequent folktales evolved. Something similar probably inspired the legends of men being turned to stone, such as the folklore surrounding the Hurlers. The Celtic word for stone was *maen,* pronounced "men," as it appears in the word *menhir.* Those who later heard the Celts refer to standing stones by this name might have assumed the local people thought the monoliths were men turned to stone.

A common theme in these folktales is that the individuals were turned to stone on a Sunday. As we have seen, the Celtic Freya Seal meant "day of the sun." With the coming of Christianity, the same words, rendered as Freyaseal, became the Celtic name for Sunday. This could mean that megalithic stones in general were associated with the sun in Celtic folklore, possibly suggesting that the stone circles were originally connected with sun worship. Maybe, rather than representing UFOs, as was suggested in the 1960s, the megalithic stone rings actually represent the sun. One of the most interesting aspects of these folktales is the recurring theme of dancing, the crime for which the perpetrators were turned to stone. Might this have been a common legend derived from the true fate of the megalithic people?

This recurring theme might be explained by examining the legend of the Giants' Dance at Stonehenge. The earliest references to Stonehenge by this name are found in Brythonic writings. Brythonic was the British language that developed as a hybrid between Gaelic, the original Celtic language, and the Latin of the Roman conquerors; this hybrid later developed into Welsh. In Brythonic works, Stonehenge was referred to as Cawr Dawns, which is more accurately translated as "giant dance" (singular, with no apostrophe). But those who committed such Brythonic phrases to writing were Latin-speaking monks.

It is possible they misinterpreted the term Cawdd Dawn. Roughly translated as "the gift of wrath," it was the name recorded by the Romans for a state of frenzy into which Celtic warriors would rouse themselves before battle. Interestingly, this Cawdd Dawn ceremony did involve ritual dancing. Perhaps the legend that dancing brought about the fate of those petrified at stone circles actually derived from an original tradition that the peaceful megalithic civilization was brought to an end by the sudden onset of the violent behavior suggested by the archaeological evidence.

Unfortunately, all the theories that have so far emerged concerning the purpose of the megalithic monuments and the mysterious fate of those who erected them are ultimately guesswork. To have any hope of discovering the truth about the end of the megalithic civilization, we need to take a closer look at what archaeology, applying the latest scientific techniques, has revealed about its demise.

5
Mass Aggression

BEFORE WE EXAMINE the violent end of the megalithic civilization, we need to appreciate just how intrinsically nonviolent it had previously been. One of the most remarkable aspects of the culture is that during its two-thousand-year history, it absorbed a number of different ethnic groups that continued to coexist peacefully for century after century. The infusion of these peoples has led archaeologists to divide the megalithic culture into three subphases: the Windmill Hill, Beaker, and Wessex periods. Nevertheless, throughout these periods, the same lifestyle and monument-building traditions not only endured but also were invigorated by the influx of these new migrants.

In Britain and Ireland, those who built the earliest megalithic structures, the chambered burial mounds, from around 3500 BC included both the descendants of those who had been living here since the end of the last ice age, around ten thousand years ago, and immigrants from northern France. It was, in fact, the people of Brittany who appear to have inspired the British and Irish to start building such tombs. This original phase of megalithic society is known the Windmill Hill period, named after the first of their settlements to be excavated in the Windmill Hill area near Avebury in the 1920s. The term can be rather misleading, as it suggests that the culture was local only to south-central England. It spread throughout the British Isles, however, as far north as the Orkney Isles of Scotland, as far west as the Land's End peninsula of Cornwall, and across the sea to Ireland.

The Windmill Hill period, from approximately 3500 to 2700 BC, is also when the first mysterious earthworks were constructed, such as causewayed enclosures, cursus embankments, and henge monuments, and when the first stone circles were erected and the huge artificial hills such as Silbury were built. Throughout Britain, Ireland, and northern France, this single culture constructed the same kind of monuments with the same innovations simultaneously during this entire period. For instance, three of the largest megalithic complexes in the British Isles, Avebury in Wiltshire, Stanton Drew in Somerset, and Brodgar-Stenness in the Orkneys, developed in tandem: the henge, followed in turn by the smaller stone circles and the artificial hills. In fact, so similar are these three complexes that they could have been planned by the same architects.

The megalithic people of the Windmill Hill period also followed the same funerary customs throughout Britain, Ireland, and northern France. The dead were interred communally, generation after generation, in stone-lined chambers at the heart of large burial mounds accessed by a single passageway, its entrance sealed with a huge slab. This practice, which originated in Brittany, is found throughout Britain and Ireland—for instance, at the Newgrange mound in County Meath, Maeshowe in the Orkneys, and the Ballowall Barrow in Cornwall.[1] A typical example is the West Kennett Long Barrow near Avebury. Excavations here discovered some forty-six bodies that had been interred over a period of around a thousand years. These barrows have also been referred to as temple tombs, because it seems that some kind of ancestor worship was practiced here. Skeletons in these burial mounds are often missing a long bone, such as the femur, and these individual human bones have been found at nearby causewayed enclosures. It is thought that the barrows were periodically opened and these bones removed for ceremonial purposes.[2]

Throughout the Windmill Hill period, the megalithic people lived in the same unusual manner. Generally, as civilizations persist, communities tend to grow; settlements become progressively larger, townships or cities develop, and temples and places of ritual observance are built within the confines of such communities. Megalithic settlements, in contrast, remained small, averaging between one hundred and three hundred people—which is strange, considering the mammoth construction projects that continually brought them together en masse. Even in the most densely populated areas, such as Salisbury Plain around Stonehenge, concentrations of smaller, separate villages existed rather than larger towns.

More puzzling still is that megalithic monuments, such as stone circles and earthworks, were exclusively constructed away from settlements. Dwellings, built of timber, stone, or both, were often set in pits with only the roof or upper part of a building above ground level; such earth-sheltering techniques provided excellent insulation against both cold and heat. In these small villages the megalithic people raised sheep, cattle, and pigs, domesticated dogs, and, in the surrounding fields, grew crops such as wheat, barley, rye, oats, and beans. During the Windmill Hill period, the same kind of tools were fashioned by communities located throughout Britain, Ireland, and northern France. For instance, stone axes and knives were made to a conventional form, and arrowheads had the same leaf-shaped design. The period's pottery was also of a collective style: vessels had lug handles (a kind of flattened knob) and rounded bottoms, and were decorated with a characteristic grooved patterning just below the rim.[3]

The best-preserved megalithic village to be seen anywhere is at Skara Brae on the west coast of Mainland in the Orkney Isles, and here we are provided with a unique insight into the daily life of the times. Radiocarbon dating has shown the village to have been occupied for about a thousand years, until 2200 BC, when it was buried by a freak sandstorm. Like a miniature Pompeii, the Roman city buried beneath the volcanic ash of Mount Vesuvius in AD 79, Skara Brae remained almost perfectly preserved until another freak storm uncovered the ruins in 1850. Astonishingly, not only the buildings but also their furnishings remained just as they were left when the village was abandoned over four thousand years ago.[4]

Skara Brae was a settlement of eight similar dwellings, built largely below ground level, linked by a series of stone-lined trenches that served as alleyways. The roofs of these dwellings were originally thatched and covered with turf, while the interconnected passageways were covered with stone slabs. Each house, averaging around 130 square feet in size, consisted of a large square room with rounded internal corners lined with drystone (uncemented) walls. The houses had central fireplaces, and around the walls there were rectangular niches that served as cupboards, as well as additional stone shelving where pottery and other household utensils were stored. There were also stone dressers, benches, and box beds set into the walls, which would have been filled with straw or heather mattresses and covered by blankets of sheep- or deerskin. The village even had a sophisticated drainage system of shallow stone-lined trenches linked to an area of each dwelling that may have functioned as an early form of toilet facility.

One of the eight houses was set out to a different plan and was divided into separate cubicles. It is thought that this building served as a workshop where tools such as bone needles were made. The village is estimated to have been inhabited by between fifty and one hundred people at any given time, and was just one of a number of similar-sized megalithic settlements on the island.

The social arrangement of megalithic life on the Orkney Isles is typical of that found in Britain, Ireland, and northern France. People lived in small villages scattered throughout the area and were formed from family groups, or they might even have been communes. Although they lived in separate communities, the people of the Orkneys came together to build and utilize—for whatever purpose—their local concentration of megalithic monuments. Together with their neighbors, the inhabitants of Skara Brae were the people who built the monuments of the Brodgar-Stenness stone circle complex five miles to the southeast. These were not only built to the same style as monuments throughout the megalithic world, but they were also constructed in the same contemporary stages. Moreover, the local people would have required the help of communities elsewhere to have raised these monuments. A specific caste must have been established to orchestrate such activities nationally, and one theory is that some manner of wandering priesthood, living outside daily routine, coordinated megalithic society as a whole—perhaps something similar to the social role of Buddhist monks in more recent Tibet.

Around 2700 BC, new immigrants began to arrive in France and then Britain from what is now Spain. These were the Beaker People, named after their distinctive inverted bell-shaped drinking cups. Their pottery was generally more elaborate than what is found at earlier megalithic sites; it took the form of what has been called corded ware, bowls of vessels decorated by a series of lateral rings. Until this point, the megalithic culture had remained firmly in the Stone Age, but the Beaker People had developed metalworking and made utensils from copper and ornaments from gold. By 2600 BC, these technologically superior people had spread across Britain and Ireland and could easily have supplanted the native culture—but the very opposite occurred.

The Beaker People were not only integrated into the indigenous culture; they also worked alongside its people to bring a vibrant new phase to megalithic civilization. Not only did their additional manpower and expertise help make existing megalithic monuments more elaborate, but new and much larger structures were built as well. The first stone circle was built at Stonehenge, and nearby the massive new henge monument was built at Durrington Walls. At Avebury, too, the colossal outer circle was erected around the existing smaller rings, and the gigantic henge was constructed outside that. In fact, much larger stone circles were erected everywhere, such as Stanton Drew in western England, the Ring of Brodgar in Scotland, and the Castleruddery stone circle in Ireland. But it didn't end there: a couple of centuries later, this same unified culture added stone avenues to existing stone circles, such as Avebury and Stanton Drew, and built causeways such as those at Durrington Walls and that linking the Ring of Brodgar to the Stones of Stenness. What might so easily have been a violent clash of cultures was a peaceful amalgamation: the megalithic people learned metallurgy from the newcomers, but the newcomers adopted megalithic beliefs and lifestyle.

Around 2100 BC, Britain and Ireland saw the influx of yet another people, this time from what is now Germany. Because they first settled in south-central England, an area later known as Wessex, they have somewhat misleadingly been termed the Wessex Culture. Technologically, they were far in advance of the megalithic civilization of the time, in that they had learned to smelt copper and tin to cast bronze, a much harder alloy than either tin or copper alone. As we have seen, the metallurgical skills of the Beaker People could have led to their culture supplanting the megalithic culture, but the Wessex People, with their far superior Bronze Age technology, could have completely swamped it. Copper and tin alone are of little use in fashioning weapons of war, but bronze is an entirely different matter. Just as the later Iron Age Celts easily overwhelmed the Bronze Age cultures of northwest Europe, the Bronze Age Wessex Culture could readily have conquered the megalithic people of the British Isles. But they didn't. Instead, they settled as peacefully alongside them as had the Beaker People.

Once again, the newcomers not only adopted megalithic culture, but their more sophisticated building techniques also enabled innovative modifications to existing megalithic monuments. The Sarsen Circle and Trilithon Horseshoe, with their impressive lintels, were erected at Stonehenge, and new stone circles, such as the northern circle at Stanton Drew and the Sanctuary at Avebury, were built. Additionally, more sophisticated Woodhenge-type structures were erected as far apart as Wiltshire, Cornwall, Scotland, and Ireland. Interestingly, bronze tools do not appear to have been employed in the construction of the more elaborate stone monuments, the archaeological evidence indicating that the same old antler picks, stone axes, and cattle-bone shovels were used. It may be that some manner of ritual tradition was being observed. Nonetheless, it seems to have been the Wessex Culture's more advanced construction techniques that made it possible to hoist the lintel blocks on top of the upright monoliths at Stonehenge.[5]

Twice the megalithic civilization, originally itself consisting of two separate ethnic groups, absorbed a mass influx of other, more technologically advanced peoples. This brought more sophistication to various aspects of life, such as farming, building, and the manufacture of work implements and household utensils, but the culture itself endured. Settlements continued to exist as collections of small, separate villages—a mode of living that the immigrants themselves adopted—and exactly the same monuments were revered. Whatever belief system inspired such a lifestyle, the construction of the megalithic monuments, and the periodic mass mobilization of workforces, it was readily embraced by both the Beaker People and the Wessex Culture. We can only assume that, whatever this was, it must have been pretty persuasive. The most remarkable thing of all is that throughout this entire two-thousand-year period, there is no evidence whatsoever of internal feuding, ethnic conflict, or organized violence of any kind.

There is a saying that absence of evidence is not evidence of absence. This old adage may hold true for some scenarios, but when warfare occurs, because of its destructive nature, it cannot help but leave behind evidence; and if none is found, we can be fairly certain that it did not occur. Warring requires weapons of war, but the weapons of the megalithic era never developed beyond what was suitable for hunting, even after the coming of bronze. For example, bows were short and never evolved into the taller, longer-range bows necessary for shooting at targets that could shoot back; knives never evolved into swords; and maces and battle-axes never evolved at all. Indeed, the precise opposite occurred in the case of the Wessex Culture: The bronze swords they had made in their homeland of Germany were quickly abandoned once they settled in Britain.

Warfare also leaves behind casualties, and no large numbers of simultaneous burials have yet been found; it also leads to wounds, and no skeletons from the megalithic period have been found with the kind of smashed skulls or crushed and lacerated bones that would be evident following death in battle. Battles themselves require warlords, but the megalithic civilization appears to have had no warrior elite. The West Kennett Long Barrow is the largest megalithic tomb in the Avebury area and was used for an entire millennium. The generations after generations who were buried here must have been the community leaders and their immediate families.

The same goes for the largest burial mounds within other megalithic complexes elsewhere, such as Newgrange in Ireland, Maeshowe in the

Orkneys, and the Ballowall Barrow in Cornwall. In none of these tombs do we find evidence that these rulers were warlike. It is not only that the bones exhibit no battle scars but also there are none of the usual funerary trappings normally associated with a warrior class. Although many of these bodies were interred with grave goods like pottery jars, bowls and cups, gold or copper buckles and bracelets, necklaces of various semiprecious stones, and bone pendants, ornaments, and dress pins, none of them was buried with weapons. Knives and daggers were sometimes included among the grave goods, but these were simply tools for daily use such as skinning animals or cutting meat.[6]

Even if the megalithic people participated in disorganized conflicts, and fought with totally unsuitable arms, and somehow disposed of their war dead in places not yet discovered—all of which seems highly unlikely—their battlefields would be revealed by fallen and broken weapons. Yet no such evidence of contemporary battles has been found around any megalithic settlement yet excavated. The fact that these settlements lacked any kind of fortification shows that they survived without their inhabitants ever having to defend themselves. Although the people were quite capable of building huge earthworks, they never built defensive ramparts around their settlements. Circular ditches and banks were built around megalithic monuments, but these henge structures were completely unusable for defensive purposes: not only were they impractically large, but they also had too many entrances and often had the ditch on the wrong side; excavations have discovered no telltale evidence that the megalithic people built stockades along the embankments.

If the megalithic civilization had ever waged civil, tribal, or international conflicts, then its people would have been well capable of building moats, defensive ramparts, and stockades around their settlements—but they never did. The very fact that the megalithic people continued to live in small villages, rather than band together for protection in numbers, is evidence in its own right that they never lived in fear of conflict. None of this is to say that no one ever raised a hand in anger or killed a neighbor with malice aforethought, but what can be said with certainty is that they never fought with one another or against anyone else in collective warfare.

But then, after two thousand years of peace, everything suddenly changed.

Somewhere around the year 1500 BC, give or take fifty years for the accuracy of radiocarbon dating, the last of the megalithic monuments was built. It wasn't that the monuments gradually fell into disuse; construction abruptly ceased. Right up until this time, megalithic building projects had continued as they had for two millennia. For instance, the last work that took place at Stonehenge at this time was a major piece of engineering, when the Bluestone Circle and the Bluestone Oval were erected, and at the Brodgar-Stenness complex in the Orkneys four huge tumuli were built. Henge monuments were still being constructed right up until this time, such as Arbor Low in the county of Derbyshire in north-central England; and entirely new megalithic complexes were raised, such as the Barbrook complex, also in Derbyshire, which included three stone circles, accompanying earthworks, and additional freestanding monoliths. It wasn't just that megalithic monuments were no longer being built, they also were no longer being used: animal bones found at megalithic sites, evidence of ritual feasting, are not found after around 1500 BC.[7]

This sudden cessation of monument building was also accompanied by a simultaneous change of lifestyle. For centuries the megalithic people had lived in small villages that lacked any recognizable form of defense. At exactly the same time as construction of megalithic monuments ceased, stone walls began to be built around settlements throughout the British Isles: for example, in southwest England at Ryder's Rings and Legis Tor on Dartmoor; in northern England at Mam Tor in Derbyshire and at Grassington in Yorkshire; and in Scotland at Traprain Law in the county of East Lothian and at Jarlshof on the Shetland Isles. At some settlements more elaborate defenses were constructed, such as at Thorney Down, fifteen miles to the south of Stonehenge, where a rectangular enclosure bounded by a bank and outer ditch was constructed around a settlement of nine dwellings. At other sites throughout Britain and Ireland, archaeologists have found the remains of postholes used for timber stockades dating from this period, such as Staple Howe in the county of Yorkshire in northern England, Navan in County Armagh in Ireland, and Craigmarloch Wood in the county of Renfrewshire in Scotland.

But this was just the beginning; settlements quickly became larger. The clusters of villages of around one to two hundred inhabitants amalgamated into much more substantial settlements, and the old close-knit communities of between ten and twenty dwellings grew into townships of hundreds of dwellings surrounded by defensive ramparts. In fact, in many areas the lowland settlements were abandoned altogether in favor of more readily defendable hilltop sites where forts could be constructed. These new settlements were surrounded by rings of embankments and external ditches that, unlike the earlier henge monuments and causewayed enclosures, were clearly fortifications. They had single, narrower entrances, and excavations have revealed that timber palisades were erected along the embankments and wooden gates were constructed at the entrances.

Such hillforts, as they are called, are found scattered all over the British Isles—at Castle Hill near the village of Little Wittenham in the county of Oxfordshire in southern England; at Mam Tor in the Peak District Hills of Derbyshire in central England; at Cannington Camp in the county of Somerset in western England; and on Beacon Hill near the village of Burghclere in the county of Hampshire in southeast England, among others.[8] Exactly the same hillforts were also built in Scotland: at Eildon Hill near Melrose in the region of Scottish Borders, and at Traprain Law, a hill near Haddington in the county of East Lothian.

On average, these hillforts covered around twelve acres and were occupied by between two and three thousand people, but some, such as Eildon Hill, covered as much as forty acres and could have been occupied by as many as five thousand inhabitants. Such fortifications are clear evidence that two thousand years of peaceful megalithic culture had been supplanted by a sudden age of violence. And it was not just a localized phenomenon limited to a few areas; it was happening throughout the megalithic world.

At exactly the time that these fortifications were built, we find the first

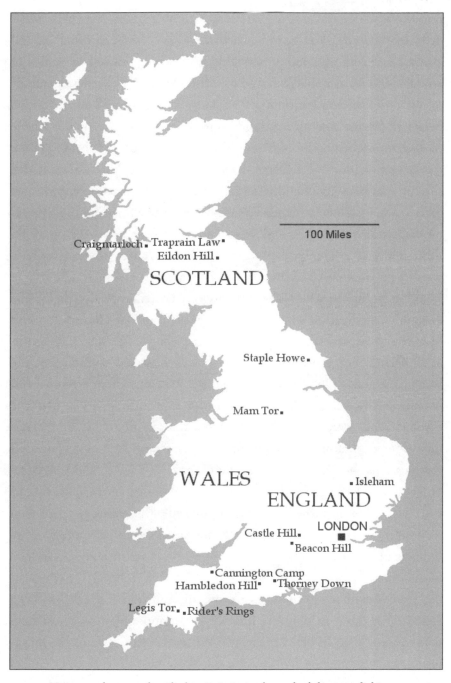

Major settlements fortified in Britain at the end of the megalithic age

purpose-made weapons of war appearing in the British Isles. The remains of bronze swords, spearheads, and battle-axes have been found in and around such hillforts, and preserved in nearby bog land, the remains of wooden and leather shields have been discovered. An excellent example of just how strife-ridden Britain eventually became is demonstrated by a hoard of Bronze Age objects found during excavations near the village of Isleham in the county of Cambridgeshire in eastern England. Among the largest quantity of artifacts from the period ever discovered at one site (around sixty-five hundred in all) were swords, arrows, spearheads, battle-axes, long daggers, and even armor. Anyone who views these pieces on display at the Moyse's Hall Museum in the nearby town of Bury St. Edmunds cannot help but be horrified at the evidence showing just how warlike the once peaceful country had become.

One of the most emotive examples of the tragedy that befell the megalithic civilization was revealed by excavations at Hambledon Hill near the town of Blandford Forum in the county of Dorset in southern England. For centuries, a megalithic causewayed enclosure at the site had been used for peaceful ceremonial feasting. Then, around 1500 BC, the earthwork was rapidly transformed into a hillfort: gaps in the embankments were filled to create continuous ramparts, and stockading was erected along the top. Unfortunately, whomever these makeshift fortifications were built to repel, they appear to have failed. Archaeologists found the charred remains of the wooden barricades, revealing they had been burned to the ground, while the bones of those who died defending the settlement were found inside. Near the gateway, the remains of one young man were found with an arrowhead still lodged within the rib cage.

Similar evidence of hillforts having succumbed to attack has been found throughout Britain and Ireland. It is impossible to say just how many people died in the carnage that occurred at the end of the megalithic age, because the long-standing custom of interring the dead in burial mounds was suddenly abandoned in favor of cremation. This abrupt change of funerary tradition from burial to cremation may indicate the extent of the violence that swept the megalithic world: perhaps there were just too many dead to bury. Only senior members of society were still buried in tombs, and the new kind of grave goods with which they were interred are clear evidence that a warrior leadership had assumed command: they were buried with such weapons as swords, shields, bows, and battle-axes.[9]

At one time, archaeologists understandably assumed that the British Isles had suffered the onslaught of a foreign invasion. A sudden similar abandonment of defenseless settlements in favor of hillforts occurred in historical times when the Romans left Britain, clearing the way for the Anglo-Saxons from Denmark and Germany to invade the country in the fifth century AD. But modern scientific techniques of examining ancient human remains, such as tooth enamel analysis and DNA testing, have revealed that the leaders interred in the burial mounds were not foreigners.

They were all descendants of the Windmill Hill People, the Beaker People, and the Wessex Culture, who had been living peacefully together for centuries. When one culture supplants another, it is also marked by new decorative styles employed in the manufacture of artifacts such as pottery, but there is no such change around 1500 BC. In fact, there is no evidence of any sort whatsoever of fresh large-scale migration into Britain, Ireland, or northern France until the coming of the Celts around 700 BC—eight centuries later. The only logical conclusion that can now be drawn is that for some reason, the megalithic people had begun to fight among themselves. But why?[10]

One scenario that could have created conditions in which such internecine strife might have arisen is a sudden change in climate. Crop failures due to colder or dryer conditions would apply pressure to society as a whole: with less crop production, people would be forced to protect what little they had from those who were going hungry. So was there a sudden climate change around 1500 BC?

The understanding of ancient climatic conditions in northwest Europe was first made possible in the late nineteenth and early twentieth centuries by the study of peat bogs in Scandinavia. Peat is a fibrous organic substance formed by incomplete decomposition of plants in wetlands. In the 1870s, the Norwegian botanist Alex Blytt, followed in the early 1900s by the Swedish botanist Rutger Sernander, examined the different-colored bands in which the peat had stratified and concluded that they were caused by variations in climate at the time the vegetation died: the darker layers were deposited in drier times and the lighter layers in moister times. If Blytt and Sernander were right, then climatic conditions had fluctuated periodically, and dramatically, during the formation of the peat bogs since the end of last ice age.[11]

Just before the First World War, the Swedish geologist Lennart von Post not only confirmed Blytt and Sernander's findings, but he was also able to elaborate upon them by studying ancient pollen preserved in these same peat bogs. Von Post reasoned that as pollen represented the type of plants that were growing at the time each layer of peat was formed, and different types of plants flourished in different climates, the pollen in each peat layer was representative of climate. After much study, he concluded that there had indeed been different climatic periods over the last ten thousand years that corresponded with those proposed by Blytt and Sernander.[12] Von Post's work concentrated on Scandinavia, but in the 1940s English botanist Harry Godwin showed that the same had occurred in the British Isles, producing a wider European evaluation of prehistoric climate variations, and in recent times radiocarbon dating has more specifically dated these climate shifts.[13]

Although the causes are unclear, we now know that around 3500 BC, northwest Europe entered a warm and dry period that climatologists refer to as the Sub-Boreal. It is probably no coincidence that this coincides with the beginning of the megalithic age. So did these pleasant conditions suddenly become harsher when megalithic civilization so abruptly ended? The answer is no. The Sub-Boreal period lasted until around 700 BC, when it gave way to the colder, wetter period known as the Sub-Atlantic. Although there is evidence that the climate became progressively wetter toward the end of the Sub-Boreal period, it did not become significantly colder. Not only was this well after the period in question, and not only did it occur gradually and not suddenly, but, if anything, it would have improved crop yield.

One theory popular in the 1980s was that a brief period of severe cold led to the collapse of megalithic culture. Even if such a cold spell lasted for just a year or two, it was argued, the resultant episode of hostilities would have destabilized long-standing community relationships, irrevocably altered society, and led to the emergence of a warrior elite.

It was suggested that such short-term climate change could be caused by contaminants in the atmosphere, similar to a so-called nuclear winter, in which it is thought that so much debris would be blasted into the atmosphere by a large-scale nuclear exchange that around the world sunlight would be reduced for months, possibly years, making temperatures plummet. A natural event that could have produced a similar effect would be an asteroid impact, such as the one that is thought to have wiped out the dinosaurs 65 million years ago, or a massive volcanic eruption, which would also have hurled dust and ash high into the stratosphere.

An example of just such a happening in historical times is the aftermath of the gigantic eruption in 1883 of Krakatau, a volcano on an island near Java. The earth's atmosphere was so contaminated by its fallout ash that throughout the world it became known as the year without summer: it snowed in faraway California, and in London the river Thames froze over.[14]

At the time the nuclear winter theory was proposed to account for the demise of the megalithic culture, there was no way of proving or disproving it; such a cold spell would not have lasted long enough for it to influence the development of peat bogs. Today, however, there is another way of knowing if such a phenomenon really occurred. A year-by-year record of contaminants in the earth's atmosphere is preserved in polar ice. Every winter a fresh layer of ice forms here, creating clearly defined strata, one for each year. Each layer contains trapped air, holding a sample of the earth's atmosphere as it was when the ice formed. Since the late 1970s, scientists have been taking core samples far down into the polar ice sheets to establish a record of the earth's atmospheric conditions going back some one hundred thousand years. Unfortunately for the megalithic nuclear winter theory, there is no evidence of either an asteroid impact or a volcanic eruption contaminating the atmosphere of the Northern Hemisphere sufficiently to cause even the briefest climate alteration around 1500 BC. The nearest such event either side of this time was a major volcanic eruption, thought to have occurred in Iceland, in the year 1156 BC.[15]

Over the years, botany, geophysics, chemistry, and geology have all combined to show conclusively that there was no manner of climate change anywhere around 1500 BC to account for the sudden mass aggression that brought about the end of megalithic culture. From the archaeology, all we can tell is that for some unknown reason, a peaceful civilization suddenly became a society of warmongers. Whatever it was that brought this about, it appears to have had absolutely nothing to do with a shortage of resources. In fact, rather than getting worse, daily life actually continued to improve right through the period around 1500 BC.

Excavations have revealed larger livestock ranches appearing at this time and more land being exploited for crops. Both pottery and metalworking saw continued advances, and the discovery of loom weights and spindle whorls from sites of this time show that woven garments were now being produced. Although the new settlements were fortified by a people clearly living in fear of hostility, day-to-day living was actually better than it had been before. All this has left modern scholars baffled by the demise of the megalithic culture.

So strange a fate befalling a civilization in northwest Europe is mystery enough; what is stranger still is that at exactly the same time, precisely the same fate was befalling another peaceful civilization over five thousand miles away on the other side of the Atlantic. The megalithic civilization appears to have left no clue as to what initiated its violent end. Could the answer lie in the ancient Americas?

6

Mystery of the Olmec

THE FIRST HUMAN SETTLERS in Central America, or Mesoamerica as the region is referred to by archaeologists, were the Stone Age descendants of hunter-gatherers from Asia who crossed the frozen Bering Strait from Siberia into Alaska before the end of the last ice age. The oldest archaeological evidence indicates that by 2000 BC, they had abandoned a nomadic existence and were living in small fishing villages in a large area that spread from the Gulf of Mexico to as far south as Honduras. They worked stone, made pottery, and used obsidian for blades. Within a hundred years, they had also started farming and had begun to domesticate a whole variety of crops, such as maize, beans, pumpkins, and cacao, made possible by elaborate irrigation systems. They also harvested latex from trees and processed it using the juice of a species of vine to produce rubber, which they used to make footwear and handles for tools. Astonishingly, these people discovered this rubber-processing technology as early as 1600 BC, predating Charles Goodyear's discovery of vulcanization by approximately thirty-five hundred years.

Like their contemporaries, the megalithic culture of northwest Europe, these people left no form of writing to give us any idea what they called themselves. For convenience' sake, archaeologists refer to them as the pre-Olmec, as they inhabited the same area as the Olmec civilization that followed them. The fact that they left no writings has also meant that it has been through scientific techniques that dating of pre-Olmec remains has been made possible. Because of Central America's humid equatorial climate, however, organic remains from the period are far less well preserved than in northwest Europe, often making carbon dating of animal or human remains difficult. Timber structures have left behind telltale signs such as postholes, but the wood itself has rotted to such an extent that dendrochronology is impossible. It is primarily, therefore, through the dating of pottery by thermoluminescence that a historical chronology of the pre-Olmec culture has been achieved.

Although the pre-Olmec did not build cities, they did have a remarkably sophisticated society. Dwellings of wood were constructed in small settlements of between one and three hundred people along the coast and the banks of the river systems of Central America. To protect the dwellings against flooding, they were erected on broad earthen platforms known as levees, some of which were comparable in size to the larger megalithic earthworks. Indeed, pre-Olmec settlements appear to have been remarkably similar to their megalithic counterparts. Villages were small but linked together into larger clusters, and their ceremonial sites were constructed outside these living areas.

Unlike the megalithic monuments, few of these were built from stone; instead they were square wooden buildings of a single room of around 100 square feet. The pre-Olmec did, however, erect artificial hills of earth and rubble, some over 50 feet high. As in megalithic Europe, there is no evidence that such temple complexes were ever occupied; rather, the inhabitants of between ten and twenty nearby villages appear to have come together at these sites purely for ceremonial activities. Also, like the megalithic people, the pre-Olmec of a particular area would have needed the help of others elsewhere both to construct the levees on which their settlements were built and for the task of building artificial mounds, many higher than Britain's second-largest megalithic mound of Gop Cairn. But this is not the only evidence of widespread cooperation among separate pre-Olmec communities.

Pre-Olmec communities spread throughout Central America, including the southern part of Mexico, Guatemala, Belize, and parts of El Salvador and Honduras, altogether an area of land almost thirteen hundred miles long and at its broadest point five hundred miles wide.

These communities, separated from one another by roughly the same distances as in the megalithic civilization, had close trading ties. Goods such as stones, shells, animal pelts, and feathers specific to these individual areas are found distributed throughout them all. For example, obsidian from the highland regions of Mexico found its way into settlements as far south as Honduras, and shells from Honduras are found in Mexico.

There is evidence not only that an elaborate trading system existed between the pre-Olmec peoples, but also that they shared a culture. The same kind of temple mounds were built throughout the pre-Olmec world, and technological innovations occurred simultaneously over the entire area, such as developments in pottery making and the various uses of rubber. Like the megalithic people of Europe, the pre-Olmec appear to have been a unified civilization without cities. Moreover, they appear to have been just as peaceful. They did not build defensive structures, nor did they manufacture weapons of war, and no evidence of organized tribal feuding has been found; that they lived in small villages rather than larger conurbations is indicative of a nonviolent culture with nothing to fear from within or from anyone else.[1]

The pre-Olmec culture may not have lasted as long as the megalithic civilization—five hundred as opposed to two thousand years—but it came to an end just as abruptly, and at the very same time. Archaeology has revealed that around 1500 BC, a new culture suddenly appeared throughout Central America. It was that of the Olmec, the first city-building people in the Americas and the mother culture of the later Maya, Toltec, and Aztec. But who exactly were the Olmec, and where did they come from?

The Aztec had been known to Europeans since the Spanish discovered Mexico in the early 1500s, and by the twentieth century much was also known concerning the older Mayan civilization. Until the 1940s, it was thought to have been the Maya who established the first Mesoamerican civilization, beginning somewhere around 400 BC and not declining until the tenth century AD, after which they were succeeded by the Toltec in the eleventh century and the Aztec in the fourteenth. The first inkling

Western scholars had of the existence of an earlier civilization in Central America did not come until the twentieth century.

In the early 1900s, ancient artifacts discovered in Mexico were first recognized as significantly different from those of other Mesoamerican civilizations, and in 1929 the American Museum of Natural History officially classified the culture that made them by the term Olmec. Olmec was a name the Aztec had used for a people who lived around the Gulf of Mexico during their own period of dominance, after the fourteenth century, and it was not until the 1940s that this newly classified culture was discovered to have been very much older. What these people had really been called remains a mystery, but the name Olmec has stuck.

The first proper excavation of an Olmec settlement began in 1938, undertaken by the American anthropologist Matthew Stirling. His team, working at La Venta, on the southernmost coast of the Gulf of Mexico, discovered the ruins of what was clearly a large Olmec city. Excavations around a 100-foot earthen pyramid uncovered the remains of a ceremonial plaza, the foundations of buildings decorated with colored clay floors, and several tombs constructed from huge basalt columns, where lavish burials were accompanied by splendid funerary goods such as jewelry, amulets, and figurines. By 1942, after four years of digging, Stirling was left seriously doubting that the builders of such a city could have coexisted with the Aztec or even the earlier Toltec or Maya, and suggested that the Olmec had predated them all. At first, his conclusions were questioned by other scholars; it was not until the 1950s that radiocarbon dating finally resolved the issue. Eventually, it was established that Olmec civilization dated back to as early as 1500 BC. Moreover, it extended far beyond the gulf coast where Stirling's original excavations had been conducted, with at least twenty-six major cities or cultural centers spread throughout Central America.[2]

Since the 1940s, many other Olmec sites have been excavated, and this ancient civilization has revealed some, but by no means all, of its secrets. The Olmec heartland was an area on the Gulf of Mexico in what are now the Mexican state of Tabasco and the southern part of Veracruz. This hot, swampy lowland was home to a number of Olmec cities, the largest of which was that excavated by Stirling at La Venta; another was at the town of San Lorenzo. These cities are typical of the other Olmec settlements found throughout Central America.

Urban districts consisted of houses with wooden walls and clay and palm roofs, which were serviced by a remarkably sophisticated infrastructure, such as paved walkways, an efficient drainage system, and even an elaborate water supply. Many Olmec centers had a network of long, U-shaped, rectangular basalt blocks, laid end to end and covered with capstones, which appear to have served as aqueducts to provide drinking water to the different areas of the settlement. At the heart of these cities there was a public precinct consisting of a ceremonial plaza surrounded by huge decorated standing stones, and at its heart was a flat-topped rectangular pyramid with a square building on top of it. No form of writing has been discovered from this early period of Mesoamerican history, but from these massive building projects, together with the remains of spectacular stone sculptures and delicately crafted artifacts of jade and other precious materials, archaeologists have reconstructed a picture of a highly organized culture with a powerful religious ideology.

The Olmec appear to have been a complex society governed by priests and kings, a seemingly hierarchical system where the elite were separated from the common people. The leadership of these Olmec cities seem to have wielded considerable, if not absolute, power, and their faces have been preserved in the form of colossal human heads. These sculptures of enigmatic helmeted figures with broad, stern-looking faces were carved from giant boulders, some of which were over 4 feet high, and probably glorified individual rulers while they were alive and served as memorials to them after death. Huge basalt thrones of Olmec chieftains have also been found, carvings on the front of them showing the ruler seated in judgment. Their tombs, richly stocked with precious burial goods, are a testament to their wealth and high status.

Some indication of the extent of the power these rulers wielded is evidenced by where the stone for many of the Olmec building projects originated. Archaeologists have determined that the stone used to make most of the monuments at La Venta and San Lorenzo came from basalt quarries in the area of the Tuxtla Mountains, some five hundred miles to the west. Here, workmen cut the rocks into their basic shapes before hauling them across hills, rivers, and swamps to the Olmec heartland. These stones were probably transported using methods similar to the ones that the megalithic people in contemporary Europe employed; the labor force required would have been considerable. This is evidence not only of Olmec organizational skills and command of logistics, but of a powerful and efficient leadership as well.

Olmec cities functioned as citadels, from which a local chieftain controlled an independent city-state. There seem to have been well over thirty of these altogether, spread out from central Mexico all the way down to Honduras. The first period of Olmec civilization, known as the Early Formative, appears to have been a time of civil strife when local chieftains fought with one another to establish authority over their newly acquired lands. Unlike the pre-Olmec, the people made weapons such as bows, spears, shields, and long swords from hard, glasslike obsidian.

They also fortified their cities, where the regional inhabitants clustered together for protection. Unlike their predecessors, the Olmec had a ruling class whose members were buried in tombs richly furnished with warrior grave goods. It is thought that the supreme power in the Olmec city-states were priest-kings who not only served as military commanders but also officiated at ceremonial activities that were in stark contrast to those of their nature-worshipping predecessors. The Olmec were to establish a tradition in Mesoamerican culture that lasted, in places, until the time of the Aztec: the practice of human sacrifice. Very different from the pre-Olmec carvings that depicted naked, benevolent-looking deities, the statues of Olmec gods had fierce, warlike faces and were portrayed wearing leather armor and brandishing weapons.

The early Olmec, however, did not war themselves to extinction. Once the regional chieftains had established their authority over a controllable area, they made peace with their neighbors and settled down to enjoy the benefits of ruling their individual city-states. Gone, however,

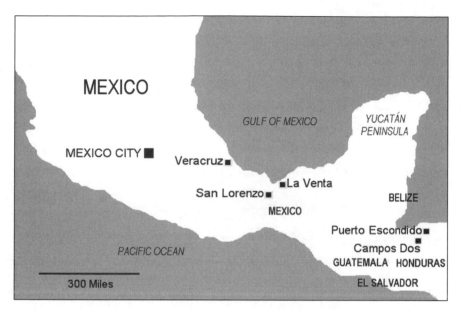

Principal Pre-Olmec sites in Central America

was the egalitarian lifestyle of the pre-Olmec, and in its place there was established a feudal society. Life in Olmec cities was rigidly formalized; the priestly and ruling classes lived in comfortable dwellings around the ceremonial centers, while the workers or peasants dwelt in suburbs of more humble accommodation. Remarkably, for such a warlike people divided into dozens of separate states, Olmec civilization lasted for centuries. Free trade and exchange of ideas led to technological advances that made possible the height of Olmec civilization between 1200 and 400 BC. Although there appears to have been no such thing as an Olmec emperor based at La Venta, there seems to have been a kind of constitutional figurehead whose role was to adjudicate in quarrels between the regional chieftains. He may have been something like the emperor of medieval Japan at a time when the real power lay with the regional samurai warlords.

Although the term *mother culture* may be an oversimplification, Olmec influence lasted long after the civilization's demise; its political system of a strongly centralized hierarchy was adopted by most other pre-Columbian Central American civilizations that followed. Even

Olmec architecture was adopted by later Mesoamerican cultures: the Olmec earthen pyramids, for example, with large houselike structures built upon them, appear to have been the model for the later stepped pyramids of the Maya and Aztec.[3]

The end of Olmec civilization began with the rise of the Mayan culture in the Yucatán Peninsula of Mexico. Beginning around 400 BC, Mayan civilization spread slowly southeastward, and by AD 250 it had reached prominence in what are now Guatemala, Belize, Honduras, and El Salvador. The birth of Mayan civilization was a gradual changeover from one culture to another, established by a new ruling class of the same indigenous peoples. In other words, the Maya were the Olmec who changed their religion and systems of beliefs, which is why they continued to hold on to some of their forebears' cultural traditions. The end of Olmec civilization was a drawn-out affair over some six centuries, but its rise had been almost instantaneous by comparison. Within just a few years, the Olmec appear to have overwhelmed their predecessors entirely, suggesting that they were foreign invaders. So where did they originate?

Although stone statues of warrior-kings and warlike gods appear right from the beginning of the Olmec period, it took time for the Olmec to develop into the civilization that left behind the kind of large and permanent stone buildings for which they are famous, from around 1200 BC. Nevertheless, the Olmec were erecting exactly the same kind of buildings, but made from wood, and exactly the same kind of pyramidal mounds, but built from earth, right at the start of their sudden rise to supremacy throughout Central America, from around 1500 BC. The implications are that the Olmec were already an established civilization right from the time of their sudden appearance. Accordingly, if they were invaders, we should expect to find evidence of this culture's previous existence elsewhere.

It was once thought that the Olmec originated in northern Mexico, or even across the border in what is now the southern United States, and had moved progressively south, invading in turn the lands of the pre-Olmec in southern Mexico, Belize, Guatemala, El Salvador, and Honduras. But despite decades of searching, archaeologists have found no evidence of this supposed Olmec homeland; nor have excavations at the other end of the Olmec area of occupation, south of Honduras in Nicaragua. At one time it seemed that the Olmec civilization simply appeared in Central America is if from nowhere. In fact, from the time of the discovery of the existence of the Olmec civilization in the 1940s, their origins were such a mystery that some scholars even suggested that they did not originate on the American continent at all. It was proposed that the strange stone heads depicting Olmec rulers had facial features that did not match the appearance of Native American peoples from North, Central, or South America. For instance, they apparently had broader noses and fuller lips than indigenous Americans. Some suggested that these features were African, and theorized that the Olmec had come from Egypt and had brought their pyramid-building culture with them. There were a number of objections to such a theory, however.

Leaving aside the fact that there was no evidence that the ancient Egyptians had ever built seagoing vessels capable of reaching the New World, if the Olmec really were Egyptians, they had somehow forgotten most of their homeland technology. Not only had they totally forgotten how to smelt bronze, they also seemed to have forgotten how to build large structures from stone. In fact, the first Olmec pyramids, built from earth, were flat-topped structures very different from Egyptian pyramids. The main objection to the theory, though, was that the stone heads actually have as many Native American features as they do African: they have the epicanthic folds, which Africans do not, and they have the rounder jaws typical of the Asiatic people who migrated to America at the end of the ice age.

Ultimately, from two completely different ends of the debate, anthropologists negated the idea that the Olmec stone heads were evidence of overseas migration. The notion of racial archetypes generally has been much discredited since the mid-twentieth century. For example, the number of facial differences that exist between groups of peoples isolated from one another is greatly exceeded by the differences that exist within such groups.[4] Other anthropologists drew attention to the fact that the stone heads closely resemble the appearance of the people who still live in the tropical lowlands of Mexico even today.[5] One way or the other, there appeared to be no evidence that the Olmec came from anywhere other than the American continent. Nonetheless, all this left the Olmec origins as mysterious as ever. If they did not originate elsewhere in the Americas, or come from across the Atlantic, then who on earth were they? The answer finally began to emerge in the 1980s.

In 1988 archaeologists excavating an Olmec site at Isla Alor near La Venta discovered that its first pyramid had been built directly over an earlier, pre-Olmec earthen mound. The original mound, around 40 feet high and dating from around 1700 BC, formed the core of the later structure some 70 feet high, built by the Olmec around 1450 BC. Surprisingly, further excavations revealed that the original pre-Olmec structure was exactly the same shape as the one that followed: it was constructed as a flat-topped, rectangular pyramid.[6] Soon after, excavations of another pyramid in the far south of the Olmec world, in the lower Ulúa River valley of Honduras, found exactly the same thing.[7]

Until this time it was thought that the pre-Olmec had built only earthen mounds and that the flat-topped, rectangular pyramids were introduced by the Olmec. These new discoveries therefore led to renewed excavations of other Olmec pyramids, and it soon became apparent that the same had happened elsewhere. Eventually, ground-penetrating radar enabled geophysicists to bypass the lengthy procedure of excavation to reveal that dozens of Olmec pyramids throughout Central America had been built over pre-Olmec originals, in Mexico, Guatemala, Belize, El Salvador, and Honduras. Moreover, the pre-Olmec pyramids even had square wooden buildings erected on top of them, something else that was previously thought to have been an Olmec innovation. It had become clear that rather than being Olmec inventions, truncated pyramids with buildings on top of them were actually pre-Olmec in origin. The Olmec structures had simply been larger, later developing into more sophisticated monuments clad with stone and with brick structures at their summits rather than wooden ones. The reason this had not been realized previously was that all but the earlier and simpler mounds had been built over in subsequent Olmec times. At the very least, this was evidence that the Olmec had adopted an important facet of pre-Olmec belief structure, or perhaps aspects of their religion. But the implications were far deeper.

Within a few years, a more comprehensive picture of early Olmec settlements in Central America had emerged. Their ceremonial complexes were built over existing pre-Olmec ones, and to the same design; their cities developed around them, absorbing what had been the clusters of earlier villages. In other words, the first Olmec cities were merely grander copies of what already existed. And it was not only the design of ceremonial structures that the Olmec adopted from their predecessors, but also their style of pottery. In the mid-1990s, excavations at Puerto Escondido in Honduras, directed by John S. Henderson, professor of anthropology at Cornell University, and Rosemary Joyce of Berkeley, found that pottery of the late pre-Olmec period decorated with a distinguishing incised design continued to be produced by the Olmecs well into their period of occupation, from around 1700 to 1300 BC.

This was quite unexpected, and most unusual. Throughout the world, archaeologists are able to determine prehistoric population movement by changes in the style of excavated pottery, referred to as ceramic sequencing. Even when immigrants adopt the religion or social structure of the indigenous culture, invariably their own style of pottery, in particular the way it is decorated, remains unchanged. This, for example, is what enabled archaeologists in Europe to determine the progression of prehistoric mass migrations such as the Celtic expansion around 700 BC.[8]

Wondering if Puerto Escondido might have been an isolated peculiarity, Henderson and Joyce excavated another site in Honduras, at Campo Dos, and found exactly the same thing, and by 1994 archaeologists working in Mexico, Guatemala, and Belize came to the same conclusions. Furthermore, scientific analysis of ceramic-paste characteristics showed that pottery had been manufactured exclusively in Central America, meaning that the early Olmec had not brought it with them from elsewhere. These discoveries that the Olmec built the same monuments and employed the same ceramic style as their predecessors, coupled with the fact that they did not bring the most essential household utensils with them from anywhere else, led to one inescapable conclusion: there had been no invasion—the pre-Olmec and Olmec were one and the same.[9]

Could the fierce Olmec really have really been the peaceful pre-Olmec after having undergone some abrupt social transformation? Some scholars, reluctant to accept that such a warlike culture could so suddenly have developed from the peaceful pre-Olmec peoples, questioned the findings. Perhaps, they suggested, the pottery thermoluminescence dating was flawed. Although there could be no doubt that the incised pottery was pre-Olmec, perhaps some of this pottery had been wrongly ascribed to the later Olmec period. What was needed to settle the issue was some means of dating other finds discovered in situ with the pottery.

Because Central America's equatorial climate caused extreme decomposition of the contemporary human remains, DNA testing and tooth enamel analysis could not be called on as they had been in Europe. Fortunately, however, advances in radiocarbon dating by this time enabled even badly decomposed organic remains of the period to be dated. Samples excavated in 1994 during excavations at La Venta by archaeologist Rebecca Gonzalez-Lauck of the National Institute of Anthropology and History of Mexico and at San Lorenzo by Professor Ann Cyphers-Guillen of the National Autonomous University of Mexico provided samples for carbon dating that provided dates which tallied precisely with those obtained for the pottery by thermoluminescence. Even given carbon dating's margin for error of around fifty years each way, there could be no doubt that the same pottery was made by both the pre-Olmec and their Olmec successors. The dates obtained ranged between 1700 BC and 1300 BC, well before and well after the period around 1500 BC when Olmec culture suddenly appeared.[10]

With no evidence of previous Olmec culture elsewhere, and their monuments and household wares being identical to those of their immediate predecessors, it seems that the Olmec were indeed one and the same indigenous people as their pre-Olmec forebears. For some reason they had suddenly adopted a more aggressive lifestyle, and competition between the new city-states had simply led to larger buildings. But the reason for this abrupt transformation left archaeologists baffled. As in Europe, there was no evidence whatsoever of sudden climate change that might account for it. In July 1996, in a feature in *Time* magazine, leading experts who had studied early Olmec culture collectively admitted to being mystified as to what had suddenly transformed a society of peaceful farmers into the warring, class-based social structure of the Olmec, and they remain so to this day.[11]

Astonishingly, around 1500 BC, at exactly the same time that the megalithic civilization suddenly ended in an unexplained epidemic of mass violence, exactly the same occurred to the peaceful peoples of Central America over five thousand miles away. Could this be just a remarkable coincidence? That the same thing should have occurred on both sides of the Atlantic is strange enough. But it doesn't end there. At this precise time, exactly the same fate was befalling civilizations on the other side of the Pacific, in southern Asia.

7

An Asian Apocalypse

AT THE SAME TIME AS THE MEGALITHIC and pre-Olmec cultures existed in Europe and Central America, a civilization flourished in southern Asia that was technologically far in advance and far older than either of them. As long ago as 7000 BC, the inhabitants of what are now Pakistan and part of northwest India abandoned a hunter-gatherer existence in favor of village life. Known as the Mehrgarh people, after the site where archaeologists first discovered their remains, they established settlements along the valley of the Indus River. Here they cultivated wheat and barley and domesticated cattle, sheep, and goats. Their settlements, which ultimately spread along almost a thousand miles of the Indus Valley, consisted of houses built from simple mud bricks with thatched roofs. Often constructed to a uniform pattern of four separate rooms, these dwellings were even carpeted by a matting of reeds.

Tools from this early period of Mehrgarh culture consisted of the kind of Stone Age utensils used by the megalithic people of Europe, such as bone needles, antler picks, stone axes, and flint blades, while vessels were made from stone and reed baskets were coated with bitumen so they could be used as buckets. Numerous Mehrgarh burials have been found, many with elaborate grave goods, such as bangles and pendants incorporating semiprecious stones like turquoise and lapis lazuli, together with simple stone statuettes, mainly in the form of women and animals.

The buildings of the first Mehrgarh settlements were not laid out in any overall plan, but by around 5500 BC they began to be constructed in a grid pattern. They were also more sophisticated, with stone foundations and more than one floor, and the walls were even painted. Pottery also appeared around this time, and detailed painted figurines made from terra-cotta were made, most of them depicting women, suggesting some form of goddess worship. In seems, in fact, that women played a dominant religious role in society as a whole, as it is only in female graves that funerary goods of this period are found.

Throughout the fifth millennium BC, considerable technological advances were made by the Mehrgarh people. They learned how to smelt metal from common ore, and copper was used for various tools; cotton was cultivated for both fiber and oil; and with the introduction of the potter's wheel, ceramics were mass produced. By 4000 BC, metallurgy had reached a remarkable level of sophistication. Copper drills, turned by bowstrings, were used to bore holes through semiprecious stones such as carnelian, turquoise, and lapis lazuli to make beads, and ordinary stones could be made to look luxurious by being varnished with a green copper-oxide glaze. Around the year 3500 BC, at the time the megalithic culture was only just getting started in Europe, the Mehrgarh people were not only already entering the Bronze Age, they were establishing one of the world's first city-building civilizations as well.[1]

Although those who built the first Indus Valley cities were the same people who had lived in the region for thirty-five-hundred years, archaeologists refer to this new phase of Mehrgarh history as the Harappan civilization, after its first excavated city, at Harappa in northeast Pakistan.

Harappa was one of seven huge cities discovered from this period; it covered almost four hundred acres, probably having as many as forty thousand inhabitants. Such cities and hundreds of smaller towns made up the Harappan civilization, which thrived for the next two thousand years along the Indus Valley, covering an area comparable to that of ancient Egypt.

Streets were wide and laid out to a uniform grid, and dwellings were large rectangular brick structures, some three or four floors high, which probably looked very similar to modern apartment buildings. Indeed, this is exactly what they seem to have been. Individual families appear to

Major Harappan cities of the Indus Valley

have occupied four or five rooms, sharing bathroom and washing facilities with other residents of the building: around four separate apartments obtained their water from a well set in a room that had laundry troughs, stone baths, and even latrines. The Harappans actually created the world's first urban sanitation system. Wastewater and sewerage were channeled from individual buildings into covered drains that lined the city streets.

Dwellings were also made as homelike as possible. Windows had shutters and drapes, internal walls were plastered, and houses were decorated with small stone figurines of everyday people, possibly friends, loved ones, and the departed, which were carved to an anatomical precision not matched anywhere in the world until the time of the Classical Greek sculptors two millennia later. Utensils were made from ornamented bronze, and pottery was lavishly painted with natural motifs such as animals, fishes, birds, flowers, and trees. Daily grooming was facilitated by household items such as finely crafted bone combs, bronze razors, and mirrors made from polished copper.

For well over a thousand years, many aspects of Harappan civilization were far ahead of the other most advanced civilizations of the contemporary world, such as Egypt and Mesopotamia (a region now occupied by Iraq and part of Syria, Turkey, and Iran). Its cities had public granaries, warehouses, and dockyards, all built with a knowledge of engineering unparalleled anywhere else in the world. There were surgeries where physicians treated the sick. Astonishingly, there were even dentists. The teeth of some human skeletons of the period have been bored, probably with bronze bow drills, and seem to have been filled with some kind of cement.

Around 3000 BC, the Harappans developed an early form of writing, and storage vessels and signboards over gates and doorways held inscriptions. This script, however, has yet to be deciphered, so unfortunately it is a mystery as to what kind of belief system inspired this civilization. Nevertheless, some idea of the nature of Harappan culture can be gleaned. To start with, almost uniquely for the ancient world, organized religion does not seem to have played a role in Harappan life. They left no buildings recognizable as temples or shrines, and although there are small statues and figurines of humans and animals, some of which may have represented gods, there are no large-scale statues usually associated with places of public worship.

There is also no recognizable evidence of any form of priesthood. In fact, society as a whole appears to have been remarkably egalitarian. Although numerous human images from the time have survived on pottery decorations and as statuettes, none of them appear to represent priests, kings, or people of obvious elevated importance. Nor have excavations of Harappan cemeteries uncovered the remains of individual burials reflecting high status. What does seem apparent is that women enjoyed a higher status in society than in many other ancient cultures: the majority of the finest cast-bronze figurines from the period depict females.

In fact, Harappan civilization might even have been the world's first democracy. Harappan cities had large complexes of adjoined buildings that archaeologists once thought were the palaces of regional rulers, but later excavations revealed that they had no living quarters. Instead, these buildings, originally referred to as citadels, are now thought to have been municipal centers consisting of assembly rooms and a forum large enough to accommodate five thousand people. They were probably an ancient equivalent of a city hall.

One of the most remarkable aspects of this urban-based civilization is that the Harappans appear to have been just as intrinsically nonviolent as their megalithic and pre-Olmec contemporaries. Archaeology has found no weapons suitable for warfare, no human remains bearing battle scars, and no evidence of armies and military leadership; no warrior grave goods have been unearthed, there are no statues depicting soldiers, and no pottery decorations have been found that portray battle scenes or even individuals fighting. Although walls were erected around some Harappan cities, they were quite impractical as defensive structures. Not only did they lack features of military architecture, such as castellation, turrets, and arrow slits; they seldom encircled the entire perimeter and were erected only across areas of low-lying land. It is thought that these ramparts were built not to repel human foes, but as barriers for diverting the floodwaters of the monsoons.

Amazingly, there is no evidence whatsoever of warfare or civil strife in the Indus Valley for fifty-five hundred years, from the very birth of the settlements around 7000 BC. But then, at exactly the time that the megalithic and pre-Olmec cultures abruptly ended in episodes of mass aggression, the peaceful Harappan civilization came to its own sudden and violent end. Whereas other ancient city-building civilizations, such as in Egypt, Mesopotamia, and China, all left their mark on all subsequent cultures, so devastating was the cataclysm that overwhelmed the Indus Valley that Harappan civilization vanished from history altogether.[2]

When the Harappa cities were being excavated in the mid-twentieth century, it was thought that they had declined gradually due to climatic change. It was suggested that a reduction of rainfall in the foothills of the Himalayas caused lower river levels, thereby destroying the irrigation system on which agriculture relied. By the 1970s, however, it had become clear that although there had been a period of less rainfall in the region toward the end of the Harappan era, this could not account for the civilization's abrupt end. Studies of the age and development of lake deposits in the Indus Valley showed that dryer conditions were well established by as early as 1750 BC.[3]

Furthermore, carbon dating revealed that although some cities suffered because of the drier conditions, many in the lower-lying areas, closer to the Indus itself, continued to thrive. It seems that although the Harappan civilization was in decline after 1750 BC, it was still very much intact as late as 1500 BC, when final disaster struck. What is indisputable from the archaeological evidence is that until this time, whatever climatic conditions existed, the inhabitants of the Indus Valley were living just as peacefully as they had for over five thousand years. But then, without warning, Harappan civilization ended in a horrific cataclysm.

Excavations of numerous Harappan settlements have revealed a thick layer of charred timbers and ash from the last period of occupation, showing that cities and towns throughout the Indus Valley had been destroyed by fire. Excavations at three of the largest Harappan cities (including Harappa itself) uncovered hundreds of human remains from the level of burning, the posture of the skeletons indicating that the cities' inhabitants either had been struck down in the streets while attempting to flee or had died huddled together in buildings. Few of them actually appeared to have died during the burning, however; analysis of the burned stratum indicates that the fires started after the citizens were killed. Moreover, the skulls and bones of many had been crushed, broken, or lacerated in a manner that could have been caused only by weapons such as battle-axes, swords, and spears, while some were found with arrowheads still embedded within the rib cage. The burning of these Harappan cities had clearly not been due to fires caused by some natural

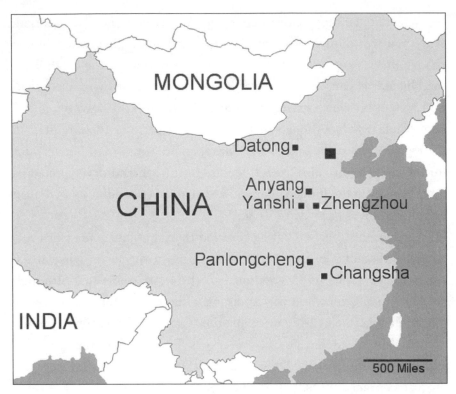

Key sites in China of the early fifteenth century BC

catastrophe, such as an earthquake or volcanic eruption; rather, they had been deliberately started after the inhabitants had been massacred. Ultimately, many other Harappan cities, towns, and settlements were found to have suffered the same fate, and even those that were spared being razed by fire were suddenly abandoned.[4]

Archaeologists have carbon-dated the burned timbers from this mass devastation to around the year 1500 BC, give or take fifty years. This is exactly the same time as violence suddenly overwhelmed the previously peaceful peoples thousands of miles away in northwest Europe and Central America. In this case, however, it was not the Harappans who had decimated one another in civil strife, but the work of foreign invaders. Among the rubble of the burned layers of these cities weapons have been found, such as battle-axes, swords, and harpoons, and even the remains of war chariots, none of which was of Harappan origin.[5]

The assault on the Indus Valley seems to have been nothing less than a mindless rampage. By the time it was over, there was nothing left of Harappan civilization for anyone to inherit. The invaders did not even attempt to reconstruct the shattered cities; instead they built nothing more than humble dwellings from the rubble of the once splendid towns. The only sizable structures they erected, which are found throughout the Indus Valley, were huge stone altars, presumably to venerate their native gods. Such systematic and frenzied attacks on settlements throughout the Indus Valley, destroying cities and butchering their inhabitants, suggests that the invaders intended not only to conquer Harappan lands but also to obliterate their civilization entirely.

This is certainly what they achieved. Until the emergence of archaeology in the nineteenth century, historians had no idea that the Harappans had ever existed. Surely the Harappan enemies had to have been the most bloodthirsty, violent, and savage peoples the region had ever known. Surprisingly, they were anything but. Those who invaded the Indus Valley around 1500 BC had previously been just as peaceful as the Harappans.

Archaeologists were first able to identify these invaders from their unique ceramic style. Pottery found directly above the level of burning, and hence from a period immediately after the carnage, was quite different from that below it. Unlike the painted Harappan designs, the new pottery was decorated with patterns in relief that were distinctive to a people known as the Aryans.

Until they swept into the Indus Valley to bring death and destruction to Harappan civilization, the Aryans were a nomadic people who lived as independent tribal groups in the mountainous regions of what is now Afghanistan. They shared an ancestry with others who migrated into the Middle East and parts of Europe in later times, also referred to as Aryans, originating on the steppes of south-central Asia. What they originally called themselves is unknown, as they had no form of writing during this early period.

The name Aryan, meaning "noble ones," comes from a name they later adopted after ultimately conquering much of India. Originally, they probably had no collective name, as the various Aryan tribes lived independently of one another. In the nineteenth century, the word Aryan became associated with twisted notions of racial superiority, due to a misunderstanding of these peoples' history.

Some of the original Aryans from the Asiatic steppes eventually migrated to the Middle East, where they came into conflict with the ancient Israelites, and by Roman times some scholars used the word Aryan as a collective term for gentiles, or non-Jews. By the twentieth century, academics had ceased using this inaccurate term, but European racial supremacists continued to use it, and by the time the Nazi Party was founded in Germany in the 1920s, the word had come to be erroneously associated with people of Nordic extraction. Those who lived in Afghanistan in the sixteenth century BC, however, were almost certainly identical in appearance to the people who inhabit the region today.

The original Aryans were not organized into any kind of civilization, although they did enjoy a common culture indicated by their collective style of pottery, hunting weapons, and nomadic form of existence. Although they appear to have been accomplished horsemen and lived a similar lifestyle to that of the Mongols of later times, they were nowhere near as warlike. In fact, until their sudden assault on the Indus Valley, they seem to have lived peacefully for centuries. Although they did not leave behind permanent cities or towns, their seasonal camps have been excavated, and the small statuettes of their gods appear to represent a people whose religion revolved purely around nature.

In many ways they were very like their contemporaries the pre-Olmec in faraway Central America, but living a nomadic rather than a settled existence. Once they moved into the Indus Valley, however, they dramatically changed. Not only did they wage total war and commit acts of mindless vandalism, they also began to practice human sacrifice. Excavations at Harappan towns have uncovered numerous decapitated human remains around the altars the Aryans built there after their conquest.[6]

At precisely the same time as the distant megalithic and pre-Olmec peoples had so abruptly changed from passive to warmongering societies, the Aryans had just as suddenly transformed from separate tribes of peaceful nomads into a mass horde of bloodthirsty maniacs. So vicious were the assaults on Harappan settlements that once the Aryans overpowered them, they slaughtered civilians and razed their cities to the ground. As they had no writing of their own, and Harappan script has not been translated, just what happened to change the Aryans so dramatically remains a complete enigma. But the Harappans were not the only civilization to perish at this time in southern Asia. Twenty-five hundred miles to the east of the Indus Valley, the Erlitou culture of China suffered a very similar fate—and ancient Chinese records of this period do survive.

Although the oldest permanent settlements in China date from around 3000 BC, the country's first city-building civilization began around 2100 BC with the start of the Chinese Bronze Age. It is known to archaeologists as the Erlitou culture, named after a site first excavated in 1959 at Yanshi near the city of Luoyang in Henan Province, east-central China. The Erlitou culture built cities and towns throughout what are now Henan and the adjacent provinces of Shanxi and Hubei, an area approximately one thousand miles long by five hundred miles wide. Within two hundred years, Erlitou cities had grown to considerable size. Yanshi was by far the largest. Covering an area of almost 750 acres, it appears to have been the capital of the Erlitou civilization.

More typical were settlements at sites such as those near modern Datong in the far north of Shanxi Province, and at Panlongcheng in southern Hubei, which covered about one hundred acres. As throughout much of China's history, even the largest buildings were constructed mainly of wood, so little remains to be seen in the form of ruins. Nonetheless, archaeology has revealed that Erlitou towns were sophisticated settlements with large public buildings; the residents enjoyed the benefits of urban society, wore silk clothing, used tools made from bronze, and turned fine glazed ceramics on potter's wheels.

The settlements of this earliest Chinese civilization were even connected by paved roads along which travelers were transported in horse-drawn carriages. Just like that of their contemporaries the Harappans, the Erlitou culture was remarkably peaceful. Despite being a Bronze Age civilization with an astonishing grasp of metallurgy, there is no evidence that they mass-produced weapons of war. Moreover, of all the hundreds of human remains excavated from graves and tombs at sites such as Yanshi, there is no evidence of a single human being having died in combat for six centuries. Then, around 1500 BC, everything changed when warfare tore the country apart.[7]

Unlike the Indus Valley, in China there was no foreign invasion. Instead, the region appears to have erupted into civil war. A layer of charred timbers, charcoal, and ash, identical to that found at Harappan cities, indicates that the city at Yanshi was burned to the ground. This was no natural disaster: human remains and discarded weapons found among this level of occupation reveal that the settlement was overwhelmed by a human foe. Although there is no evidence of such mass destruction of cities of the period as are found in the Indus Valley, existing settlements were suddenly fortified, and Chinese life transformed from a peaceful to a militaristic culture. With the destruction of Yanshi, new cities were built, such as near the modern city of Zhengzhou in Henan Province, some eighty miles to the east, which was surrounded by 12-foot walls with a circumference of over four miles. Copper-mining settlements, such as Panlongcheng, which had long been centers for the manufacture of harmless bronze tools and vessels, became industrial complexes for the wholesale production of arms. A new capital ultimately arose at Anyang, 150 miles northeast of Yanshi, and here excavations have uncovered the remains of mass human sacrifices.[8]

Carbon dating places the boundary of this abrupt transformation of culture to between 1520 and 1470 BC. Before this time, there is no evidence whatsoever that people of the Erlitou culture were engaged in any kind of warfare, but skeletons unearthed from graves of the subsequent period exhibit visible signs of battle wounds, and tombs of the ruling elite are resplendent with grave goods including sophisticated weaponry such as swords, spears, and bows, and even the remains of war chariots. As with the megalithic culture in distant Britain, DNA tests reveal that this warring society was made up of the same people as their peace-loving predecessors.

Society had clearly undergone such a radical alteration that archaeologists refer to this new militaristic phase of Chinese culture as the Erligang period, named after the site near Zhengzhou where its remains were excavated in 1951. From the archaeological record alone, the violent end of the Erlitou culture would be as mysterious as the sudden demise of the Harappan civilization. Thankfully, however, there survive ancient Chinese accounts of this period from which to learn what actually occurred.

Between 1928 and 1937, excavations led by archaeologist Lee Chi, of the Chinese Academy of Sciences, excavated the ancient city at Anyang and discovered China's oldest historical records. Dating from the late Erligang period, between 1350 and 1100 BC, they were texts inscribed on animal bones, in particular on large, flat shoulder blades of oxen and on turtle shells. More than twenty thousand were found during these first excavations alone. Remarkably, they were written in Chinese characters very similar to those still used today and so were relatively easy to translate.

The texts were in the form of astrological predictions or horoscopes prepared by priests for the ruling elite of Erligang society. Collectively referred to as oracle bones, these divinations interpreted the movement of heavenly bodies to offer advice on matters such as politics, religion, military affairs, and medicine. Providing a critical insight into the early stages of Chinese civilization, they included not only predictions of events but also later notations concerning what had actually transpired. Accordingly, they were a historical record of 250 years of early Chinese history. Furthermore, as the texts often compared contemporary matters with events of the past, they also included historical records of what had occurred in both the early Erligang period and the Erlitou period that preceded it.

From these oracle bones, now preserved at the museum of the Academia Sinica in Taiwan, historians have learned that the Anyang site had been the Erligang capital of Yin. The kings who ruled from here were known as the Shang dynasty, a family that had originally seized power from another royal lineage, known as the Xia dynasty.

It was obvious from the descriptions of lifestyle that the members of the Xia dynasty were one and the same as China's rulers during the Erlitou period. The Xia kings, it seems, had been benign constitutional monarchs who left regional government in the hands of the local inhabitants. Although there was a national army of sorts, garrisoned at the former capital at Yanshi, it was more of a police force than anything else. The various regions were governed by councils of elders, but a local clan leader had the authority of council chairman, adjudicated in legal matters, and had his own local militia to maintain law and order. He was apparently a combination of a modern judge, sheriff, and mayor.

If a dispute arose between individual clan leaders, the king would act as intermediary, being something of a cross between a modern Supreme Court judge and the secretary-general of the United Nations. Although the penal code could impose harsh penalties for legal transgressions, the system appears to have been fair and successfully maintained a peaceful society for generations. That is, until the last of the Xia rulers, King Jie, suddenly changed from a benevolent monarch to a tyrannical dictator.

Jie is said to have expanded his army, dissolved the regional councils, and imposed martial law. To consolidate his power, the king ordered the arrest of any local clan leader who spoke out against him, and rounded up and executed thousands of dissenters. And this was only the beginning. Within a year of proclaiming himself an absolute monarch, he had imposed excessive taxation, conscripted slave labor to work on fortifications, and demanded human sacrifices to glorify his name.

The oracle bones talk of a virtual Utopia being transformed into a barbaric realm where the despotic Jie reigned over a people who enthusiastically turned on their neighbors and took sadistic pleasure in the atrocities being committed. Eventually, a clan from the Mamuji region of what is now the most easterly part of Henan Province rebelled against Jie, overthrew him, and burned his capital to the ground. The leader of the victorious clan, a man named Tang, became king, and a new hereditary regime, the Shang dynasty, was established on the Chinese throne. With the old capital destroyed, the first five Shang kings ruled from various locations until the new capital of Yin was established. The Shang were still in power and reigning from there when the oracle bones were inscribed, and so these were clearly the rulers during what archaeologists had termed the Erligang period.[9]

Although the oracle-bone texts provide no specific dating when referring to the period of Jie's reign, the events described tally with what the archaeological evidence reveals about the violent end of the Erlitou culture around 1500 BC. With the advent of dendrochronology in the 1960s, however, some scholars suggested that his reign had occurred a century and a quarter earlier. Tree-ring patterns for the year 1628 BC showed that in China at the time, there had been a particularly severe winter. Chinese records dating from the period of the Qin dynasty refer to Jie's reign, saying that during his last year as king, prolonged frosts caused catastrophic crop failures. As tree samples from around 1500 BC show no such cold spell, dendrochronologists proposed that the end of the Xia dynasty did not correspond to the burning of the Erlitou city at Yanshi or with the sudden appearance of the Erligang culture. But few archaeologists agreed.

The icy period reported may have been a localized phenomenon not occurring in the region from which the tree samples were obtained. Moreover, the record itself might be inaccurate. The Qin dynasty, from which the reference dated, did not occur until between 221 and 206 BC, almost fifteen hundred years after the period in question. The much older oracle bones, dating from a thousand years earlier, indirectly imply a date for Jie's reign that corresponds with the violent upheaval the archaeological evidence indicates around 1500 BC.

Among the oracle bones there survives a horoscope cast for Tai Geng, the Shang king who founded the city of Yin, concerning the fortunes of his new capital. As an astrological horoscope, it recorded the relative positions of the sun, moon, and planets at the time it was cast, enabling a precise date to be determined for the event. The relative positions of the heavenly bodies are unique to a given moment in time, and with the aid of computer simulations, modern astronomers can accurately date such ancient astronomical observations. The date of the founding of the new city revealed by horoscope is 1351 BC. As the oracle bones also refer to King Tai Geng deciding to relocate his capital immediately on becoming king, it would appear that this was also the date of his succession.

The oracle bones also record that five Shang kings preceded Tai Geng, the first of them being the warlord Tang. Although the length of their reigns is not revealed, we can make a guess as to how long it was before the founding of Yin that Tang overthrew the Xia king Jie. From later records, we can calculate that the average reign of a king during a stable period of ancient Chinese history was between twenty-five and thirty years. If the same applied to the early Shang dynasty, the year in which Tang came to power was somewhere between 1500 and 1475 BC, which tallies with the archaeological evidence concerning the burning of the Erlitou city at Yanshi. To get a date of around 1628, as proposed by the dendrochronologists, all the first five Shang kings would have to have lived twice as long as the average. It seems far more likely that Erlitou culture ended with the reign of King Jie.[10]

One way or another, and irrespective of what caused it, the archaeological evidence reveals that violent upheaval dramatically altered Chinese civilization around 1500 BC, just as it did in the contemporary cultures of the Indus Valley, Central America, and northwestern Europe. At the time all this was happening, the civilizations from which the most comprehensive historical records survive existed in what is now the Middle East—and exactly the same thing was happening there.

8

Clash of Empires

THE OLDEST CIVILIZATION in the Middle East was in Mesopotamia, the ancient Greek name for an area made fertile by the Euphrates and Tigris Rivers. Centered on what is now Iraq, it also included eastern Syria and parts of southeast Turkey and south-central Iran. The prehistoric development of this region follows pretty much the same pattern as evidenced in the Indus Valley: hunting gathering was abandoned around 7000 BC, and by 5500 BC, villages had developed to a similar degree of sophistication.

The culture from this time until around 3500 BC is referred to by archaeologists as the Uruk period, named after a site excavated in southern Iraq. Similar to the Mehrgarh culture of the Indus Valley, the Uruk culture is characterized by large settlements up to twenty-five acres in size of multiroom mud-brick dwellings. The inhabitants manufactured painted pottery, and by 4000 BC used metal tools made primarily from copper. The Uruk culture is often credited with inventing the wheel around 4500 BC, although it appeared in the Indus Valley at the same time. Which of them really came up with the idea is still very much open to debate.[1]

The first true city-building civilization in Mesopotamia also arose about the same time as the Harappa civilization appeared in the Indus Valley, around 3500 BC, when it too entered the Bronze Age. Known as the Sumerian civilization (Sumer being the name for what is now southern Iraq), it was based around the city of Ur, some ninety miles northwest of modern Basra. Although the easternmost part of Mesopotamia is

some twelve hundred miles east of the Indus Valley, similar technological developments occurring simultaneously in the two regions imply an
interchange of ideas.

Sumerian culture, however, was very different from Harappan culture. First, Sumerians were nowhere near as egalitarian. At Ur, most
people were buried without grave goods; only a few were interred with
elaborate items, indicating a class system in which certain individuals
enjoyed higher status in society than others. Second, organized religion
played a far greater role. Most settlements had large buildings decorated
with statues and carvings of deities that were clearly places of public
worship. And third, they were not nearly so peaceful. The Sumerians
made weapons such as swords, daggers, spears, and maces, and even
armor from bronze.

We also know more about the nature of Sumerian than Harappan
society, as the Sumerians developed a form of writing that was readily
decipherable. They invented a script known as cuneiform, which consists of elongated triangular characters impressed into wet clay tablets
with a bone, metal, or wooden stylus. So easy was this form of writing
to master that it continued to be used not only in Mesopotamia but elsewhere in the Middle East as well until the first century AD. Because of
later references to it by the Greeks and Romans, it did not become a forgotten script like that used in the Indus Valley. Cuneiform texts on clay
tablets survive from the time of the Sumerian civilization, and from them
we can glean a fairly comprehensive outline of the civilization's history
from around 2900 BC. We know, for example, that for the next fifteen
hundred years, Mesopotamian civilization revolved around the ascen-
dancy of various cities spread along the Euphrates and Tigris Rivers.

Around the year 3000 BC, the seat of power shifted from Ur to the
city of Adab (modern-day Bismaya), some seventy miles to the north,
when the Sumerian king Lugal-Anne-Mundu formed the first Mesopotamian empire by extending his influence throughout the region. Over
the following centuries, the Sumerians continued to dominate Mesopotamian life until around 2350 BC, when power shifted to the region of
Akkadia in central Iraq.

The 15-foot standing stones of the Ring of Brodgar on the Orkney Isles, one of the hundreds of mysterious megalithic monuments still standing in Britain after 4,500 years. Why such monuments were built is one of the world's great unsolved mysteries. (Photograph by Deborah Cartwright)

The Avebury stone circle in the English county of Wiltshire. At well over 1,000 feet in diameter, almost ten times bigger than Stonehenge, it is Britain's largest megalithic monument.

The 130-foot-high Silbury Hill, near Avebury, is one of the hundreds of artificial mounds built during the megalithic age. Its purpose remains an enigma. (Photograph by Deborah Cartwright)

The Rollright Stones in the English county of Oxfordshire are typical of the hundreds of stone circles erected throughout Britain, Ireland, and northern France between 5,500 and 3,500 years ago. (Photograph by Louise Simkiss)

Dating from 2000 BC, the 13-foot-high Callanish Stones on the Isle of Lewis, off the west coast of Scotland, are one group of thousands of such standing stones, known as menhirs, erected by the megalithic people of northwest Europe. (Photograph by Deborah Cartwright)

Stonehenge, in south-central England, is the most famous monument to survive from the peaceful megalithic age, which lasted for 2,000 years. Shortly after Stonehenge was completed, around 1500 BC, the civilization that built it abruptly and mysteriously tore itself apart.

Between 3500 and 1500 BC, the megalithic peoples of the British Isles lived in unbroken harmony; then, virtually overnight, they became a society of warmongers. The 5,000-year-old megalithic settlement of Skara Brae in Scotland was suddenly abandoned when catastrophe struck. (Photograph by Deborah Cartwright)

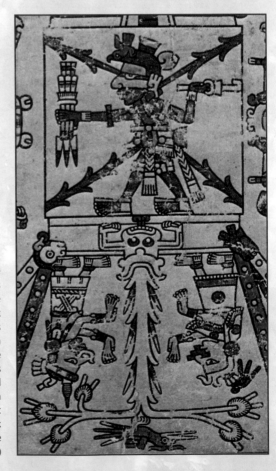

In Aztec mythology, the serpent-bodied goddess Coyolxauhqui, queen of the stars, is said to have brought warfare to the harmonious paradise that once existed in ancient Mexico. Could the representation of the goddess (lower center) have depicted a comet? Illustration from the fifteenth-century Aztec hide manuscript the Codex Fejervary-Mayer. (Merseyside County Museum, Liverpool)

Legends of the Maya, who emerged in Mexico 2,400 years ago, held that a fire demon appeared in the skies when Central America's first civilization was destroyed. Third-century Mayan carving from Palenque, Mexico. (National Ethnology Museum, Berlin)

Women enjoyed a higher status in Harappan society than in many other ancient cultures until the Aryan invasion in the fifteenth century BC. One of the hundreds of 4,000-year-old terra-cotta female figurines unearthed during excavations at Mohenjo-Daro in the Indus Valley. (National Museum of India, New Delhi)

Despite their remarkable grasp of metallurgy, the Chinese Erlitou culture between 3000 and 1500 BC made no weapons of war. Around 1500 BC, with the emergence of the Erligang culture, an ancient armament industry suddenly flourished. A 3,500-year-old bronze ax head and jade dagger found in tombs of the Shang capital of Anyang. (Réunion des Musées Nationaux, Paris)

In 1486 BC, the pharaoh Tuthmosis III led his army on a rampage of Middle Eastern conquest. Basalt statue of Tuthmosis III found during excavations of ancient Thebes. (Luxor Museum, Egypt)

In 1486 BC, the Mitannians of Syria embarked on a mindless suicide attack on the Egyptians in Canaan. Contemporary relief from the Temple of Karnak showing an Egyptian soldier slaying a Mesopotamian warrior. (Jane Ryder Picture Library)

In 1486 BC, after coexisting peacefully for generations, the
Middle Eastern kingdoms of the Hittites, Mitanni, and Assyria
fought one another with unbridled savagery. A palace relief
found at Nineveh shows an Assyrian war chariot, the ancient
equivalent of a tank. (British Museum, London)

The Egyptian Aten disk, long believed
to have symbolized the sun, may well
have represented the massive comet that
appeared in 1486 BC. (Cairo Museum)

Around 1486 BC, the Hittites of what is
now Turkey began to depict a winged disk
hanging in the skies over battle scenes. Relief
found during the German excavations of
Hattusas in 1905. (Altes Museum, Berlin)

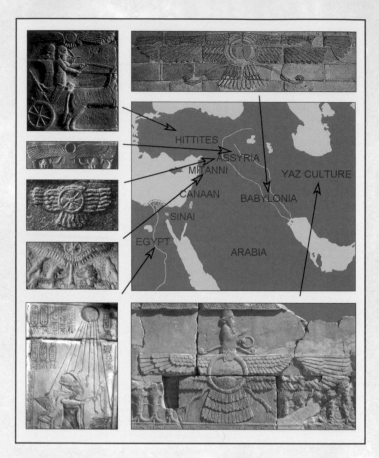

From the early fifteenth century BC, civilizations throughout the Middle East began to represent their principal deities by a celestial disk. Could these symbols have represented the huge comet recorded by the Chinese around 1486 BC?

HITTITES

ASSYRIA

MITANNI

YAZ CULTURE

CANAAN

BABYLONIA

SINAI

EGYPT

ARABIA

Graham Phillips outside the Vatican Archives. Here he discovered the vital clue to solving the mystery of the sudden epidemic of violence that swept the ancient world. (Photograph by Steve Bacon)

The symbol for the Chinese god Lao-Tien-Yeh from a ceramic fragment dating from around 1450 BC, unearthed during excavations at Anyang. (Museum of the Academia Sinica, Taiwan)

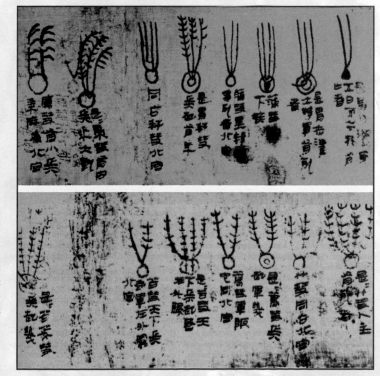

Page from the 2,300-year-old Mawangdui Silk Almanac depicting comets observed by ancient Chinese astrologers from as early as 1500 BC. It records that a huge, ten-tailed comet appeared around 1486 BC. (Hunan Provincial Museum, Changsha)

For almost two millennia following the fifteenth century BC, ancient civilizations throughout the Middle and Near East used the celestial disk as a symbol for warrior kingship, such as in this third-century Persian bas-relief from the Naqsh-e Rajab valley in Iran. (Photograph by Mark Cockle)

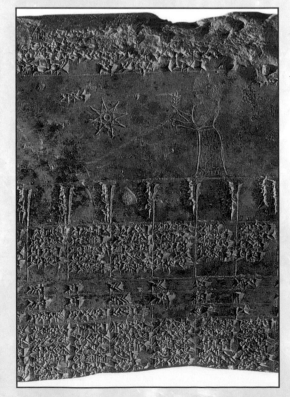

Babylonian astrological tablet from the third century BC shows the "new star" that is said to have brought disaster to Mesopotamia twelve centuries earlier. (The Louvre, Paris)

Throughout ancient Mesopotamia, comets became associated with warfare, violence, and political upheaval. Does this stone tablet found in southern Iraq, dated to between 2300 and 1400 BC, show the breakup of the comet of 1486 BC as described by the ancient Egyptians? (The Louvre, Paris)

When Halley's Comet appeared in 1910, it had five tails and was the most spectacular to appear since the invention of photography. (Conroy Carter Astronomical Archive)

The seven-tailed De Cheseaux's Comet of 1744 was the
largest recorded since the birth of modern astronomy. The
ten-tailed comet of 1486 BC was far bigger, and fragments
of it may even have exploded in the atmosphere.
Woodcut from Amedee Guillemin's Heaven's Gate shows
the tails of the 1744 comet displayed above the horizon.
(Conroy Carter Astronomical Archive)

Artist's impression of the
ten-tailed comet of 1486 BC.
(Catherine Knight)

When a cometary
fragment exploded over
the Tunguska region
of Siberia in 1908,
it devastated 1,000
square miles of forest.
Photograph taken in
1927 of a few of the
estimated 80 million
trees flattened by the
event. (Conroy Carter
Astronomical Archive)

The pharaoh Akhenaten made
monotheistic Atenism Egypt's
national religion. (Cairo Museum)

During the reign of Tutankhamun, Atenism was abandoned in favor of the old gods, but monotheism survived in the religion of the contemporary Israelites. Image from Tutankhamun's throne shows the young pharaoh and his queen beneath the Aten symbol. (Cairo Museum)

The rock dwellings of the Korma Mountains in Turkey. The ancient Cappadocians lived peacefully here for centuries until abruptly, in the early fifteenth century BC, they began to fight among themselves in a psychotic frenzy of self-destruction. (Photograph by Deborah Cartwright)

A new Mesopotamian empire, based around the city of Akkad on the Tigris River, was established by a king known as Sargon the Great. Sargon established an Akkadian dynasty that lasted for approximately two hundred years. For around a century, from 2150 BC, power swung back to the Sumerians, and Ur regained its influence as Mesopotamia's principal city.

This period, sometimes referred to as the Sumerian Renaissance, saw the emergence of a religion that was to dominate central and southern Mesopotamia for the next fifteen hundred years. Sumerian mythology included a pantheon of gods and goddesses and the concept of demons and angels later adopted by the ancient Israelites. The Akkadians also developed creation stories very similar to those found in the Bible, such as the Garden of Eden and the Great Flood, which some scholars believe may also have influenced the early Hebrews. The most spectacular monument to Sumerian religion was the Ziggurat, a massive terraced or stepped pyramid with a base measuring some 210 by 150 feet. Still surviving as a ruin today, it originally consisted of successively smaller brick-built platforms rising to a height of about 65 feet. (Another such ziggurat, built later at the city of Babylon, is thought to have been the origin of the biblical story of the Tower of Babel.) As grand as it was, the Ziggurat of Ur was merely a part of a large temple complex that also served as an administrative center for the city.

By 1950 BC, Sumerian influence had again declined, and power shifted back to central Mesopotamia, this time to the city of Babylon, on the Euphrates River, about fifty miles south of modern Baghdad. At the same time, the city of Assur, on the Tigris River, in northeastern Mesopotamia also rose to prominence, leading ultimately to two separate Mesopotamian kingdoms: Babylonia, centered on Babylon in the central and south part of the region, and Assyria, centered on Assur in the north. By 1600 BC, a third Mesopotamian kingdom had arisen in Mitanni, in the northwestern part of the region. This kingdom of Mitanni grew to absorb all of what is now northern Syria and had its capital at Washukanni in the Khabur River basin in what is now the Syrian region of Al Hasakah.[2]

Although various cities, states, and kingdoms rose and fell through-out two thousand years of recorded Mesopotamian history, and armed conflicts among them sometimes occurred, for most of the time they lived together in peace. The rise in influence of the city-states had been primarily through control of commerce, industry, or raw materials. Although various kings left behind inscriptions recording magnificent victories, the archaeological record suggests that most wars had been limited to localized battles in which no more than a few hundred people died. In fact, so as not to bring devastation to their hard-earned civilization, the ancient Mesopotamians evolved a tradition of fighting in which only small armies, and in some cases single champions, fought to resolve disputes.

Indeed, other civilizations in the Middle East later copied this custom, and such a scenario may have been behind the biblical story of the Philistines and Israelites resolving a conflict with the single-combat clash between David and Goliath. By the all-important period around 1500 BC, Mesopotamia was enjoying such an era of peace that the three kingdoms of which it was by then composed—Babylonia, Assyria, and Mitanni—had never fought seriously with one another. In fact, times were so peaceful that one of them, Mitanni, hadn't even bothered to form an army.[3]

To the north of Mesopotamia, sharing borders with Assyria and Mitanni, was the kingdom of the Hittites. It occupied an area known as Asia Minor, what is now Turkey between the Mediterranean and the Black Seas. Although they were indigenous to this region, the Hittites had adopted much from Mesopotamian civilization. They built ziggurats and erected temples similar to those in Mesopotamia, adopted cuneiform writing, and laid out their cities in the same designs. The Hittite kingdom was founded around 1750 BC, and within 250 years it was just as prosperous as its Mesopotamian neighbors.

Its capital at Hattusas, near the modern-day village of Bogazkale in north-central Turkey, rivaled many of the cities in Babylonia, Assyria, and Mitanni. It is estimated to have covered over a square mile and was inhabited by as many as fifty thousand people. Because the Hittites adopted Mesopotamian writing, much of their history has been preserved in the form of inscribed clay tablets (around thirty thousand have been recovered from the ruins of Hattusas alone), and from such texts we know that for the first 250 years of its existence, the Hittite kingdom had few disputes with its Mesopotamian neighbors.[4]

To the south of Mesopotamia was the huge Arabian Desert, and to the south of Syria there was a further wilderness in the area of what is now Jordan. Along the eastern coast of the Mediterranean, however, there was a fertile strip of land that ran through modern Lebanon, Israel, and Palestine. Known as Canaan, this region consisted of dozens of separate tribal areas controlled by hilltop settlements. Although these settlements, often referred to as citadels, were fortified, the various tribes appear to have lived in relative harmony. They were certainly no threat to the contemporary kingdoms adjoining Canaan to the north Mitanni and to the south the most notorious civilization of the ancient world, the kingdom of Egypt.[5]

The first permanent settlements were established in Egypt by 5500 BC, and just over two thousand years later, city-building civilization had developed along the fertile banks of the Nile River. Originally these were two separate kingdoms, known to Egyptologists as Upper and Lower Egypt, respectively the south and north of the country (the terms *upper* and *lower* referring to the course of the Nile). By the end of the fourth millennium BC, the Egyptians had developed writing in the form of hieroglyphics, and from hieroglyphic inscriptions we know that around 3100 BC Egypt was united into a single kingdom, and a ruling dynasty was established at the city of Memphis, twelve miles south of modern Cairo. It was not until around 2686 BC, however, that Egyptian civilization really came of age, with the beginning of the so-called Old Kingdom.

From the very start, the ancient Egyptians were so obsessed with religion and the afterlife that they never bothered to build an empire or attempt to conquer their neighbors. Despite the Hollywood image to the contrary, for most of its existence Egypt had no time or interest, or the remotest desire, to fight with anyone; all it wanted was to retain its independence. To understand this, we need to appreciate the extraordinary nature of Egyptian religion.

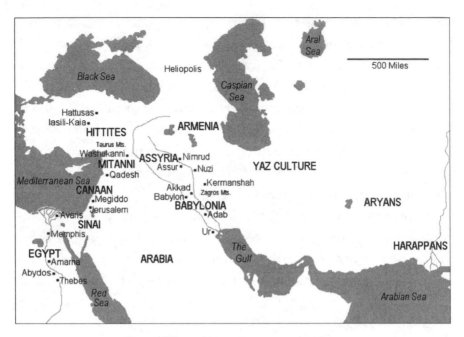

The Middle and Near East around 1500 BC

In ancient Egypt religion was everything, but it was unlike any religion that survives today. Although Egypt had a pantheon of gods, the principal deity was the sun god Re (also called Ra), for whose worship a massive religious center had grown up at Heliopolis, some thirty miles to the north of Memphis. It was believed that Re had once ruled over Egypt personally but, wearied by the affairs of humankind, had retired to the heavens, leaving the kings, ultimately known as pharaohs, to rule in his stead. Called "the son of Re," the pharaoh was considered a half-human, half-divine being through whose body Re himself could manifest. Only the king could expect an individual eternity with the gods; everyone else could only hope to participate vicariously, through contributions to his well-being. In other words, to get to heaven, you worshipped the king.

This applied as much after the king's death as it did during his life. It was believed that the dead pharaoh's spirit would survive only if it periodically returned to earth for sustenance, in the form of food, drink, and other material offerings—something that necessitated having a body to return to. The process of mummification was therefore developed by preserving the body with natron, a dehydrating agent applied to the skin beneath bandages. The king was then entombed with his possessions to be utilized in the afterlife, and surrounded by religious illustrations to ensure his power and protection in the next world. These elaborate interments were originally housed in so-called mastaba tombs, a series of chambers cut down into solid rock, above which stood a brick-built superstructure resembling a miniature royal palace. The entire area was then enclosed by a defensive wall and guarded around the clock. The mastaba tombs were therefore not so much final resting places as they were dwelling places of the dead.

Although it seems that devotion to the king could ensure his subjects a place in next world, the quality of the afterlife depended on what they took with them. This meant that the nobility were also mummified and entombed as elaborately as possible. They constructed their smaller mastaba tombs around that of their beloved pharaoh, in the belief that they would continue in his service in the life to come. Consequently, a great necropolis—a city of the dead—grew up near Memphis at Sakkara, and to cater the opulent funerary activities, a massive industry developed. In addition to the ever-growing priesthood, who attended to the dead by receiving offerings and carrying out unceasing rituals, a wealthy middle class emerged: the craftsmen who built the mausoleums and the artisans who produced the exquisite jewelry, amulets, and burial equipment that furnished them. Remarkably, by far the finest, most lavish, and most numerous objects manufactured in Egypt at this time were intended only for the tomb.[6]

As the funerary industry grew, so did organized crime. Despite the vast numbers of guards and others in attendance at Sakkara, gangs of ingenious robbers still managed to plunder the tombs. To counter this menace, safer and altogether more imposing tombs were conceived— the pyramids. The first of these was designed and built by the royal vizier, or chief minister, Imhotep for the pharaoh Zoser around 2650 BC. This huge construction, which still dominates the ruins of Sakkara, was originally designed as a mastaba tomb, but later alterations and additions created a stepped pyramid in which a series of six mastaba superstructures of decreasing size where placed one on top of the other. It was not long before the more familiar, smooth-sided pyramids began to appear. Various explanations have been offered to account for this development. It may have been an architectural device to conceal the entrance from thieves—who nevertheless managed to plunder them all—or it may have represented a sun's ray, symbolizing the power of the principal god, Re.

Modern commentators have attributed to the pyramids astrological, mystical, or even alien significance; the only thing we can be sure of, however, is that they were seen as a link between heaven and earth. *Pyramid* is a Greek word, and was the term the Greeks used when they first encountered these monuments; the Egyptian word for these structures was *mer*. Meaning "place of ascension," this name clearly implies that the Egyptians of the Old Kingdom saw the pyramids as a means by which the pharaoh could ascend to the realm of the gods. In these new constructions, the king was no longer buried underground, as had been the procedure with the mastaba tombs, but in a chamber within the pyramid itself. Nevertheless, like the earlier tombs, the pyramid was still adjoined by a mortuary temple where offerings could be received.

Around the middle of the third millennium BC, the Old Kingdom reached the zenith of its achievements with the construction of the great pyramids at a second necropolis, near Memphis at Giza. It was once believed that the great pyramids were constructed by huge armies of slaves, but it now seems far more likely that they were the work of a willing populace. The construction of the royal pyramid complex became the focus of society, of paramount importance not only to the king but also to all his subjects, whose quality of existence in life and after death depended on his soul's survival. The largest and most spectacular of these was the pyramid of Cheops, built for the pharaoh Khufu around 2580 BC. Described by the ancient Greeks as the First Wonder of the World, it was originally around 480 feet high—the tallest building on earth until the nineteenth century. Incredibly, its base covered thirteen acres, an area so vast it could accommodate the cathedrals of Florence,

Milan, London's St. Paul's and Westminster Abbey, and St. Peter's in Rome and still have room to spare.

Exactly how it was constructed is even now something of a mystery. From excavating contemporary habitations at Giza, archaeologists have estimated the maximum possible size of the workforce that cut and hauled its thousands of tons of rock into place. Equipped only with simple tools, it should have taken them generations to build the pyramid of Cheops, yet the whole gargantuan undertaking was apparently completed during Khufu's reign of just twenty-three years.[7]

The national obsession with the royal dead finally brought about the end of the Old Kingdom. The incredible drain on the economy required to build, furnish, staff, and maintain these enormous burial complexes, ever growing with the death of each successive king, finally bankrupted the country. Even the monarchy was ruined: in addition to preparing his own burial complex, the king was expected to repair and provision those of his predecessors, as well as provide tombs for his own family and court. Before the Old Kingdom ended in political fragmentation around 2181 BC, however, considerable military and technological advances had been made. Seagoing vessels traded the Mediterranean, and learned scribes were writing with ink on papyrus sheets manufactured from reeds. Sadly, this finely balanced, well-ordered society collapsed into the chaotic conditions of an era now called the First Intermediate.

Around 2040 BC, after about a century and a half of decline, a fresh era emerged, initiated by a strong line of rulers from the city of Thebes, modern Luxor, in southern Egypt. In essence, the Middle Kingdom was a watered-down version of the Old Kingdom: the pharaohs were still buried in pyramids, although less opulent, and they were still expected to funnel wealth to the priesthood. The main expenditure during this period, however, shifted from necropolises to temples. Not only did the temple of Re at Heliopolis, the temple of the creator god Ptah at Memphis, and the temple of Osiris at Abydos require the king's financial support, but he had to fund the massive Temple of Karnak that the newly powerful sect of the wind god Amun had built at the city of Thebes.

Before the Middle Kingdom began to decline, around 1782 BC, the country enjoyed the benefits of significant technological innovations. The invention of the furnace bellows and the smelting of bronze made for better tools; a clever device developed for lifting water increased the efficiency of irrigation; and with the invention of the horizontal loom came an impressive range of fabrics. The Egyptians of the period were even supplied with copious quantities of alcohol, thanks to the introduction of new agricultural methods and the mass cultivation of grapes. Eventually, however, the Middle Kingdom was bankrupted by all this expenditure, like the Old Kingdom before, and Egypt entered another Dark Age known as the Second Intermediate, when tribal peoples from Canaan moved into northern Egypt and established their own kingdom there for a while. Ultimately, around 1600 BC, an Egyptian prince from Thebes named Amosis reunified Egypt and instigated a fresh era of prosperity and a new dynasty. Thus began the so-called New Kingdom, the period into which the famous Tutankhamun was later born.

Despite the fact that the obsession with religion and the afterlife had twice bankrupted the nation, the Egyptians of the New Kingdom continued to pursue it. The capital remained at Thebes, and here a new necropolis was located in the bleak western hills. In this barren gorge, known today as the Valley of the Kings, the Egyptians abandoned their earlier custom of building pyramids, perhaps because of their vulnerability to tomb robbers, and opted instead for deep rock-cut tombs.

It has been suggested that the area was chosen as the royal burial site because the valley is overlooked by a natural cliff formation that resembles a pyramid. It was more likely chosen for practical considerations, however, the narrow valley being relatively easy to guard. Here the tombs, consisting of a series of stairwells, corridors, and chambers cut into the mountainside, were ingeniously designed to defeat the tomb robbers. By this time the god Amun had become the chief god of Egypt, and the king was now regarded as this deity's son.

As the Old Kingdom had been obsessed with the dead and the Middle Kingdom with temples, the New Kingdom became obsessed with the worship of this principal deity, and the Temple of Karnak was expanded to an unprecedented size. Although the New Kingdom did nothing to rival the construction achievements of the great pyramid, this huge temple complex of shrines, courts, halls, and processional ways covered hundreds of acres. It is estimated that it was staffed by an astonishing sixty thousand people—a multitude of priests, scribes, servants, and religious officials whose essential purpose it was to conduct the intricate daily rituals deemed necessary to ensure the blessing of Amun and the continued prosperity of Egypt. But this extravagant obsession with the god Amun did not bankrupt the New Kingdom. By now the country could afford it. During this period, it was more prosperous than it had ever been. Its colossal works of art, temples, palaces, and monuments are the most numerous of any era. And just like their ancestors, the Egyptians of the New Kingdom were too fixated on their own internal affairs to wage war.[8]

By 1500 BC, despite the fact that the kingdom of Egypt had existed for over fifteen hundred years, the Egyptians had never once attempted to build an empire. In the popular Hollywood image, Egypt is often portrayed as a country of slavery, invading armies, and bloodthirsty pharaohs. As we shall see, there was a period when Egypt became like this, but that was not until over a century after the start of the New Kingdom. Until that time, there appears to have been no such thing as slavery in Egypt, and armed conflicts were limited to the occasional border dispute. The only period of real warfare was the struggle to win back northern Egypt at the end of the Second Intermediate.

Egypt had an army; it was large, well trained, and equipped with the finest weapons of the day, but it was purely a defensive force. It existed to maintain law and order and to secure and patrol borders, but one of its chief functions was to guard temples, palaces, and tombs. The Egyptians were too wrapped up in their own idiosyncratic existence to be bothered with anyone else. That is not to say that ancient Egypt was any kind of Utopia. It was about as far from democracy as you could hope to get; its rigid class structure was firmly maintained, and the system dealt severely with dissenters and those who transgressed religious or civil laws. Nonetheless, even the most humble Egyptian citizens appear to have supported the system that kept them employed, fed, and sheltered, and in a lifestyle enviable throughout the contemporary world.[9]

This, then, was the state of affairs in the Middle East at the close of the sixteenth century BC: its kingdoms were prosperous, stable, and at peace. But then, suddenly and quite inexplicably, the entire region simultaneously erupted into an unparalleled era of violence. An exact date for this abrupt outbreak of hostilities is difficult to determine. Although the Hittites, Mesopotamians, and Egyptians all left behind written records of this period, it is difficult to establish precisely how they correspond to the years of our modern calendar, because events were usually only recorded to have occurred during a particular year of a king's reign. Nevertheless, by cross-referencing such records and comparing them with the results obtained from thermoluminescence, dendrochronology, and radiocarbon dating, a rough chronological framework of ancient Middle Eastern history has emerged, and from this it is clear that the violence all began somewhere within twenty years of the year 1500 BC.

The most comprehensive records we have of this sudden era of aggression survive from Egypt. Toward the end of the sixteenth century BC, the pharaoh Tuthmosis III ascended the Egyptian throne, but as he was just a baby, his mother, Queen Hatshepsut, ruled as regent. For two decades the country remained at peace and continued to prosper. But then, in the twenty-second year of his reign, shortly before he would have automatically assumed full kingship, Tuthmosis seized power from his mother in a palace coup. No records survive to explain Tuthmosis's actions. Perhaps Hatshepsut had decided to retain power for herself. Whatever the reason, the coup succeeded; Tuthmosis probably had his mother executed, as she is never mentioned in the records again, and he ordered the deaths of all who opposed him. There may be nothing unusual about this seizure of power, but what happened next was unprecedented in Egypt's long and colorful history.

Although Tuthmosis quickly and effectively achieved his objective, firmly securing the reins of power, he initiated an almost Stalinist reign of terror. Supported by the elite palace guard, the pharaoh purged the civil service, the priesthood, and even the army; regional government was abolished; and show trials and executions were publicly staged throughout the county. Previous pharaohs had enjoyed absolute power in principle, but for all intents and purposes, they played no part in secular activities. In essence, they were sacred icons.

Deemed living gods, Egyptian kings were kept in the lap of luxury, their every whim catered to, but their activities were almost exclusively religious and ceremonial. Worldly affairs and matters of government were left to ministers, civil servants, and regional nobles. What emerged within a few months of Tuthmosis III's solo reign, however, was nothing short of dictatorship. So tyrannical was he that he may even have been the pharaoh who enslaved the ancient Israelites. Despite the common misconception, for the first fifteen hundred years of its history, Egypt did not conscript vast armies of slaves (evidence shows that the pyramids, as noted, were built by paid workers or willing volunteers). It was during Tuthmosis's time that the first records of slaves are found in Egypt. He enslaved thousands of foreigners from Canaan who had been settled for generations in northern Egypt, which may well have included the Hebrew tribes.[10]

The moment he secured his hold on power, Tuthmosis set about establishing Egypt's first empire, and began by marching the biggest army the world had ever seen into the region of Canaan. The devastation unleashed against one of the tribal citadels in the region was so severe that its name has come to be associated with total carnage ever since. The citadel was called Megiddo; the Greek rendering of the name by which it is more commonly known is Armageddon. (When the Bible's Christian Scriptures were composed in the first century AD, the Book of Revelation prophesied that the end of the world would start here with another apocalyptic battle.) But Tuthmosis did not stop there.[11] After conquering Canaan, his armies swept into Nubia to the south of Egypt and into Libya to the west. This was to be the single greatest expansion of Egyptian power in the entire thirty-five hundred years of the kingdom's existence, leading many historians to refer to Tuthmosis III as the Napoleon of ancient Egypt. Tuthmosis III, however, was not the only king in the Middle East of the time who suddenly became a tyrant with imperial pretensions.[12]

If Tuthmosis III was the Napoleon of ancient Egypt, his contemporary the Hittite king Hantili II was the Adolf Hitler of Asia Minor. At precisely the time that Tuthmosis III began his campaign into Israel, Hantili II initiated a preemptive strike south against his neighbors the Assyrians, a people with whom the Hittites had peacefully coexisted for generations. Inscribed clay tablets of this period uncovered by archaeologists from the Hittite capital of Hattusas show that King Hantili was also a ruthless monarch at home. He established what can only be described as the world's first concentration camps, in which both foreign captives and domestic opponents were worked to death in mines.

Previously the Hittite kingdom had enjoyed a remarkably lenient penal system, with terms of imprisonment being the norm for most crimes other than murder. Hantili II, however, changed all this, instigating new and barbaric forms of punishment for even the most trivial of crimes: flaying alive, drawing and quartering, and crucifixion, to name but three.[13]

At exactly the same time as Hantili II was invading northern Assyria and persecuting his own people, Mitanni, the hitherto passive kingdom in Syria, had its own ideas of grandeur. Its king, Shaushtatar, led a surprise attack against southern Assyria, quickly occupying those areas that were not being conquered by the Hittites. Some historians have suggested that this unusual act of aggression by a previously peaceful kingdom might simply have been an act of expediency: Shaushtatar had merely taken advantage of the weakened state of Assyria. Shortly after he marched against the Assyrians, however, Shaushtatar led his army south on what amounted to a suicidal rampage against the mighty Egyptians occupying Canaan. Vastly outnumbered by the technologically superior Egyptians, the Mitannian army was all but obliterated.

Egyptian tomb inscriptions of this period note with amazement how the Mitannian hordes charged mindlessly toward the Egyptian army in waves, only to be repeatedly cut down by showers of arrows. There was absolutely no sense or precedent for this bizarre Mitannian behavior. Suicide troops, such as the Japanese kamikaze pilots in the Second World War, are not unknown to history, but Japan had a history of military zeal. Mitanni, on the other hand, had been an ancient equivalent of modern-day Switzerland. In fact, the Mitannians had previously had no standing army at all; Shaushtatar had conscripted his soldiers in just a few months. The Mitannian attack on the Egyptians was as pointless and as unlikely an event as the Swiss attacking the Soviet Union at the height of the Cold War.[14]

Nothing is known of what happened in Babylonia during this time, as no records survive from the period because the city, perhaps the largest in the world at the time with around one hundred thousand inhabitants, was razed by fire. Archaeological excavations have revealed that around 1500 BC, the city suffered such carnage that it would be centuries before it again rose to greatness. From Egyptian, Mitannian, Assyrian, and Hittite records, there is nothing to indicate that any of these kingdoms were responsible for what happened in Babylon. In fact, they were too busy fighting each other. It seems more likely that Babylon was sacked by the Kassites, who occupied the Zagros Mountains to the east, between what is now Iraq and Iran, as they later occupied Babylonia for four centuries.[15]

In the kingdoms of Egypt, Mitanni, and the Hittites, there seems to have been a mass epidemic of violent hysteria. As far as we can tell, the abrupt desire of these kingdoms to build empires, and their sudden acts of aggression, domestic tyranny, and civil conflict, was instigated separately. The rulers of these various nations suddenly decided to commit acts of savagery and wage their wars independently of one another. Whatever caused all this may have had a common origin, but the historical records of the period to offer no obvious clue as to what this might have been. We can be sure of one thing, however: it had nothing to do with climate change. In the Middle East we don't need archaeology to reveal that there were no crop failures or famine, nor any form of pestilence or plague. Texts and inscription from the time reveal that the entire region was enjoying a period of unequaled prosperity.

So there we have it. At exactly the same time as the megalithic civilization in northwest Europe was tearing itself apart, the pre-Olmec civilization in Central America abruptly descended into savagery, China erupted into civil war, the Aryans frenziedly wiped out the Harappans in the Indus Valley, the Middle East exploded into warfare and mass destruction—and for no apparent reason. As in the rest of the world, there was absolutely nothing to gain and everything to lose from such violence.

Surely all this synchronous brutality and homicidal frenzy cannot be coincidence. There had to have been a common cause for this global epidemic of savagery. But what could it have been? These centers of civilization were scattered around the world, separated by thousands of miles, and in most cases completely unaware of the others' existence. Before seeking answers, there is, however, another aspect of this global insanity that needs to be appreciated. Just as abruptly as it began, it came to a sudden and simultaneous end.

9

A Sudden Calm

BECAUSE THE MOST comprehensive historical records of the period have survived from the countries of the Middle East, let's begin by examining what happened here. A great deal is known about the campaigns of Tuthmosis III since his royal scribe, an Egyptian noble named Thanuny, was also a general in the army. Not only did Thanuny write a firsthand account of Tuthmosis's military exploits, but it was inscribed for posterity on the walls of the Temple of Karnak, where it still survives. Early in his sole reign, after he had secured Canaan, Tuthmosis could easily have advanced his forces into northern Syria and overrun the kingdom of Mitanni. Not only was the Egyptian army in the region larger and vastly superior, but also its Mitannian counterpart was a ragtag affair, hurriedly and only recently assembled.

To add to this, half the Mitannian army had been wiped out during Shaushtatar's crazed assault on the Egyptians in Canaan, and the rest was occupied in Assyria. Tuthmosis decided instead to march east toward southern Mesopotamia, however, in the hope of conquering Babylon, at the time the largest city in the world. But the plan went badly wrong. Tuthmosis's forces became bogged down fighting a guerrilla war with the Semite tribes indigenous to the mountains east of the river Jordan. They surprised the Egyptians with their fanatical resistance, and so impeded their progress that Tuthmosis was ultimately beaten to Babylon by the Hittites.[1]

Hittite records of the period are found among the thousands of inscribed clay tablets uncovered at Hattusas, now preserved at Turkey's

Ankara Museum. From these we learn that the Hittite king Hantili II had attacked northeast Assyria a few months earlier, but even when his forces were still engaged fighting the Assyrians, he divided his army and led half of it south to invade Babylonia, reaching Babylon without serious opposition. Under normal circumstances, the Egyptian army would have been more than a match for the Hittites, but it was already worn down, having fought its way through Jordan, and was gravely in need of fresh supplies.

There is no reference in the Hittite texts concerning an engagement with the Egyptians at this time, and the inscriptions from the Temple of Karnak contain little detail about Tuthmosis's foray into southern Mesopotamia. Tuthmosis most likely decided against engaging the Hittites and opted to abandon his Babylonian campaign. The outcome was that he retreated to Canaan, consolidated his hold on that region, then returned to Egypt and concentrated his efforts against Nubia and Libya. The Hittites also withdrew from Babylonia. When Hantili reached Babylon, he found it already sacked, presumably by the Kassites from the Zagros Mountains. With little to plunder and his forces stretched perilously thin along a five-hundred-mile front, he made a strategic withdrawal back to Assyria. It seems that once the Hittites withdrew, the Kassites swept down from the mountains to overwhelm Babylonia. Hittite records reveal that they were firmly entrenched there within a decade, and after a brief period of struggle with the Jordanian Semites, they remained in control of the region for the next four centuries.[2]

No native Mitannian records of this period have yet been found, and so what we know about the kingdom of Mitanni at the time comes from contemporary Hittite and Egyptian sources, and in particular Assyrian cuneiform texts on tablets found during excavations of the ancient city of Nuzi, just southwest of what is now Kirkuk in northern Iraq. The so-called Nuzi Tablets, now in the British Museum, record that the Assyrian king Puzur-Ashur III was completely surprised by the Hittite attack on his country, and could do little to stop their advance south along the east bank of the Tigris. Eventually, Puzur-Ashur mobilized his forces and dispatched an army under the command of his son Enlil-Nasir to engage the invaders.

The king remained at Assur, making ready to defend his capital against the Hittites should the counterstrike fail, but was ill prepared when the city came under surprise attack by the Mitannians. Even though Shaushtatar's army was little more than an undisciplined, disorganized rabble, it caught Puzur-Ashur off guard. With most of his forces sent to oppose the Hittites, and the city as yet unready for siege, Assur was overwhelmed and its king was killed.[3]

Meanwhile, although Enlil-Nasir's army successfully engaged the Hittites fifty miles northeast of Assur, they too were taken by surprise when they were outflanked by Hantili's unexpected return from Babylon. Caught between two Hittite armies, the Assyrians were badly beaten, and Enlil-Nasir was forced to retreat back across the Tigris. When the prince returned home, he was astonished to find that Assur had already fallen to the Mitannians. Enlil-Nasir still had a sizable army, but without a capital and faced with a war on two fronts, he proposed a treaty with Shaushtatar. The Mitannian king, however, would have none of it. Realizing their hopeless predicament, the Assyrian officers brokered their own deal with Shaushtatar: they offered him the Assyrian crown, swore their allegiance, and handed him Enlil-Nasir in chains.

The king of Mitanni now had command of a disciplined, professional army that, in collusion with his own, was sufficiently equipped to repel any further Hittite advance into Assyria. Enlil-Nasir was returned a prisoner to the Mitannian capital of Washshukanni, the Assur royal palace was stripped of its gold and silver to buy the continued support of the Assyrian troops, and the local populace was enslaved en masse to supply Shaushtatar's war machine. For the next couple of decades, Assyria remained divided between Shaushtatar and Hantili, the Hittites occupying the land to the east of the Tigris, the Mitannians controlling the west, with the two kings engaged in repeated battles from which neither emerged as decisive victor.[4]

Ten years after his retreat from Babylon, Tuthmosis III again attempted to conquer Mesopotamia. Rather than a repeat campaign in the Jordanian mountains, he instead moved north through southern

Syria with the intention of swinging east. Here, however, he came under attack by Shaushtatar, and quickly realized that the campaign's success would necessitate neutralizing the kingdom of Mitanni. He therefore continued north into the region of Nuhashshe, in central Syria, where he found the Mitannian army a much more formidable opponent than the disorganized horde that had foolishly attacked him a decade earlier. It was not only that Shaushtatar's army was better trained, and included Assyrians; his troops were now seasoned veterans, having spent the best part of ten years fighting the Hittites.

Nonetheless, the Egyptian army was still superior, and could probably have defeated Shaushtatar had Tuthmosis not made the mistake of dividing his forces. In an attempt to assault the Mitannian capital from two sides, he sent half his army north along the Mediterranean coast to the Taurus Mountains. But the Taurus Mountains were Hittite territory, and here the Egyptians were attacked by the Hittite forces and their advance stalled. With insufficient numbers, Tuthmosis's southern army was forced to abandon its assault on Washshukanni. Only just avoiding being surrounded by a Mitannian attack to the rear, Tuthmosis retreated into southern Syria, where he met up with his northern army and ordered his forces to dig in.

Over the next ten years, there were periodic engagements between the Egyptians and Mitannians in the region of Nuhashshe, but the situation remained a virtual stalemate. Tuthmosis's main fields of military activity were south of Egypt and in the Libyan desert, although he was continually forced to return to Canaan and southern Syria to suppress revolts. Shaushtatar's joint kingdom of Mitanni and western Assyria was locked in repeated battles with the Hittites, while Babylonia became a killing zone where the mountain peoples, the Kassites from the east and the Semites from the west, fought savagely over the spoils of what had once been the cradle of civilization. For two decades the entire Middle East was consumed by warfare, tyranny, and chaos—but then suddenly and quite mysteriously, everything changed.

Twenty years after he had seized power from his mother, Tuthmosis III found his forces in southern Syria under direct attack by the Mitannians, who rapidly overran a number of cities in the region. From the Nuzi Tablets we can gather that Shaushtatar, determined to expand his empire, reckoned he was now strong enough to take on the Egyptians in an offensive capacity. With an old score to settle, Tuthmosis returned to Syria to personally conduct the new war with Mitanni and quickly retook the lost ground. After forcing back the Mitannians from most of southern Syria, Tuthmosis prepared to attack the strategic city of Qadesh, where Shaushtatar had his military headquarters.

Everything was poised for a final showdown between two of the most ruthless warrior-kings of the era. Tuthmosis went on the offensive, destroying three surrounding Mitannian garrisons, and was about to attack Qadesh when something—and the inscriptions at the Temple of Karnak provide no clue as to what made the pharaoh halt in his tracks and return to Egypt. What is even more remarkable is that although southern Syria was now wide open for Shaushtatar's taking, the Mitannian king also decided to return home, to his capital at Washshukanni. Amazingly, at precisely the same time, the Hittite king Hantili suddenly lost all interest in empire building and ordered his occupying army to withdraw from eastern Assyria.[5]

Historians have suggested that some kind of peace conference was brokered and that all sides agreed to a cessation of hostilities. There is no contemporary reference to such an accord, however. If there was an arranged armistice, it was a most unusual one for the period. At a time when there was no such thing as international law or a United Nations, there was no reason whatsoever for the three parties to trust one another. The history of the ancient Middle East is full of examples of nations using peace treaties to play for time, redeploy troops, or rearm. Nevertheless, all three kings returned home and withdrew their armies from the relevant theaters of conflict.

Even if there had been some kind of truce that everyone for some reason honored, it would not explain the simultaneous benign behavior of two of these previously despotic monarchs on their home soil. After having kept the Assyrian prince Enlil-Nasir captive in Washshukanni for twenty years, Shaushtatar not only ordered his release and let him return home to Assur but also allowed him to be crowned Assyrian king. Stranger still, at exactly the same time, he freed the Assyrians he had enslaved in Assyria two decades before. As Enlil-Nasir I, the new Assyrian king was still subordinate to the Mitanni king, and his country remained a vassal state; nonetheless, this was an astonishing change of heart by the ruthless Shaushtatar. The Hittite king Hantili also behaved in a completely uncharacteristic manner: immediately after ordering his troops home from Assyria, he abolished the forced labor camps he had set up twenty years earlier and reestablished the lenient penal code his country had at that time enjoyed.[6]

What followed was an era of peace that lasted for almost a century. Although Tuthmosis held on to his gains in Canaan, Nubia, and Libya, from then until his death twelve years later he was again involved in only a single campaign, and this was little more than a border dispute in Nubia. His immediate successors withdrew most of Egypt's occupying armies and, for no obvious military reason, virtually abandoned the hard-won empire altogether. Hittite power fell into total obscurity, only reemerging with the reign of Tudhaliya I around 1400 BC; and although the Mitannians continued to retain military control of Assyria for the next hundred years, domestic administration was returned almost entirely to the Assyrians themselves. And it was not only the main players in the Middle East who suddenly abandoned hostilities. In Babylonia, the Semites withdrew into the Jordanian mountains, leaving the Kassites to establish a dynasty of kings in central Mesopotamia who remained harmoniously enthroned for generations. Throughout the Middle East, something most unusual in world history seems to have occurred: peace appears to have broken out.[7]

It is puzzling enough that an unprecedented two-decade era of violence, cruelty, and oppression should have ended so abruptly in the Middle East. What is even more mysterious is that exactly the same appears to have happened elsewhere in the world.

Although far less is known about what happened in China during the period around 1500 BC, as no contemporary records survive, the oracle bones discovered at Anyang, dating from a century and a half later, contain numerous references to Tang, the first of the Shang kings who overthrew the dictatorial rule of the Xia King Jie. Archaeologists do not know the exact date of the destruction of the Shang capital at Yanshi; what the oracle bones do reveal, however, is that for fourteen years after its destruction, the new king Tang was permanently engaged in conflict. It was not only forces loyal to the old Shang dynasty that kept him occupied—in fact, these seem to have been dealt with fairly quickly—but also the various regional clan leaders who had become formidable warlords in their own right.

The wars in which Tang's forces became embroiled were not merely armed struggles to fill an internal power vacuum; well before his civil authority was even remotely secured, the new king attempted to build an empire by leading his troops into what is now the province of Jiangxi south of the Yangtze River and north in a vain endeavor to conquer the fierce nomadic tribes of Inner Mongolia. But then, just as in the Middle East, hostilities abruptly ceased.[8]

Unfortunately, there is no reference in the oracle-bone texts as to precisely what brought about the end of fighting; all we know is that Tang abandoned his pretensions of empire building and came to an agreement with the Chinese warlords to establish a government along similar lines to what had existed during the Xia period. The archaeological evidence also points to an era of peace at this time, with a grand new city being built at Zhengzhou, eighty miles east of Yanshi, which appears to have been the new Chinese capital. The new Shang dynasty was far more autocratic than its predecessors—armies remained standing and cities were fortified—but an era of internal peace returned to China that would last until the last Shang king committed suicide after his army was defeated by the Iron Age Zhou people of what is now Shaanxi Province to the west in 1046 BC. Going by the oracle-bone texts, which reveal that Tang rose in revolt just over five years after Jie dissolved the regional councils and imposed martial law, and that Tang's period of armed conflict lasted for a further fourteen years, the period during which China was consumed by violence coincides almost exactly with the two decades of aggression in the Middle East.[9]

Far less is known about the Aryans who annihilated the Harappan culture around 1500 BC, as no historical records relating to this period of Indian or Afghan history survive. The archaeological evidence shows that these previously peaceful inhabitants of Afghanistan banded together and swept into the Indus Valley to wipe out its civilization. The Harappans were massacred and their cities destroyed, and over the ruins altars were erected where mass human sacrifices took place. Archaeology also reveals, however, that this barbaric behavior did not last long. At excavations of Harappan settlements, such as Harappa itself, only the soil stratum immediately above the level of carnage contains the remains of the decapitated sacrificial victims.

In fact, the historical evidence that does exist from later times suggests that the Aryans rapidly abandoned their bloodthirsty activities completely. Although it was many years before the Aryans built their own civilization in the Indus Valley, what eventually emerged was one of the most spiritually inclined societies in the history of the world. It was the Aryans who founded what became Hinduism. From studies of the origins of Hinduism, it seems that the religion had its pacifist origins within a very few years of the Aryan invasion of the Indus Valley. The oldest Hindu texts are known as the Rig-Veda, a collection of Sanskrit hymns dedicated to gods who are still revered by Hindus today.

Although the oldest surviving copies of this work date from many centuries later, because of astronomical references and allusions to contemporary life in the text, linguists have localized their composition to the Punjab region of the upper Indus Valley, and have dated them to the early fifteenth century BC. If this is correct, then the Aryans appear to have abruptly reverted to a peaceful culture within a couple of decades of their sudden transformation into a horde of mindless killers.[10]

What is known about the contemporary historical periods in northwest Europe and Central America comes totally from archaeology. There were no written records from Britain, Ireland, or France until Roman times, fifteen centuries later, and no known form of writing existed in Central America until around 500 BC. The archaeology in northwest Europe has revealed that the sudden cessation of monument building by the megalithic civilization was accompanied by a simultaneous change of lifestyle. Settlements became very much larger, surrounded by defensive ramparts, and new hillforts were built containing entire towns.

Following this abrupt change in culture, the descendants of the megalithic people (referred to as the Late Bronze Age culture) continued to live primarily in these fortified settlements, the grave goods of the ruling classes indicating an unbroken line of leadership, until the coming of the Celts around 700 BC.

After the sudden and violent transformation of society from pre-Olmec to Olmec culture in Central America, everything settled down here too. The Olmec civilization continued to exist and flourish until its eventual decline around 400 BC. In neither of these areas of the world can we tell just how long the era of violent upheaval lasted, but from the archaeological evidence it appears that in both cases it was a one-off phenomenon that could not have lasted much more than a generation. Thereafter, despite the fact that society had been irrevocably altered, the inhabitants of Central America and northwest Europe continued to exist in relative harmony for centuries.

As we shall see, there were other places in the world where cultures succumbed to a brief upsurge in violent activity around 1500 BC. For example, archaeology has shown that a people from what is now Armenia suddenly invaded northeastern Iran and established a proto-civilization in the area that scholars refer to as the Yaz culture.[11] At the same time, some calamity overwhelmed an emergent culture in Japan. The contemporary Japanese Jomon people may not have built cities, but they led an urban lifestyle in sophisticated timber towns.

Furthermore, at this time they were manufacturing some of the most advanced pottery in the world. Like the Olmecs, the Jomon people survived for many years after 1500 BC—but only just. Excavations have shown that around 1500 BC, Jomon towns throughout Japan suffered pillaging and burning, suggesting some kind of mass civil upheaval. Judging by the numbers of Jomon graves discovered from periods immediately before and after this event, this ancient Japanese population appears to have mysteriously decimated itself.[12]

It is overwhelmingly clear that around 1500 BC something quite extraordinary was happening to human beings all over the world. Something—and it wasn't overpopulation, famine, lack of resources, or climate change—was driving even the most peace-loving peoples to shocking acts of barbarism, violence, brutality, and frenzied bloodlust. But this is only half the astonishing picture that emerges. After a couple of decades, as far as can be established, just as suddenly as it began, these unprecedented acts of aggression appear to have simultaneously ceased.

All this raises the question as to why this extraordinary global synchronicity has not been the subject of scholarly study. What we have to remember, however, is that both history and archaeology are remarkably selective subjects: archaeologists and historians concentrate on a specific region or culture. Nevertheless, they do share a bewilderment at what could have caused the sudden violence that enveloped or annihilated the civilizations they have studied. The fact remains that very few researchers have examined the overall picture. It is problematic enough that archaeologists and historians cannot explain the demise or acute transformation of the particular culture about which they are authorities, let alone to make matters worse by trying to explain what happened to other cultures outside their field of expertise. If pushed, however, they tend to put it all down to coincidence. Surely, though, this is straining the concept well beyond its breaking point. Yet if there was a common cause, what could it possibly have been?

10
When and Why

AROUND THIRTY-FIVE HUNDRED YEARS AGO, what can only be described as an epidemic of mass aggression suddenly seems to have erupted on a global scale. The big question is, why? So far, our dating of this event has been based primarily on scientific techniques, such as radiocarbon dating and thermoluminescence, none of which provides a precise date for the abrupt onset of the carnage; that can be determined only to within approximately fifty years either side of 1500 BC. Before we can attempt to discover the cause, we need to establish a more exact date, and for this we require historical records.

Unfortunately, few cultures in the world at that time had developed writing, and most texts from those that had have either remained undeciphered, are fragmentary, or have been lost over time. Luckily, though, one civilization from which numerous translatable and well-preserved writings of the period have survived is ancient Egypt. Egypt did not escape the bout of violence that swept the world—as we have seen, the pharaoh Tuthmosis III seized power from his mother and initiated an unprecedented reign of international hostility—so perhaps Egyptian records can reveal exactly when it all began. Before we examine Egyptian records, however, we must consider the controversial question of Egyptian dating itself.

The ancient Egyptians covered their monuments, temples, tombs, and palaces with carved inscriptions in a form of pictorial writing known as hieroglyphics, and Egypt's dry desert climate has meant that many of these inscriptions have remained clearly preserved. For centuries, however, no one could read them. Ancient Egyptian has not been a living language since Egypt came under the sway of the Arab world in the second half of the first millennium AD and Arabic became the national tongue. For years, the translation of Egyptian hieroglyphics defied all attempts, and it was not until the end of the eighteenth century that it was at last made possible by the discovery of the Rosetta Stone.

This slab of black basalt, found near the town of Rosetta at the mouth of the Nile in 1799, bore a lengthy inscription dating from 196 BC. As the same text was included both in Egyptian hieroglyphics and in a known language, Greek, it enabled the French scholar Jean-François Champollion to work toward a complete decipherment of hieroglyphics by the mid-1820s. Nevertheless, even though it has been possible for scholars to read hieroglyphics for almost two centuries, enabling us to learn much about ancient Egypt's colorful past, a massive problem remains, and that concerns dating.

When ancient Egyptian scribes dated an event, they did so by referring to it as having occurred in a particular year of a king's reign. This was all very well for the ancient Egyptian, but for us to determine how these dates relate to the modern calendar, we need to know the names of the kings that reigned, for how long, and in what order. A comprehensive list of Egyptian kings is something we do not have, and so even today Egyptologists are still arguing about how Egyptian history fits into a modern chronological framework. We know, for example, that Tuthmosis III seized power from his mother and began to wage war on his neighbors in the twenty-second year of his reign, but what year was this BC?

A rough chronology of Egyptian history has been made possible from five known inscriptions that reveal the names and order of succession of many of Egypt's pharaohs. The Palermo Stone, a black diorite slab dating from around 2470 BC, recorded a series of early kings; the so-called Royal List from the Temple of Karnak at Thebes included the names of those who preceded Tuthmosis III around 1500 BC; and another Royal List, from the city of Abydos, made by the pharaoh Seti I around 1290 BC, named the seventy-six kings who preceded him, as did two duplicates made by his son Ramesses II.

Unfortunately, as a historical chronology, these lists are almost use-less on their own, as they fail to provide the length of each reign. Luck-ily, however, one ancient text survives that does: a list of some three hundred kings written on a long sheet of papyrus dating from around 1200 BC. Now in the Turin Museum, in Italy, the so-called Royal Canon not only gives the kings' order of succession, but also provides the exact period of each reign, right down to the months and days. The problem, however, is that there is no way to directly relate the list to the mod-ern calendar. Which year BC did the list start, and which year BC did it end? It fell to astronomy to eventually resolve the matter. Some of the pharaohs' reigns could be precisely dated due to ancient astronomical observations and a lucky mistake in the Egyptian calendar.

The ancient Egyptians believed that the year consisted of exactly 365 days, and were unaware that the true year (the time the earth takes to orbit the sun) was in reality approximately 365¼ days. Today we know this, which is why we add an extra day (February 29) every fourth or leap year. The ancient Egyptians made no such adjustment, so their calendar gradually moved out of alignment with the true solar year by a day every four years until, after 730 years, their midsummer's day ended up falling in the middle of winter. Because they had no idea that the year was determined by the length of time it took the earth to orbit the sun, this discrepancy perplexed the ancient Egyptians, who every few centu-ries would find the seasons apparently reversed.

Only every 1,460 years would the calendars properly align. This Egyptian calendar was known as the civil calendar, as it was used to orga-nize civic activities, such as administrative meetings, tax collections, and censuses. The Egyptians did have a second calendar, however, known as the celestial calendar, which was used to plan religious events. Religious activities were tied to celestial events, such as the rising of certain stars and constellations at particular times of the year. These events were, of course, determined by the true solar year, which meant that the celestial calendar would move out of alignment with the civil calendar by a day every four years and coincide only once every 1,460 years.[1]

When the Egyptian calendar was first drawn up, in the third

millennium BC, the civil and celestial calendars aligned, and the Egyptian New Year's Day was determined to be the day of the heliacal rising of the brightest visible star, Sirius: this was the day of the star's annual reappearance after some months below the horizon in what is now early July. From then on, the civil calendar was arranged so that New Year's Day fell on the same day every year—every 365 days. It was not long before the Egyptians realized that the heliacal rising of Sirius was occurring one day later every four years.

It was 1,460 years before the heliacal rising of Sirius again occurred on the civil calendar's New Year's Day, and when it did a special festival took place that was thought to mark the beginning of a new astrological eon called the Sothic cycle (after Sothis, the ancient name for Sirius). Thanks to the later Romans, we know exactly what years, relating to our modern system of dating, these Sothic cycles began. Such an occasion is known to have been celebrated by the Romans who occupied Egypt in 139 AD, as a coin was issued to commemorate the event. As this occurred only every 1,460 years, by counting backward we can work out that the Egyptian civil and celestial calendars had previously aligned in the years 1321 BC and 2781 BC.

Against these important dates, specific years in the reigns of kings from the Royal Canon can be determined. For example, one of the kings included in the list is a pharaoh named Senusret III, and a contemporary inscription records that in the seventh year of his reign, the heliacal rising of Sirius occurred on the 226th day of the civil calendar. As it took four years for the calendars to move out of alignment by one day, for the calendars to be out of alignment by 226 days meant that 904 years (226 × 4) must have transpired since the beginning of the last Sothic cycle, in 2781 BC. Accordingly, the seventh year of Senusret III's reign must have been 1877 BC. With these and other such records, it is possible to date the reigns of a number of kings recorded in the Royal Canon.

As this list gives both the successive order of the kings and the length of their reigns, by counting backward and forward from the known dates, it is possible to work out when each king's reign began and ended. For example, if the seventh year of Senusret III's reign was 1877 BC, his reign must have begun in 1884 BC; the recorded nineteen-year reign of his predecessor, Senusret II, must therefore have begun in 1903 BC; the recorded thirty-four-year reign of this king's predecessor, Amenemhet III, must have begun in 1937 BC, and so on.[2]

Although the Royal Canon and other king lists linked with the recorded heliacal risings of Sirius have made a rough chronological framework of Egyptian history possible, academic arguments still continue. Unfortunately, even today the full list of Egyptian kings is incomplete, and the length of time that many of the pharaohs reigned is unknown. Consequently, Egyptologists can disagree with each other by thirty years or so concerning events in later Egyptian history, and sometimes by as much as a century regarding earlier times.[3] So can the Sothic cycle actually help us narrow down, any more precisely than the scientific means of dating, exactly what year Tuthmosis III seized power from his mother and seemingly the epidemic of global aggression began?

Luckily, one Egyptian record of the heliacal rising of Sirius dates from only a few years before Tuthmosis III's reign. The various Egyptian king lists record the three pharaohs that reigned immediately before Tuthmosis III: Tuthmosis II, Tuthmosis I, and Amenhotep I. It was during the reign of Amenhotep I that the event is recorded. An ancient Egyptian scroll dating from his reign (the Papyrus Ebers, now in the University of Leipzig, in Germany) records that the heliacal rising of Sirius occurred on the 309th day of the civil calendar in the ninth year of Amenhotep I's reign.[4]

Knowing that the last time the civil and celestial calendars had aligned was in 2781 BC, and that it took four years for the calendars to move out of alignment by one day, for the calendars to be out of alignment by 309 days meant that 1,236 years (309 x 4) must have transpired since that time, meaning that the ninth year of Amenhotep's reign had to have been 1545 BC. Egyptian texts record the length of Amenhotep's reign as twenty-one years. Nine from twenty-one is twelve, so his reign ended twelve years later, in 1533 BC. Amenhotep's successor, Tuthmosis I, ruled for twelve years, and his successor, Tuthmosis II, reigned for thirteen years, meaning that the reign of Tuthmosis III began twenty-five years later, in 1508 BC.

All this means we can conclude that the twenty-second year of Tuthmosis III's reign—that crucial year when he overthrew his mother and began his military campaigns—was 1486 BC. If the hostilities in Egypt coincided with the epidemic of aggression elsewhere in the world, as seems to have been the case, it would appear that whatever occurred to drive the world into a frenzy of violence happened in or very close to this specific year.

Having established a likely date for the outbreak of global hostility, we can now address the all-important question of what might have caused it. Do ancient Egyptian records hold any clues as to what instigated the violence that erupted around 1486 BC?

In ancient Egypt, day-to-day records were kept on papyrus (an early form of paper made from reeds), many of which have perished over time. The vast majority of the records that survived are those carved on stone monuments, but these concern chiefly religious matters or the accomplishments of the ruling elite. As such, they reveal little about what occurred from a wider perspective. Unfortunately, the majority of records concerning Tuthmosis III's reign are of this latter type. Accounts of the pharaoh's seizure of power and his subsequent military campaigns, for example, preserved on the walls of the Temple of Karnak, provide no hint as to the motivations behind the king's actions.

All we can tell is that hostilities began abruptly in the twenty-second year of his reign.[5] If we are to attempt to solve the mystery, therefore, we must go about it indirectly by asking another question. Is there a record of anything else unusual happening in or around that year which might provide some clue? In fact, there is, and it concerns the sudden appearance of a radically new religion.

For over fifteen hundred years, Egyptian religion had remained virtually unaltered. Like the ancient Greeks and Romans, the Egyptians had many gods that were revered and worshipped in prescribed ways laid down by ancient law. The only real changes to religious practices concerned which of these deities was considered the principal god. At one time it had been the sun god Re, and later it had been Osiris, the god of the dead; by the time of Tuthmosis III, the chief deity of Egyptian state religion was Amun, a god whom the later Greeks associated with their own deity Zeus, the father of the gods.[6] For centuries little changed, until suddenly, during Tuthmosis III's reign, a new religion sprang into existence that was totally unlike anything Egypt had seen before.

Known as Atenism, this innovative sect worshipped a completely new god called the Aten. Atenism was not just a new slant on traditional Egyptian religion, with a different god being regarded as the principal god; it was entirely revolutionary. Not only were this sect's religious practices at variance with usual Egyptian religion, but also its philosophy was totally new: the Aten was regarded as the only god. In fact, the Atenists believed that all other Egyptian gods were false. Today we are familiar with the concept of a single deity, or monotheism, as it is called, but in Egypt thirty-five hundred years ago, the idea was unheard of. The only other people in the world so early on to have embraced the notion of a single god were the Israelites, and the archaeological evidence indicates that even they had not adopted such a concept as early as the fifteenth century BC. (The time of Moses, when, according to the Bible, the Hebrew religion first became established, does not appear to have been until at least a century after the time of Tuthmosis III.)

Another aspect of Atenism that was so different from other religious practices of ancient Egypt was that it forbade the making of idols. Traditionally, in Egypt, an effigy or statue of a god was an essential part of cultic practice. The Egyptians believed that the deity actually inhabited the image, and rigid rules for making such images were set forth in ancient texts. Exclusively in the history of ancient Egypt, Atenism diverged from this practice: Atenism forbade the making of any idols or effigies of the Aten.

Another unique aspect of the new sect was that its god had no name. In usual Egyptian religion, the god's name was as important as its effigies and was used to summon the deity's presence. The term the Aten, which the Atenists used for their god, was not actually the deity's name; rather, it was a description, meaning "the Disk." It seems that Atenist dogma concerning their god's form of address was similar to that of later Jews and Christians, who referred to God simply as God, rather than

Jehovah or Yahweh. If the Aten did have a name, it was considered too sacred ever to be written down.[7]

The first evidence we have of this new religion is found in the tomb of an Egyptian official named Djehuty at Deir el-Bahari, just outside the ancient city of Thebes. Texts decorating the tomb walls reveal that Djehuty had been inspired to venerate the Aten, whom he regarded as the supreme god of Egypt. Egyptian tombs were often prepared years before the occupant died, and Djehuty's was no exception. From builders' graffiti in the tomb, which provide datable years from Tuthmosis III's reign, we know that the tomb was decorated between the twenty-first and twenty-third years of the king's reign.

The reference to the Aten dates from the twenty-third year (1485 BC), but earlier inscriptions refer to Djehuty's devotion to Egypt's official principal god, Amun. The inference is, therefore, that Djehuty converted to Atenism sometime between these dates.[8] As there has been found no reference to Atenism anywhere in Egypt, or elsewhere in the world, earlier than that in Djehuty's tomb, it seems that the religion came into existence at the very time, or at least very close to the time, that Tuthmosis began his solo reign during his twenty-second year on the throne, in what now seems to have been 1486 BC.

The history of ancient Egypt began over fifteen hundred years before the reign of Tuthmosis III, and in all that time Egyptian religion had remained virtually unaltered. There is not one shred of evidence to suggest that any radical religious cults developed anywhere in the country during all that time. Then, around the twenty-second year of Tuthmosis III's reign, a completely revolutionary form of religion, one that proclaimed the sole existence of a completely new god, suddenly sprang up, seemingly from nowhere. For over fifteen hundred years, despite its wealth and economic influence, Egypt had never sought to build an empire. Yet in the twenty-second year of Tuthmosis III's reign, the Egyptian army suddenly set out to conquer half the Middle East. Surely there has to have been some connection between these two events.

One possibility to be considered is that Tuthmosis III himself converted to Atenism, which somehow inspired him to build an empire. If so, then the sudden spread of the new religion would be directly linked with Tuthmosis's seizure of power and his military campaigns, perhaps something similar to the rapid spread of Islam with the Arab conquest of the Middle East in the seventh century AD. This cannot have been the case, however. Tuthmosis III remained as committed to traditional Egyptian religion as any of his predecessors. He not only continued to venerate the chief god, Amun, but at the god's main temple at Karnak, he also ordered the building of a new inner sanctuary, the walls of which he had inscribed with accounts of his military achievements.

Whatever made Tuthmosis III seize power from his mother and initiate his military expansionism, it was not a result of a conversion to Atenism. But might it have been the other way around? Was Atenism a foreign religion brought to Egypt with captives returned from Tuthmosis's campaigns? This too is an unlikely scenario. Atenism began far too early in Tuthmosis's solo reign for it to have been established in Egypt by such prisoners of war. When all the evidence is examined, it seems that Atenism did not instigate Tuthmosis III's military campaigns; nor did his conquests bring Atenism to Egypt. Could there have been another common trigger for both scenarios—something that was intrinsically connected with the sudden epidemic of global aggression?

We have already seen that there are no records from which to determine what set Tuthmosis on his path to war; perhaps, though, we might find some evidence as to what instigated Atenism. Sadly, no records have been found directly concerning the inception of Atenism, so we are left to conduct an exercise in historical detective work.

From the reign of Tuthmosis III, Atenism flourished, spreading rapidly throughout Egypt until the mid-fourteenth century BC, when a pharaoh called Akhenaten (whose name means "servitor of the Aten") ultimately proclaimed it as the country's state religion. Atenism disappeared from Egypt as quickly as it appeared, however: following Akhenaten's death, during the reign of the famous Tutankhamun around 1340 BC, the country abandoned Atenism and reverted to the old pantheon of gods. Atenists were persecuted to extinction, Atenism ceased to exist, and the religion was forgotten for over three thousand years.[9]

The best-preserved and most-numerous Atenist monuments are found from Akhenaten's reign, in a remote location called Amarna, in central Egypt. Here Akhenaten built a city, which he intended to be the country's new capital. After Akhenaten's death, when the country reverted to the old gods and modes of worship, Amarna was abandoned to the desert until its ruins were eventually rediscovered by British explorers in the early nineteenth century. The first scholarly account of the site was made by the British explorer John Gardner Wilkinson in 1824, when he surveyed a number of rock-cut tombs discovered in the hills to the east of the ancient city.

Although the tombs' hieroglyphic inscriptions could not yet be read, Wilkinson nevertheless realized that the accompanying decorations were unlike any previously found in Egypt, differing markedly from the traditional religious decor. The priests and royal family were depicted not engaged in the solemn cultic practices usually found in ancient Egyptian art, but in an altogether more dynamic and joyful attitude of worship. Likewise, the common people, who would usually have been portrayed as somber onlookers, were shown as an ecstatic congregation, joining in with the devotions, waving palms, and dancing.

Strangest of all, even the usual gods were absent from the scenes. It was quite clear that the people of Amarna had customs and religious beliefs very different from those practiced elsewhere in ancient Egypt. So different, in fact, that Wilkinson concluded that the inhabitants of ancient Amarna had not been Egyptians at all, but rather foreign settlers who had merely adopted the Egyptian language. Something that particularly mystified Wilkinson was that nearly every tomb illustration depicting the Amarna people involved in their religious practices included a strange glyph or symbol that seemed to be the object of veneration. It was a disk, below which emanated a fan-shaped series of straight lines, each ending in a hand holding an ankh (the ancient Egyptian symbol of life). Eventually, assuming that this symbol represented the sun with its rays shining down below it, Wilkinson concluded that the inhabitants of Amarna had been sun worshippers.[10]

This strange disk symbol, unique to the Aten religion, was later found inscribed in further Atenist tombs, and on monuments, amulets, and various artifacts discovered at other contemporary sites in Egypt, where accompanying inscriptions identified it as the glyph that represented the Aten itself. As Atenism forbade the making of effigies, it seems that this symbol was chosen to represent the new god rather than the human or animal-headed figures that usually represented the gods of ancient Egypt. Accordingly, many subsequent scholars concluded that the Aten was a sun god and agreed with Wilkinson that the Atenists were indeed sun worshippers.[11]

If the sudden emergence of the Aten religion around 1486 BC was in some way linked to the abrupt outbreak of hostilities that erupted at the same time, does the possibility that Atenism was sun worship hold some significance? Sun worship is not unknown among ancient peoples, but for a long established civilization like that of the ancient Egyptians to have temporarily abandoned its deeply entrenched religious practices so abruptly in favor of sun worship might imply that something extraordinary was seen to have happened to the sun. If the life-giving sun had suddenly altered in appearance, for instance, such as by changing its color, might some ancient Egyptians have taken it as an astrological portent to wage war, while others interpreted it as a sign that the sun was a deity in its own right and that it was demanding veneration, adulation, and worship?

It is certainly possible for the sun to change color, due to contaminants in the atmosphere caused by large volcanic eruptions. After the gigantic eruption of Krakatau, a volcano on an island near Java, in 1883, the earth's atmosphere was so contaminated by its fallout ash that blue-and-green sunsets were seen all over the world.[12] Such a phenomenon might have given rise to a sun-worshipping cult like Atenism, but it is difficult to see how it would lead to a global bout of violence. The leaders of some civilizations might take the sun's change of appearance as an omen to wage war, but surely not all. There are certainly no records from ancient Egypt to suggest that Tuthmosis III's actions were dictated by some astrological portent.

As we have seen, he certainly did not change his religion. Beside which, strange-colored sunsets caused by volcanic contaminants have been recorded many times in the history of civilization. The ancients may not have known what caused the phenomenon; they may even have interpreted it as a sign from the gods. But there is no known instance of such observations heralding a rampage of mass aggression.

In fact, although Atenism might provide a vital clue as to what unique event occurred around 1486 BC, there are grounds to question the long held notion that the Aten had anything at all to do with the sun.

It is understandable that early Egyptologists interpreted the Aten symbol—a disk with a fan of lines radiating out below it—as an artistic representation of the sun, and that the Aten was a sun god. As the nineteenth century progressed and hieroglyphics were better understood, however, it became apparent that the Egyptian sun god was not called the Aten, but was instead a deity called Re (sometimes rendered as Ra). Moreover, in ancient Egyptian art the sun was usually represented by a winged disk.[13] Most significantly, it was discovered that the Egyptian word for the sun itself was *on*.[14] The rayed-disk symbol clearly represented what the devotees of this new religion called the Aten, and it seems to have been some heavenly body (as it was depicted shining from above), but was it really the sun? If the Atenists were sun worshippers, then why did they not represent their deity as a winged disk, refer to it by the name Re, or call it the On? In fact, in ancient Egyptian the direct translation of the word *aten* is "disk," and it is found in Egyptian writing in reference to circular objects such as mirrors.[15] All we can say with absolute certainty, therefore, is that the Atenists' god was represented by a disk. It presumably also shone, not only because the lines emanating below it appear to represent rays, but also because the phrase "radiance of the Aten" is often found in inscribed Atenist prayers.

But if the Aten symbol did not represent the sun, what else could it have been? The only other heavenly body permanently close enough to the earth to be seen with the naked eye as a disk is the moon. (Ancient civilizations often described the full moon as a disk rather than a globe or sphere, because there was no way to perceive it in three dimensions with the naked eye.) It seems most unlikely that the Aten glyph represented the moon, however, as Egyptian art depicted the moon in the form of a crescent, and the word for moon was *io*.[16] Remarkably, though, at the very time Atenism first seems to have sprung into existence and the world was plunged into its unprecedented era of violence, the Egyptians recorded that a new shining disk appeared in the skies.

11
The Celestial Disk

ACCORDING TO AN EGYPTIAN TEXT known as the Tulli Papyrus, dating from the reign of Tuthmosis III and now preserved in the Vatican's Egyptian Museum, "In the year 22, in the third month of winter, in the sixth hour of the day, the scribes of the House of Life noticed that there was a disk of fire coming from the sky." The House of Life was part of the Temple of Karnak where royal scribes kept official records, and "the year 22" referred to in the account was the twenty-second year of Tuthmosis III's reign. Whatever this object was, it frightened the wits out of the observers: "The hearts of the scribes became terrified and confused, and they laid themselves flat on their bellies." The text records that nothing like the phenomenon had ever been seen in Egypt. It is described as "a marvel never before known since the foundation of this land."[1]

This "disk of fire" is recorded as appearing early in the very year that Tuthmosis overthrew his mother and plunged his country into a period of unprecedented hostility, evidently 1486 BC. Moreover, it is just one year before Atenism makes its first appearance. Whatever this object was, could it have been what was represented by the Atenists' symbol for their deity? Was this celestial phenomenon taken to be a new god, the Aten—"the Disk"? There is no way, from this Egyptian account alone, to know what this phenomenon might have been. If certain Egyptians did interpret it as the arrival of a new god, however, they may not have been the only ones. In a number of other Middle Eastern countries, at the very same time, new gods are recorded that were represented by a disk symbol that also appears to have depicted some new celestial object.

In northern Syria, at the same time that King Shaushtatar suddenly attacked Assyria and then embarked on his crazed assault on the Egyptian army, we find the first records of a Mitannian god named Ir, "the Bringer." Very little is known about this god, as his temples suffered plundering and desecration and were defaced by the Assyrians when they rebuilt their empire in later times. One thing we do know is that unlike Tuthmosis III and the Aten, Shaushtatar did embrace the cult of this new deity. During Shaushtatar's reign, Mitannian forces seized an area known as Arrapha, in what is now northern Iraq, from the Assyrians, and here the king built the new regional capital of Nuzi, just southwest of what is now Kirkuk.

Nuzi was excavated in the 1930s by an American expedition from Harvard University under the directorship of archaeologist R. F. S. Starr, and during excavations of what had been the local administrative palace, a letter from Shaushtatar to the provincial governor of Arrapha was found that dated from a few months after Mitannian forces occupied the area. The letter was in the form of an inscribed clay tablet bearing the seal of the king, and within the seal design was the symbol for the chief Mitannian god, Ir. The royal seals of Shaushtatar's predecessors included the usual depictions of traditional Mitannian gods, but this one showed only the symbol for the god Ir, indicating that the king had not only embraced the new cult but had also adopted its deity as the supreme national god.[2]

Since the 1930s, other excavations elsewhere in what had been the Mitannian kingdom have uncovered other references to the god Ir, and in each case he is represented only by the same symbol that appeared on Shaushtatar's seal. Just like the Egyptians, the Mitannians usually represented their gods in human form, or in the guise of animals or mythical beasts. But like the Aten sect in Egypt, the cult of Ir seems to have uniquely departed from this tradition by representing its god with a symbol. In this case it was a pair of bird wings and tail surmounted by a circle. When the symbol was first examined by scholars in the 1930s, it was suggested that it might represent an eagle deity, but a curious feature of the glyph is that within the circle there is an eight-pointed star. The wings certainly imply that Ir was a sky god, but most scholars eventually interpreted the inclusion of the star to mean that the deity was associated with some heavenly body, either a star or one of the planets.[3]

Could it, however, have represented the celestial phenomenon recorded by the Egyptians? The Tulli Papyrus describes the phenomenon as a disk, and the circle around the star in the Ir symbol does suggest that the object of veneration was starlike, although large enough to be seen as a disk. Whether or not it represents the same celestial incident recorded in Egypt, this Mitannian deity does have remarkable similarities to the Egyptian Aten. The cult of Ir makes its first appearance at the same time as the Aten sect appeared in Egypt; Ir was regarded as the supreme god and was represented by a glyph rather than a traditional animal, human, or mythical beast; and the god was represented by a symbol that seems to depict a shining heavenly disk.

The simultaneous appearance of so similar a deity in Syria is interesting enough, but at precisely the same time very similar deities appeared in at least three other countries in the Middle East alone.

Excavations in the Assyrian city of Nimrud (some twenty miles southeast of Mosul in what is now Iraq) have unearthed stone monuments carved with a symbol very similar to the Mitannian Ir glyph. It depicts a circle with a starlike design at its center, on either side of the circle there are wings, and below it is a tail. The only difference from the Mitannian Ir symbol is that the wings and tail are attached to the disk.

The oldest such examples were discovered during excavations in the 1940s led by British archaeologist Max Mallowan. These were dated to the reign of the Assyrian king Enlil-Nasir I, who is known to have been Shaushtatar's contemporary. So as far as we can tell, this Assyrian winged disk first appeared at the same time as the Mitannian Ir glyph. Earlier excavations had uncovered later versions of the same symbol, dating from a century and more after Enlil-Nasir I's reign, being used to represent Shamash, the sun god, by that time the chief Assyrian deity.

The older inscriptions discovered at Nimrud, however, show that the symbol was originally associated with a different god, called Antum (whose name means "from heaven"). The cult of Antum does not seem to have lasted long. When Assyria eventually gained independence from Mitanni in the early fourteenth century BC, Antum was relegated to a lesser deity, the consort of the goddess Ishtar; nevertheless, his symbol was retained and used to represent the new supreme god, Shamash. From various finds at the site, Mallowan's expedition concluded that for a while, during the reign of Enlil-Nasir I, Antum was regarded as the supreme Assyrian god. The Mallowan team immediately recognized the similarity to the contemporary Mitannian Ir glyph, and surmised that Antum was the Assyrian rendering of the new Mitannian god that had been introduced into Assyria after Shaushtatar's conquest of the country.[4]

More recent evidence, however, suggests that both the cult of Antum and its winged-disk symbol evolved separately from Mitanni influence. In the mid-1970s, Polish excavations at Nimrud led by Janusz Meuszynski, of the Polish Center of Mediterranean Archaeology, unearthed inscriptions referring to Antum as the chief Assyrian deity dating from the reign of Enlil-Nasir's immediate predecessor, Puzur-Ashur III.[5] This king is known to have died fighting Shaushtatar when his army first moved into southern Assyria, meaning that the Antum cult was in existence before the Assyrians were conquered by the Mitannians.

Less is known about the short-lived cult of Antum than of the cults of Ir or the Aten, but even so, we can see that there were remarkable similarities to both. Antum was represented by a symbol that seems to have depicted a shining heavenly disk; he was considered the supreme god; and his cult makes its first known appearance at the same time that the Ir and Aten sects appeared in Syria and Egypt.

An almost identical symbol to the Antum glyph suddenly shows up at exactly the same time in the Hittite homeland in what is now Turkey. The earliest examples of the Hittite use of this symbol date from the reign of the Hittite king Hantili II, who, as we have seen, made a preemptive strike against the Assyrians at the same time that Tuthmosis III was invading Canaan. First discovered during excavations of the ancient Hittite capital of Hattusas by the German archaeologist Hugo Winckler in 1905, the symbol depicts a star surrounded by a circle, with wings to each side and a fan-shaped tail beneath.[6]

At Hattusas the glyph was found inscribed on a number of clay tablets dating from Hantili II's reign, but the same symbol has since been discovered on stone reliefs from excavations elsewhere in Turkey dating from the high point of Hittite civilization in the fourteenth and thirteenth centuries BC. On such reliefs, the winged disk is usually carved above the head of a Hittite king depicted as riding his chariot into battle, which would suggest that, by this time, at least, the god it represented was a particularly important Hittite god. In fact, the symbol seems to have represented the supreme Hittite deity, Kumarbis. A vast rock-cut shrine dating from the fourteenth century BC was discovered in cliffs at Iasili-Kaïa in Cappadocia (southern Turkey) in the 1890s. Here a sculptured relief of Kumarbis (in human form) is accompanied by the same winged disk.[7] Unlike the Ir, Antum, or the Aten, however, Kumarbis was the chief god of the Hittites before the fifteenth century BC. Nonetheless, it was only during the reign of Hantili II, a contemporary of Shaushtatar and Puzur-Ashur III, that this chief Hittite deity came to be represented by the winged disk.

Yet another Middle Eastern religion that seems to have had its origins at the same time is Zoroastrianism, in what is now Iran. Unlike Atenism and the cults of Ir, Antum, and Kumarbis, this religion has survived to modern times. Zoroastrianism, which proclaims the existence of a single god called Ahura Mazda, "the Wise Lord," is said to have been founded by an ancient Iranian prophet named Zarathustra. Zarathustra is generally accepted to have been a historical figure, but over the years the period during which he lived has been variously dated to between the eighteenth and thirteenth centuries BC. Modern archaeological evidence suggests that Zarathustra had to have lived after 1500 BC.

The oldest parts of the Zoroastrian holy book, the Avesta, are called the Gathas, eighteen religious poems said to have been composed by Zarathustra himself, and these provide descriptions of the lifestyle and cultural practices of Zarathustra's contemporaries. These descriptions closely match what archaeology has revealed about the Yaz culture, an early Iron Age people of eastern Iran who did not arrive in the area from their original home in Armenia until around 1500 BC.[8] (One example is the practice of sky burials, a funerary custom of leaving the body on an exposed mountaintop to be devoured by birds of prey, which was unknown in Iran before the arrival of the Yaz people.) Linguistic evidence, on the other hand, points to a date of composition, and hence the inception of Zoroastrianism, within half a century of 1500 BC. The Gathas are written in a language known as Old Avestan, which had adopted Sanskrit characteristics brought to the area by Aryans who first invaded, then integrated with, Yaz culture during the mid-fifteenth century BC. After around 1450 BC, Old Avestan had adopted more Sanskrit characteristics than are generally found in the Gathas.[9]

The Yaz culture did not leave behind the kind of stone monuments dating from this period that are found in Egypt, Syria, Iraq, or Turkey, so we cannot know for sure how the Zoroastrian Ahura Mazda was originally depicted. The oldest surviving evidence, however, suggests that, once again, Ahura Mazda was symbolized by a winged disk. The Persians, a later Iranian civilization that adopted Zoroastrianism as its national religion, left behind many stone monuments. From these we know that by the seventh century BC, Ahura Mazda was being represented by a symbol called the Faravahar, a glyph depicting a human figure standing in a winged disk with a fan-shaped tail spreading out beneath it.

Modern Zoroastrians still use this glyph to symbolize the devotee's path toward enlightenment, but it is clear that in earlier times, it was used to represent Ahura Mazda himself. Zoroastrianism was established as the national religion of Persia during the reign of the Persian king Darius I, who ruled between 549 and 485 BC, and it is from his reign that the oldest representations of the Faravahar as we now know it survive. The earliest example accompanies the so-called Behistun Inscription located near the city of Kermanshah in western Iran. This huge inscription, 17 feet high by 28 feet wide, was carved into the limestone over 100 feet up the side of a sheer cliff.

The text, which in part concerns Darius's devotion to the Zoroastrian faith, is accompanied by carved reliefs of the king standing before his conquered enemies, and above the scene hangs the Faravahar. From the context of the inscription, it is clear that Darius regarded this symbol as a representation of Ahura Mazda. Interestingly, earlier examples of the winged disk have been found from areas of Iran where Zoroastrianism flourished immediately before Darius's time, but they differ from the Faravahar of the Behistun Inscription in that there is no human figure within the disk.[10]

It seems that these various sects, each with a celestial disk to represent its particular deity, could all have come into existence at the same time, the earliest historical evidence for each dating to within just a few years of one another. The earliest evidence of Atenism and its rayed disk in Egypt comes from the twenty-third year of Tuthmosis III's reign, which would seem to have been 1485 BC. In Syria, Ir became the chief god of the Mitannians, with a winged disk representing him, by the time Shaushtatar invaded the Assyrian province of Arrapha. From Mitannian inscriptions we know that within a year of Shaushtatar's annexation of Arrapha, the Mitannians embarked on an ill-fated attack on the Egyptian army in southern Syria, and the records of Tuthmosis's campaigns at the Temple of Karnak reveal that this battle occurred in the twenty-fourth year of Tuthmosis III's reign, apparently 1484 BC.

As with the first evidence of Atenism in Egypt, therefore, the oldest known records of the cult of Ir and the Mitannian use of the winged disk also appear to date from 1485 BC. The oldest known depictions of the Antum winged disk in Assyria cannot be so precisely dated, but they do appear in the reign of the Enlil-Nasir I, a known contemporary of Shaushtatar. Although it was once thought that Antum was an Assyrian rendering of the Mitannian god Ir, introduced to the country after Shaushtatar's invasion, thanks to the Polish excavations of the Nimrud we now know that Antum had already become the supreme god of the Assyrians during the reign of Enlil-Nasir's immediate predecessor, Puzur-Ashur III. As Puzur-Ashur reigned for only about five years and died fighting Shaushtatar during the first Mitannian offensive into his country, it means that the oldest known reference to the cult of Antum can be dated between 1491 and 1486 BC.

The earliest examples of the Kumarbis winged disk employed by the Hittites dates from the reign of King Hantili II, who is known to have invaded northern Assyria immediately before Shaushtatar attacked southern Assyria and Tuthmosis invaded Canaan. Once again, we have a date somewhere around 1486 BC. It is difficult to determine exactly when the Zoroastrian Faravahar winged disk first came to represent Ahura Mazda in Iran, but the most likely period during which Zarathustra founded Zoroastrianism is somewhere between 1500 and 1450 BC.

It seems most improbable that all this was mere coincidence. Just look at how close to one another these events occurred:

c. 1500–1450 BC   Zoroastrianism, which employed a winged disk to represent Ahura Mazda, is founded in Iran.

c. 1491–1486 BC   The cult of Antum, which represented its deity by a winged disk, is first referenced in Assyria.

1486 BC   The Kumarbis winged disk is first employed by the Hittites.

1485 BC   Atenism, which represented its god by a rayed disk, is first recorded in Egypt.
The earliest evidence for the cult of Ir and the use of the winged disk symbol to represent him is found in the Mitannian kingdom.

In every case, these sects and the use of the heavenly disk to represent their gods could well have originated immediately after the appearance of the "disk of fire" recorded by the Egyptians in 1486 BC. So was this event—whatever it might have been—their common inspiration?

Unfortunately, no texts have been discovered from any of these civilizations to directly explain the advent of these new sects or the inception of the glyph they adopted. In each case, however, the disk symbol does appear to have represented a celestial object, or at least something seen in the skies. In the kingdoms of the Mitannians and the Hittites, as in Assyria and Iran, the symbol included wings, which would suggest the deities were associated with the sky. The same seems true of the Egyptian Aten. In ancient Egyptian art, importance was usually depicted by scale: gods were larger than humans, except for the king, who was considered a god himself. Nevertheless, the gods were pictorially represented on the same horizontal plane as mortals. Atenist art diverged from this convention by depicting the Aten above the heads of its devotees; even the king is shown below the Aten symbol, which appears to be shining in the skies above him.

The sudden appearance of a new heavenly body might indeed be regarded as the arrival of a new god. Moreover, the rarity of such an event could well have inspired separate cultures independently to regard such a god as the supreme deity. In fact, it is difficult to envision what else could have been responsible for the sudden and simultaneous emergence of these extraordinarily similar religions and their almost identical symbols.

It certainly seems highly unlikely that these various sects and their disk symbols derived from a shared cultural source. If they had come into existence a few years later, this might have been a possibility. Egypt invaded part of Syria, the Mitannians of Syria invaded part of Assyria, and the Hittites invaded another area of that same country; the Hittite homeland was in what is now Turkey, and it was from Turkey that the Yaz people originated before they migrated into eastern Iran. But evidence for the first use of the celestial disk symbol and/or the sect that employed it dates from immediately before these invasions occurred. Consequently, at the time in question, for a single new religious concept to be disseminated throughout the countries of the Middle East, it would have to have been spread peacefully, rather than being imposed by conquest. And this seems an equally unlikely scenario.

Fifteen centuries later, Christianity spread through much of the Middle East and Europe, but that was possible only because the area was already part of a single domain, the Roman Empire. During the early fifteenth century BC, Egypt, Assyria, the kingdoms of Mitanni and the Hittites, and the Yaz people of eastern Iran were distinct cultures with very different cultic practices, traditions, and modes of worship. For a single innovative religious belief to have influenced each of these separate cultures to the extent the evidence implies would have taken decades, if not centuries. Yet, as we have seen, it occurred almost overnight in historical terms. Even Christianity took almost three hundred years to establish itself as the principal religion of the Roman Empire. At the time in question, these new sects were being embraced by not just a few common people, or even a handful of high-status individuals, but by kings and the ruling elite. During the Roman Empire, in contrast, it was three centuries before one of its emperors converted to Christianity.

A single new concept might spread far and quickly today with mass communications, but we are talking of a period without television, radio, the Internet, or telephones, and centuries before the invention of printing. Ideas were disseminated by word of mouth, and this meant travel, at a time when journeys were either on foot or, if you were lucky, by ass caravans or ox-drawn cart. Even camels were not domesticated as beasts of burden for another six hundred years. Given the lack of common infrastructure and the methods of travel, and bearing in mind the inhospitable desert through which devotees of any new religion would have had to pass, it seems impossible that a single new religious concept established itself over such a huge area in so short a time.

Just consider the distances involved. Let's take the kingdom of Mitanni as a geographical point of reference. The southern boarder of the Mitannian kingdom was over seven hundred miles northeast of the Egyptian capital at Thebes, and the Hittite capital of Hattusas was another five hundred miles northeast of Mitanni's northern border. As for Zoroastrianism, that makes its first appearance a thousand miles to the east of the Mitannian kingdom. These distances may not seem that significant in the modern age of jet travel, but thirty-five hundred years ago, they were vast.

Such distances are nothing, however, compared to the remoteness of yet another uncannily similar sect that appeared at the same time. Once again, the sect proclaimed the existence of a new god; once again, it was a god considered the supreme deity; and, once again, it was endorsed by a king. Most remarkable of all, the god was represented by yet another celestial disk. Astonishingly, this occurred four thousand miles from the kingdom of Mitanni, in faraway China.

We have seen how astrologers during the Chinese Shang dynasty kept detailed astronomical records in the form of horoscopes, together with notations concerning such matters as military and cultural events considered relevant to their interpretation. The earliest were inscribed on animal bones and turtle shells. Between 1928 and 1937, excavations led by archaeologist Lee Chi of the Chinese Academy of Sciences unearthed over twenty thousand such artifacts among the ruins of the Shang capital of Yin, near modern Anyang in Henan Province. Although the artifacts dated from the later Shang period, around 1350 BC, they included references to horoscopes and divinations made for earlier kings who ruled at the beginning of the Shang period over a century earlier, between approximately 1500 and 1450 BC.

One such inscription on a turtle shell, now preserved at the museum of the Academia Sinica in Taiwan, refers to Zi Sheng, the third king of the Shang dynasty, attributing the success of the Shang clan in overthrowing the Xia rulers to their devotion to a new god called Lao-Tien-Yeh—"the Great God." From the context of the inscription, it appears that Lao-Tien-Yeh not only was a new deity adopted by Tang, the first Shang king, shortly before he usurped the Xia rulers, but also considered the supreme god, as it is referred to as "the ruler of the universe." It is interesting enough that a new chief deity should appear in China at the same time as the new gods were appearing in the distant Middle East, but what is truly remarkable is that Lao-Tien-Yeh was represented by a glyph almost identical to the rayed disk that symbolized the Aten in Egypt. It was a circle with a series of straight lines radiating in a fan shape beneath it.[11]

It might just have been possible—although highly unlikely—for the various countries of the Middle East to have derived their new supreme deities and their celestial disks from each other, but for any of them to have inspired a new sect in China is completely out of the question. It would be centuries before the Chinese had any idea the nations of the eastern Mediterranean even existed, and vice versa, let alone could have been influenced by them. Even Alexander the Great, who conquered part of India well over a millennium later, and the mighty Roman Empire, had no direct contact with China.

Although archaic civilizations had many gods, and new gods were often added to their ancient pantheons, for a new supreme deity to be independently introduced by so many different cultures at the same time is far too unlikely an event to have been coincidental. Surely, some related event must have inspired them. In fact, the use of such a similar symbol to represent these new deities makes it fair to assume that they were inspired by the same event. And one type of event that could have been witnessed as far and wide as the Middle East and China would be an astronomical event, which seems to have been what the Tulli Papyrus recorded in Egypt in 1486 BC. But if these celestial disks were inspired by the object described by the Egyptians as "a disk of fire," what could it have been?

The Aten symbol appears to have represented a shining disk, but, as we have seen, it may not have been, as long thought, the sun or even the moon. Nonetheless, if it did represent some celestial object, it was large enough to be seen as a disk rather than a shining point of light, such as a star or even a planet seen with the naked eye. The Mitannian, Hittite, and Assyrian symbols all included a star within the disk, which is intriguing. Why is the god depicted as both a star and a disk? Perhaps the object originally appeared as a starlike point of light that then grew larger, or vice versa.

One rare but natural celestial phenomenon that should be considered is a supernova—an exploding star.

A supernova occurs when a massive star collapses under the force of its own gravity, or undergoes runaway nuclear fusion at its heart, resulting in an explosion that expels its stellar material millions of miles into space. If it happened to our own star, the sun, which is thankfully not massive enough to threaten such an event, it would destroy the entire solar system. The energy released during a supernova is truly staggering: a typical star like our sun would have to shine for 10 billion years to produce the energy output of a supernova. Amazingly, a supernova briefly outshines all the other stars in an entire galaxy combined.

Such events are common throughout the billions of galaxies of the known universe, but are comparatively rare in our own galaxy. In fact, the last was in 1604. In all recorded history, there have been only a couple of dozen supernovae near enough to Earth to be visible with the naked eye, but they have been spectacular. The brightest of these, astronomers believe, occurred in the year AD 1006. Although observers at the time had no idea what it was, they recorded it throughout Europe and in China, Japan, and Egypt. These records refer to it as the appearance of a new star that shone brightly for many months before fading away. In China, it was recorded as being bright enough to read by at night, and an Egyptian astrologer named Ali bin Ridwan recorded it as being "one quarter the brightness of the full moon."[12]

There is a problem, however, attributing the object described in the Tulli Papyrus and the depictions of the various celestial disk symbols to a supernova. As spectacular as supernovae are, those for which historical records survive were not close enough to Earth, or bright enough, to be described as or depicted as disks. None of the historical records of what astronomers now know to be supernovae describe the phenomena as disks; instead they are referred to as new and very bright stars. To be seen as a celestial disk, presumably a bright spherical object observed without three-dimensional perspective, whatever it was, it must have been something much bigger or a lot closer to Earth.

We can speculate forever about what the disk of fire described in the Tulli Papyrus might have been, or what the various celestial disk images that appeared in the Middle East at the same time might have represented. But records do survive from the astrologically obsessed ancient Chinese to reveal exactly what their Lao-Tien-Yeh rayed disk represented. Between 1972 and 1974, excavations by the Institute of Archaeology of the Chinese Academy of Sciences made a sensational discovery. At Mawangdui, an archaeological site at Changsha, the capital of Hunan Province in south-central China, three tombs dating from the time of the Han dynasty (206 BC–AD 220) were uncovered.

The tombs belonged to a local clan leader and two members of his family, and in one of the tombs, dating from 168 BC, there was an entire library of books over two thousand years old. Known as the Mawangdui Silk Texts because they were written on silk as opposed to paper, many concerned military, medical, and mathematical matters, but the most interesting, from our current perspective, were those that dealt with astrology. One such work, known as the Mawangdui Silk Almanac (now preserved in the Hunan Provincial Museum in Changsha), was an illustrated text concerning various astronomical observations together with their astrological interpretations. Although this almanac dated from around 300 BC, it included copies of astronomical observations going back well over a thousand years, and one of the very first listed a new celestial object that suddenly appeared in the skies in the early fifteenth century BC.

In fact, it must have appeared either at the very end of the Xia period or the beginning of the Shang dynasty, because the text makes reference to a warlord named Chieh who fought alongside Tang, the first Shang king, when he seized power. Not only was this during the same period that the rayed-disk symbol first appeared in China (and the new religions and their disk symbols appeared in the Middle East), but also the object was given the same name as the Chinese deity the symbol represented—Lao-Tien-Yeh. Moreover, a simple illustration of the object that was observed actually appears in the text: it is exactly the same as the symbol for the god, a circle with a series of straight lines in a fan shape beneath it.

This shows categorically, in this instance at least, that the new god was inspired by the appearance of a new heavenly body, and that the disk symbol representing the god was a depiction of that same object. Most important of all, however, is that the text tells us exactly what this celestial object was—a comet.[13]

12
Brush with Death

BEFORE WE CONTINUE, it is important to understand what comets actually are. Comparable in size and shape to asteroids, they are sun-orbiting objects left over from the formation of the solar system some 4.5 billion years ago. Sometimes likened to dirty snowballs, these irregular-shaped heavenly bodies are composed of particles of matter and various gases held together in water ice and frozen carbon dioxide. They average between half a mile and fifteen miles in diameter, although some can be as large as two hundred miles across.

This might not sound big by our planetary standards—Earth, for example, has a diameter of around eight thousand miles—but it would be disastrous if one collided with us. It is estimated that the Earth-colliding object that killed off the dinosaurs 65 million years ago was only around six miles in diameter. (It is thought to have been an asteroid, but a comet of equal size would have had pretty much the same effect.) The dinosaur killer exterminated around 75 percent of life on Earth; it is estimated that a comet any larger than twenty miles across would wipe out every living thing on the planet.[1]

Fortunately, although there are thought to be millions of comets orbiting the sun, most are a safe enough 6,000 billion miles away in a cometary belt known as the Oort cloud (named after the twentieth-century Dutch astronomer Jan Hendrick Oort). Sometimes, however, comets can collide and be knocked out of the Oort cloud to fall toward the inner solar system. The result is that they end up in eccentric elliptical orbits that take them repeatedly close to the sun and then far back out into space. Such orbits can take millions of years (Earth, by comparison, orbits the sun every 365 days), but some comets, deflected by passing close to a planet, can have their trajectories altered so that their orbits are much tighter. For example, Comet Hyakutake, seen in 1996, takes 9,000 years to orbit the sun; Comet Hale-Bopp, seen in 1997, takes 2,400 years; and Halley's Comet, last seen in 1986, takes only 76 years. Most of the time, even short-orbit comets are invisible to the naked eye, existing as dark objects hurtling through the cold, empty reaches of space.

But when they swing in closer to the sun, they warm up, the surface ice vaporizes, and discharged into space are dust and gases that glow with the sun's reflected light. This shining aura of dust and gases, called the coma, is typically a few hundred thousand miles in diameter and can therefore often be seen from Earth. While the solid body of a comet, referred to as the nucleus, is generally less than fifteen miles across and invisible to the naked eye, the vastly bigger coma can be seen from millions of miles away. As the comet continues in toward the sun, some of the coma is stripped away by the solar wind—a stream of high-energy subatomic particles emanating from the sun—to form the familiar comet's tail. Contrary to what might be expected, a comet's tail is not like the vapor trail of a jet streaming out behind it, but points only away from the sun, regardless of which direction the comet is traveling. This tail, referred to as the dust tail, can be millions of miles long, and dependent on circumstances can appear straight or curved. Also illuminated by the sun, the tail can be clearly visible from Earth. Comets have an additional tail called the ion tail, visible only in some very bright comets, which is caused by fluoresced ionized gases escaping from the coma.[2]

Comets visible with the naked eye appear on average about once every ten years, and in the modern era have traditionally been named after their discoverers, such as Halley's Comet, for the English astronomer Edmond Halley in the eighteenth century. If the comet has more than one discoverer, their names are combined, such as Comet Hale-Bopp, named after it was discovered by two independent American observers, Alan Hale and Thomas Bopp, in 1995. If the same astronomers have discovered more than one comet, a sequential number is added to distinguish them, such as the famous Comet Shoemaker-Levy 9, which collided with Jupiter in 1994.

Today, so many new comets are being found far out in space by corporate-owned observatories that this convention has proved impractical, so new comets are now usually given only an alphabetical, numerical designation, such as Comet C/2001 Q4, discovered in 2001. Comets can manifest very differently with each new appearance, depending on various factors such as solar activity and the comet's proximity to Earth. The orbit of the same comet brings it varying distances from Earth on each journey through the inner solar system, depending on where Earth happens to be in its orbit around the sun at the time. The circumference of Earth's orbit is about 583 million miles, so the distance can vary considerably (which is why even those comets whose orbits cross our own are unlikely to collide with us). Halley's Comet, for example, whose orbit is seventy-six years, was magnificent when it came within 13 million miles of Earth in 1910, but its reappearance in 1986 was far less dramatic, as it only came within 38 million miles.[3]

When a large comet moves well inside the orbit of Earth, and hence closer to the heat of the sun, so much material evaporates from its surface that you have the potential for a really massive coma and an extremely long tail. Some comets even develop a number of tails (which led, incidentally, to the Greek word for "comet," *kometes,* meaning "stars with hair"). For example, Comet West, which appeared in 1976, had three tails; Halley's Comet when it appeared in 1910 had five; and De Cheseaux's Comet of 1744 had seven. A cometary tail always points away from the sun, but depending on its relative position with respect to us, and our relative position with respect to the sun, as observed from Earth the tail can stream in any direction relative to the horizon: up, down, left, right, or anything in between. The comet the Chinese recorded as appearing around 1500 BC must have been an outstanding spectacle: it is depicted with ten tails spreading out below it in the shape of a fan.

The ancient Chinese had no idea what comets really are, regarding them as gods or other mythical creatures that had appeared in the sky as astrological omens. The Mawangdui Silk Almanac therefore contained a section specifically devoted to recording them. It included simple drawings of each comet's appearance: a circle depicting the coma and a line or series of lines, either curved or straight, representing the tails. The Chinese gave comets names, but unlike the modern convention of naming comets after astronomers, a comet was named after the god or mythical creature it was thought to represent.

Only the more spectacular ones tended to be named after gods, however, and the fact that the one around 1500 BC was called Lao-Tien-Yeh—"the Great God"—suggests that it was a particularly impressive one. The Mawangdui Silk Almanac also included written captions concerning what various comets were thought to portend. The relative length of the tail, its direction, and whether it was curved or straight were deemed to have specific meanings for the future; but most significant was the number of tails. Comets were generally considered to herald bad fortune, and the more tails they had, the worse the events to be expected. For example, a two-tailed comet foretold civil unrest, a three-tailed one augured political turmoil, a four-tailed comet signified disease, and comets with five tails or more were associated with war and devastation. The one recorded around 1500 BC had ten tails.[4]

In his book *Comet,* published in 1985, the famous astronomer Carl Sagan drew attention to this comet observed by the Chinese around 1500 BC, suggesting that it had to have been one of the most spectacular seen in recorded history. As it appears to have been the first comet the Chinese recorded, it may actually have started the fascination with these heavenly bodies for centuries to come.

Comets are comparatively common occurrences, and the ancient Chinese, just like us today, could expect to see one, on average, every decade. For them to have suddenly begun to record them, and in particular associate them with disaster, suggests that the tradition was started by the appearance of a particularly spectacular comet that was followed by a period of considerable disorder or catastrophe. Sagan does not propose that the comet itself was directly responsible for any calamity on Earth, merely that turmoil coincidentally occurred in China at that time, and that the Chinese astrologers imagined such a connection. Sagan was considering only China, however. Knowing the wider picture of a contemporary global epidemic of violent and aggressive human behavior, is it possible that the comet was somehow responsible?[5]

The comet observed by the ancient Chinese somewhere around 1500 BC could well have been the same celestial phenomenon described as a "disk of fire" observed by the Egyptians in 1486 BC. Although the Mawangdui Silk Almanac provides dates for later cometary appearances, those from the earlier period, such as the one in question, are only approximately datable by accompanying textual references to contemporary events or historical figures. We know that the Lao-Tien-Yeh comet appeared during the life of Tang, the first Shang king, who appears to have lived at the same time as the Egyptian pharaoh Tuthmosis III, during whose reign the Tulli Papyrus records the event.

In Egypt, the object it is said to have been seen in the third month of the twenty-second year of Tuthmosis's reign, immediately before he seized power from his mother and all hell broke loose in the Middle East. The Lao-Tien-Yeh comet could well have been recorded at the time that the Xia king Jie began his despotic reign, leading to Tang's rebellion and the subsequent pandemonium in China, which would appear to have been the same time.[6] In fact, because the Middle East and east-central China share the same latitude—meaning that a comet visible to one area would have been visible to the other—it is a fairly safe bet that the particularly spectacular Lao-Tien-Yeh comet and the exceptional celestial object described in the Tulli Papyrus were indeed one and the same.

What the Egyptians observed in 1486 BC is described as a disk of fire, yet comets are neither a disk nor on fire. Nevertheless, this is exactly how the ancient Chinese described them. Although toward the rim, the comet's coma is transparent and fuzzy, the Chinese astrologers nonetheless described the larger comets as disks, just as they did the moon. And they also described comets as fiery: they thought they shone because they were burning, which is why many were likened to fire-breathing dragons. In fact, it was not only in ancient times that comets have been described as disks of fire. In 1910, when Halley's Comet appeared, various newspapers around the world were criticized by astronomers for erroneously describing the spectacle as a fiery orb. In fact, even today, many ordinary people assume that a comet has a tail because it is burning like a shooting star—a meteor entering Earth's atmosphere. The ancient Egyptians, therefore, might well have described a comet as a fiery disk.[7]

If the celestial phenomenon described in the Tulli Papyrus was a comet, it must have been an extremely impressive one. Like the Chinese, the Egyptians would have been used to seeing comets, and so for this one to be described as "a marvel never before known since the foundation of this land" suggests something exceptional. In fact, the text actually reveals the object's apparent size: "Its body was one rod in length and one rod in width . . . and extended to the limits of the four supports of heaven."[8]

The Egyptian rod was around 170 feet, which appears to imply that it wasn't very big at all—at least by comet standards. But these measurements do not refer to the true size of the object, which the Egyptian observers had no way of knowing. They measured instead the apparent size of, or space separating, heavenly bodies by markers placed in the ground at a certain distance from the observer, and it was this distance between these markers that was recorded. (As long as the markers were always set the same distance apart, and at the same distance from the observer, a standard relative distance between heavenly bodies when close to the horizon could be determined.) We don't know exactly where these markers were set out around the Temple of Karnak, where the observations were made, but we can make a comparison of the object's size, as the Egyptians describe the full moon as being 5 cubits wide. As 100 cubits made up a rod, it seems that the object described in the Tulli Papyrus was twenty times the diameter of the full moon as seen from Earth.

Today astronomers describe the perceived size of celestial objects in terms of degrees of arc. With an unobstructed view of the horizon, you can see about 180 degrees of the night sky at once, and there are 90 degrees from the horizon to the zenith, the point directly above your head. By this standard, the full moon is about half of a degree of arc, or 30 arc minutes, a degree being 60 minutes of arc. (The sun, incidentally, is approximately the same apparent size.) What the Egyptians saw was evidently 10 full degrees of arc. If this is right, and it was a comet, it would have been a truly breathtaking display.

Comet Hyakutake, of 1996, had one of the largest comas, as perceived from Earth, to make an appearance in recent years. At its largest it was almost 2 full degrees of arc, about four times the size of the full moon, although not so bright. The largest comet coma recorded since the birth of modern astronomy in the seventeenth century was De Cheseaux's Comet of 1744, also known as the Great Daytime Comet, because it was so bright it could be seen in broad daylight. Shining brighter than the moon, its coma measured just over 4 degrees of arc, meaning that it appeared approximately eight times larger than the full moon. The object seen by the Egyptians in 1486 BC was apparently over twice as big. The comet of 1744 also had seven tails that fanned out across the sky to an additional distance of almost 35 degrees of arc.

To envision this, imagine you are standing looking toward a clear, unobscured nighttime horizon: if the heart of the coma was just over a third of the way up from the horizon to the position above your head, its tails would appear to reach the ground. Now imagine a ten-tailed comet over twice as big: its magnificent tail array would stretch out almost across the entire horizon. This may have been what the author of the Tulli Papyrus meant when he described the phenomenon as extending "to the limits of the four supports of heaven."

Because there has not been such an impressive comet in living memory, we tend to imagine comets with just one, two, or perhaps three tails, and visible only in a relatively local area of the sky. This presumably would also be what the ancient Egyptians and Chinese were used to seeing when comets appeared. They may have thought that comets were divine or magical, and they may have considered them portents, but they would nonetheless have been a part of normal experience. Like De Cheseaux's Comet of 1744, the one that appeared in 1486 BC would almost certainly have been outside the experience of anyone alive. It was much larger than the sun and moon combined, and its tails stretched far across the sky. At a time when heavenly bodies were thought quite literally to be just that—the physical manifestations of divine beings—such a spectacle might indeed have been interpreted as the appearance of a new god, and a particularly important one at that. In fact, this is precisely what seems to have happened in China: the comet was given the name Lao-Tien-Yeh—"the Great God"—and King Tang and the early Shang dynasty subsequently regarded this god as the supreme deity.

As we have seen, at exactly the same time, a new deity appeared in Egypt: the Aten, which many Egyptians also regarded as the principal god, and it too was represented by a symbol astonishingly similar to the Lao-Tien-Yeh glyph. The Aten and Lao-Tien-Yeh were both represented by a disk with a series of straight lines radiating out in a fan shape beneath it, which is exactly how the comet is depicted in the Mawangdui Silk Almanac.[9] There can be little doubt, then, not only that the comet observed in China somewhere around 1500 BC and the celestial object observed in Egypt in 1486 BC were one and the same, but also that its appearance was interpreted as the manifestations of the gods Lao-Tien-Yeh and the Aten, respectively.

The comet, however, would have been visible not only in Egypt and China, but also through the entire Middle East. In the Middle Eastern kingdoms of Mitanni, Assyria, Iran, and the Hittites, new and important gods also make a sudden appearance at this time, and they too were represented by celestial disks. It would seem very likely that these were also inspired by the same astronomical event. In Mitanni we have the god Ir, represented by a winged disk encompassing a star with a fan-shaped tail beneath. This would be an excellent portrayal of the comet—the wings symbolic of its appearance in the sky, the tail representing what we know to have been a fan-shaped cometary tail, and the star in the center of the disk would be an appropriate depiction of the coma.

Unlike the moon, which is solid, the cometary coma would be more diffuse toward the edges and therefore appear brighter toward the center. What better way to illustrate such a phenomenon in a stone carving than a star within a disk? The Assyrians and the Hittites both represented their new supreme deities Antum and Kumarbis with a virtually identical symbol, the only difference being that the wings and tail were attached to the disk; and in Iran we have another winged disk with a fan-shaped tail representing the new and sole divinity Ahura Mazda.[10]

No records or imagery exists from this period in northwest Europe or Central America to determine whether the megalithic people or the pre-Olmec culture might similarly have been inspired by the comet, but the Rig-Veda, seemingly composed by the Aryans shortly after their conquest of the Indus Valley, does contain evidence of just such a scenario. One of the most important deities of the Rig-Veda is the god Agni, whose name means "fire," and he appears to have been the Aryans' chief deity at this time. The Rig-Veda consists of hymns to many gods, but the fact that the very first hymn is dedicated to Agni would suggest that he was originally regarded as the supreme god. He was certainly the god who was said to span the gulf between heaven and Earth, and to be the envoy of all the other gods. Furthermore, he was the god of sacrifice, who received offerings on behalf of all the gods. In later times animals were sacrificed, but shortly after they arrived in the Indus Valley, the Aryans practiced human sacrifice.

When we consider this together with the fact that the Aryans also burned every Harappan city they conquered, and then erected sacrificial altars on the sites, it seems very likely that the fire god Agni, the god of sacrifice, was the deity they were venerating. The hymns of the Rig-Veda contain many descriptions of Agni's appearance. He is described as the charioteer of the skies, and the one who shines in the heavens.[11] When he was born, we are told, he filled the space between heaven and Earth with light[12], his head was in the sky[13], and he had long flaming hair[14] that is likened to the tail of a horse.[15] These and other descriptions throughout the Rig-Veda are apt poetic imagery of a comet such as the one that seems to have appeared in 1486 BC.

Clearly, the comet that appeared in 1486 BC was so different and so much more spectacular than any celestial manifestation previously known that it had a profound effect on many civilizations. It inspired new gods, new cults, and new religious movements. And if the Egyptian account is anything to go by, it also terrified people. But could it also have been responsible for the sudden outbreak of global aggression? Even in recent history, comets have been the cause of mass hysteria. When De Cheseaux's Comet appeared in 1744, there was a widespread belief that the world was coming to an end. In England, thousands of people gathered on hilltops in the hope of salvation; in the panic, dozens were killed or injured. When Halley's Comet appeared in 1835, Zulu warriors in Africa took it as a sign to massacre 280 Boers; and in Mexico, an Aztec revival cult interpreted it as a sign to attempt to overthrow the government. Even in recent years, comets have inspired people to commit acts of insanity. When Comet Hale-Bopp appeared in 1997, members of the Heaven's Gate cult in the United States took it to be a sign that they should commit mass suicide, and on March 26 of that year, thirty-eight of them killed themselves in a rented California mansion.

But none of this compares to the mass epidemic of violent behavior that occurred around the world in 1486 BC. On the contrary, as we shall see, most of the religions that came into being at the time of the comet's appearance and that seem to have been inspired by it were intrinsically nonviolent—Atenism, Zoroastrianism, and the Hindu faith, to name but three. Indeed, although in some areas, such as the Indus Valley, atrocities may have been committed in the name of the comet-inspired god, in other areas, as far as we can tell, this was certainly not the case. Tuthmosis III, for instance, never had anything to do with the new Aten sect; in fact, he continued to venerate the traditional gods of Egypt until his death, which is why his campaigns were recorded on the walls of the Temple of Karnak. If the comet was somehow responsible for the spate of worldwide aggression for around two decades following 1486 BC, it would have to have been directly responsible. One obvious way in which this might have been the case is if the comet had collided with Earth. A cometary impact would have devastating effects on the environment: resultant crop failures would cause famine and greater competition would lead to hostility. So did the comet of 1486 BC actually hit Earth?

Before considering that question, we need to appreciate how close comets are known to have come to us. The comet of 1744 was perhaps the most spectacular since the birth of scientific astronomy, but it was not the closest to Earth. Modern astronomical observations, coupled with computer simulations, are able to identify comets observed in the past and to calculate their orbital periods and trajectories within the inner solar system. Halley's Comet is an excellent example. It is named after the astronomer Edmond Halley, as he was the first to recognize its seventy-six-year orbit in the early 1700s, but he was not the first to observe it. It had, in fact, been seen by people throughout the world for centuries.

Until the time of Halley, however, no one realized that the same comet kept returning. Now we know not only that it returns, but also that its proximity to Earth varies with each orbit. On some occasions when it swung into the inner solar system, it was far from Earth and went by unnoticed; at other times, its orbit brought it much closer, and it was clearly visible in the night sky. When it appeared in 1986, it came within 38 million miles of Earth, but it was far more spectacular in 1910 when it came within 13 million miles. Both these were relatively distant passes considering that in AD 374, and again in AD 607, it came to within 9 million miles. The closest approach to Earth by Halley's Comet was in AD 837, when it came to within a little over 3 million miles. That might sound like a great distance, but by astronomical standards it was a near miss. Put into perspective: the moon is approximately 239,000 miles from Earth, a little over a quarter of a million miles, and the sun is 93 million miles away. But the close encounter of AD 837 was not the nearest cometary miss in historical times. That was in 1770, when Lexell's Comet came to within just 1.39 million miles of Earth.

That the comet of 1486 BC was spectacular and had ten tails, and that its coma evidently covered 10 degrees of arc, would appear to suggest that it came very close to Earth. This does not necessarily follow, however. The magnificence of the display could be due to other factors. Comet Hale-Bopp in 1997 was probably the most widely observed comet of the twentieth century, and one of the brightest seen for many decades; it was visible to the naked eye for a record eighteen months, twice as long as the previous record holder, in 1811. But it only came within

122 million miles of Earth, over three times farther away than Halley's Comet of 1986, which was far less spectacular. The reason Hale-Bopp was more impressive is that its nucleus has a diameter of about twenty-five miles, nearly three times the size of Halley's, and also that its surface contained materials that made it more active.

Another comet in recent years was particularly impressive for a different reason. In 1996, Comet Hyakutake was especially bright, with an extraordinarily long tail; it was far more spectacular than Halley's Comet in 1986. Its nucleus, though, is only about a mile and a quarter in diameter, compared with Halley's of just over nine miles. The main reason Comet Hyakutake put on a better show is that it warmed up more because its orbit took it closer to the sun—to within 22 million miles, as opposed to Halley's 54 million miles. So there are a number of factors that make comets more or less spectacular. Their comas can appear large and their tails long, not necessarily because they are closer to us than other, less impressive comets, but because their orbit takes them nearer the sun, thus venting more cometary material into space, or because their nucleus is larger or has a more active surface.[16]

From the historical evidence we have examined so far, therefore, it is difficult to determine just how close the comet of 1486 BC actually came. It seems most unlikely that it actually hit Earth, because if it did, we wouldn't be here to think about it. It is not only the size of a comet, but also the speed it would be traveling when it hit Earth that would release so much devastating energy. Average-sized comets, such as Halley's Comet at around nine miles across, traveling at around twenty miles a second (72,000 miles an hour), would create an explosion 15 billion times that of the Hiroshima bomb. On impact, it would create a fireball almost two thousand miles wide and have a blast radius of twenty-five hundred miles.

In the hours following the impact, the rest of the world would be showered in burning hot debris and would experience earthquakes, hurricanes, and tsunamis worse than any on record. Dust thrown high into the stratosphere would block out the sun for months on end; any animal life that managed to survive the initial effects would have to endure week after week of arctic conditions, and plants would die, unable to photosynthesize. And if you managed to survive all that, you would have to face a world whose ozone layer had been virtually destroyed, where acid rain fell for years, and where the entire planet would subsequently suffer a massive greenhouse effect in which temperatures would rise for centuries. The asteroid that is thought to have killed off the dinosaurs 65 million years ago is believed to have been only six miles in diameter. The chances are that if a comet the size of Halley's hit us, as much as 90 percent of all life on Earth would become extinct. If a twenty-five-mile-diameter comet the size of Hale-Bopp hit us, it would probably wipe out every living thing.[17]

It is obvious that no sizable comet collided with Earth in 1486 BC, but what about a smaller one? Even a relatively small comet, such as Comet Hyakutake, with a diameter of just over a mile, would have catastrophic results if it hit our planet. It would create a fireball of 150 miles wide and have a blast radius of 250 miles. For weeks after, the skies would be darker than the thickest cloud cover, and for the next couple of years, we could expect no summer. Although there would be far fewer initial fatalities due to the impact than from a comet the size of Halley's, the consequence of long-term colder conditions would be crop failures and result in famine that would decimate the world's population.

It is clear that nothing like that happened in 1486 BC either. Evidence of such global food shortages would be found in the historical texts of the Middle East; there would be indications of harsh conditions in contemporary tree-ring samples; and there would be ice-core evidence from the Arctic revealing atmospheric contaminants from the time. Furthermore, there would be physical evidence. If a projectile just the size of an apartment block, say two hundred feet wide, hit the ground at twenty miles a second, it would annihilate a large modern city and leave a crater almost a mile wide; but no sizable impact crater from that period has been found.[18] There is, however, another possibility: the comet broke up, and only part or fragments of it entered the atmosphere. When recording the "disk of fire" of 1486 BC, the Egyptian Tulli Papyrus goes on to describe what sounds very much like a comet breaking apart. The disk is said to have divided into smaller fiery disks, until, "after several days had passed, they became more numerous in the sky."[19]

In modern times, a number of comets have been observed to break up into separate fragments. For example, in 1965 Comet Ikeya-Seki was visible to the naked eye when it broke into three pieces on October 21 of that year, and the famous Comet Shoemaker-Levy 9 broke into hundreds of pieces, which were observed by astronomers the world over as they slammed into the atmosphere of Jupiter in July 1994. The fragments of neither of these comets came anywhere near Earth, but in 1846 Comet Biela was observed to break apart, and fragments from it, thankfully very small, subsequently cascaded into Earth's atmosphere as a meteor shower.

Individual meteors, or shooting stars as they are commonly called, are usually small particles of interplanetary dust, smaller than a grain of sand, that enter Earth's atmosphere at extremely high speeds, burning up and appearing as a brief streak of light. (A meteorite, by the way, is a large meteor fragment that manages to hit the ground.) A meteor shower occurs when a number of meteors are seen within a short period, and these are generally caused by Earth passing though the orbit of a comet. Each time a comet swings by the sun, it leaves behind dust particles that eventually spread out along its path, forming what is known as a meteoroid stream. When Earth passes through this stream, for a few days at around the same time each year there will be a meteor shower.

One annual meteor shower that peaks around August 12 (with a meteor appearing about once a minute) is called the Perseids and is caused by Comet Swift-Tuttle; and another, called the Leonids, around November 17, is caused by Comet Tempel-Tuttle. (The Perseids and Leonids are named after the constellations of Perseus and Leo, the area of sky from which they appear to radiate.) The meteor shower caused by the breakup of Comet Biela, however, was far more spectacular. The fragments that entered the atmosphere were much larger than the usual dust particles and therefore appeared in the form of what are called bolides, which are much bigger and brighter, appear slower, and last longer than usual meteors.[20] Going by the Tulli Papyrus, this appears to have been what was observed in 1486 BC.

After describing the breakup of the disk of fire into separate, smaller disks, the Tulli Papyrus account goes on to say: "The disks grew in size . . . they shined in the sky more than the brightness of the sun . . . and fish and birds rained down from the sky."[21] This may well be a description of the separate cometary fragments drawing closer to Earth, before some entered the atmosphere to become bolides. Before the birth of modern astronomy, observers often described bolides in terms of preternatural fish and birds. Because of their glowing trails, medieval paintings often depicted them as airborne fish, while the ancient Greeks called bolides firebirds.[22] Luckily, none of the Comet Biela bolides of 1846 was big enough to survive being burned up in the upper atmosphere, but the cometary event of 1486 might have been a different matter. So what would happen if cometary fragments did make it through the upper atmosphere?

The Perseids and Leonids meteor showers are caused by dust-particle remnants of a comet's tail; another annual meteor shower, however, is caused by a comet having broken up in the past. This is the Beta Taurids meteor shower in late June and early July, which is associated with Comet Encke. Encke is believed to be a part of what was once a larger comet that has broken up over the last few thousands of years, the Beta Taurids being made up not only of dust particles, but also of pebble-sized relics of this breakup. This meteor shower would be particularly spectacular if it occurred at night, but because it comes from the sun-facing side of Earth, it cannot be observed visually by day. (We know of it because of radar and satellite observations.) In fact, Encke is still breaking up, and a large fragment of it is actually thought to have hit our planet as recently as 1908.

Around 7:15 on the morning of June 30, 1908, at the height of the Beta Taurids meteor shower, the inhabitants of the Lake Baikal region of south-central Russia observed a column of bluish light, nearly as bright as the sun, moving across the sky. About ten minutes later, a thousand miles to the north, there was a massive explosion in the Tunguska region of central Siberia. Luckily, this remote forested area was unpopulated, and as far as is known nobody died. Nevertheless, the explosion flattened an estimated 80 million trees over an area of almost a thousand square miles. At the time, scientists were sure that the event was caused by a large meteor or bolide impact, yet they were mystified when no crater was found at the epicenter of the explosion. Instead, there was just mile after mile of flattened trees radiating out from a central point.

It is now thought that the cause was a fragment of Comet Encke that exploded with an estimated blast of twenty megatons—or that of a large nuclear weapon—within the atmosphere, but between three and six miles above Earth's surface. Scientists believe it exploded in the air because of the oblique angle of its atmospheric entry. Even though the fragment is estimated to have been around two hundred feet in diameter, large enough to have left a crater almost a mile wide if it had come in at a sharper angle and hit the ground, the aerial explosion did not create a crater, and it did not blast debris into the atmosphere to darken the skies.[23] If a fragment, or fragments, of the 1486 BC comet had similarly exploded in such an airburst, there would remain no physical evidence of the event, nor would there have been collision fallout or debris blasted into the stratosphere to cause temporary climate change or crop failures. There might, however, have been another effect of such an event that directly influenced human beings—one that caused them to exhibit violent and aggressive behavior.

13

The Birth of Monotheism

BEFORE WE CONSIDER HOW THE COMET of 1486 BC could directly have caused the global epidemic of mass aggression that followed its appearance, we need to examine its single most enduring effect on civilization. Although after two decades of worldwide upheaval, everything suddenly calmed down, civilizations everywhere had been irrevocably altered. Cultures had changed, societies were restructured, and new empires and ruling dynasties were established. Moreover, new religious sects had emerged, such as Hinduism in the Indus Valley and Zoroastrianism in Iran.

Most significantly, however, the comet seems to have been responsible for initiating a religious concept that completely altered the course of history. As we have seen, the unprecedented astronomical event was so dramatic that it appears to have been interpreted by many cultures as the manifestation not just of a new god, but of a supreme god. In two instances, Zoroastrianism in Iran and Atenism in Egypt, the unparalleled magnitude of the celestial phenomenon even resulted in the deity being regarded as the only god. These are, in fact, the first examples of monotheism—the theological concept of a single, universal deity—known to history. It would seem, therefore, at least as far as we can tell from any records that survive, that the comet actually brought about the birth of monotheism.

But it goes further. One ancient monotheistic religion fundamentally helped shape Western civilization, and that was the religion of the Israelites: it eventually evolved into Judaism, and from Judaism sprang

Christianity. Astonishingly, it seems that this too originated as a direct result of the comet's appearance. Although there is no archaeological or historical evidence for the emergence of the Hebrew faith itself as early as 1486 BC, one of the monotheistic sects inspired by the comet's appearance is so similar to the early Israelite religion that they must have had a common origin—and that is Atenism.

The earliest evidence for the existence of Atenism and its veneration of the rayed disk dates from the very time of the comet's appearance. Over the following century, Atenism grew to completely dominate Egyptian religion to such an extent that around 1364 BC, the pharaoh Amenhotep IV came to the Egyptian throne, changed his name to Akhenaten (meaning "devotee of the Aten"), and made Atenism the country's state religion. It is from this time that the most comprehensive records concerning Atenism survive. The first person to draw scholarly attention to the astonishing similarities between Atenism and the early Hebrew religion was the Austrian psychoanalyst Sigmund Freud, in his book *Moses and Monotheism,* published in 1939. Freud pointed out that not only did both the Atenists and the Israelites venerate a single deity that they believed to be the only god, but also their deities were nameless and could be referred to only by titles.

Jehovah, the name for God familiar to Christians today, is actually a Greek rendering of the Hebrew YHVH or Yahweh, which is a shortened form of the title "I am and always will be." Even this was not allowed to be spoken aloud. The ancient Israelites usually referred to God by the Hebrew words Adonai, or Lord; and El, or God—*the* God. No matter how reverently, in Egypt gods were addressed directly and by name. Indeed, the name of the god was thought to invoke its presence. The god of the Atenists, however, was a singular exception.

As we have seen, the term "the Aten" was not actually the god's name, but rather a description of the symbol used to represent him: it simply means "the Disk." Like the Hebrew God, the Aten had no name and was addressed only by titles, such as Neb, or Lord; and En-ger, or God. (Freud was not actually the first to suspect a link between Atenism and the religion of the early Israelites. As early as 1909, the American archaeologist

James Breasted noticed that Psalm 104 in the Bible and the Hymn to the Aten, an Atenist equivalent to the Lord's Prayer, were almost identical in parts.) Another unique similarity Freud observed between the God of Israel and the Egyptian Aten was that neither deity was permitted to be represented by a graven image. According to the Bible, Israelite religion proscribed the making of effigies of God. In Egypt, however, an effigy or statue of a god was an essential part of cultic observance. In all of ancient Egyptian history, only Atenism diverged from this practice, forbidding the making of idols.[1]

Perhaps the most compelling evidence that Atenism and the religion of the Israelites were related came with an archaeological discovery made in 1989. In that year, at Sakkara near Cairo, the French archaeologist Alain Zivie discovered the tomb of an important Egyptian official named Aper-El. Tomb inscriptions revealed that he was Akhenaten's grand vizier (chief minister) and high priest of the Aten religion. Surprisingly, DNA tests on Aper-El's mummy revealed that he was a native of Canaan, as were the Israelites, which in itself would have been unusual enough.

More remarkably, however, he actually seems to have been an Israelite. His name, Aper-El, was a title meaning "servitor of El." El, Alain Zivie realized with surprise, was the Hebrew word for God. Remarkably, it seemed that this man was not only a high priest of the Aten—an Atenist equivalent of an archbishop—but he also venerated the Hebrew God. Both these deities were regarded by their worshippers as the only god. That Aper-El recognized both implies that he and the Atenists regarded the Aten and the Hebrew God as one and the same.[2]

There can be little doubt that both religions were originally very similar, but did they really emerge at the same time? Until recently, it was thought that the religion of the ancient Israelites did not originate until well after Akhenaten's time. Recent archaeological evidence, however, indicates that it originated precisely during Akhenaten's reign—not only a time when Atenism was at its very height, but also when the Israelites were actually in Egypt.

According to the Bible, the early Israelites had existed as tribal people in the area of Canaan until a famine forced them to move west into

Egypt and settle in the land of Goshen in the northeast Nile Delta. For many years, we are told, they lived peacefully alongside the Egyptians until a despotic pharaoh had them enslaved. Although the Bible does not provide dates or name the pharaoh concerned, many biblical scholars believe that the story reflects the historical events of the early fifteenth century BC, when Tuthmosis III formally introduced the practice of slavery to Egypt. The Bible goes on to say that some generations after the original enslavements (unfortunately, we are not told how many), Moses was born the son of an Israelite slave but was adopted by an Egyptian princess and raised at court as a prince of Egypt.

When he became a man, Moses's sympathy for the Israelite plight made him an enemy of the pharaoh, who forced him into exile in the Sinai wilderness to the east of Egypt. It was while Moses was in exile that God is said to have spoken to him and told him to return to Egypt and free the Israelites, which he eventually did, in the events referred to as the Exodus. It was only at this time that Moses revealed God's existence to the Israelites and lay down the Hebrew religious laws. Although the Bible propounds that God created the world and had always existed, it does not portray a Hebrew religion—the prescribed worship of God— until the time of Moses. God is said to have spoken individually to a few of the early Hebrew ancestors, but the Israelites as a whole had no idea that God even existed. In fact, we are told, even Moses had never heard of God before his calling. In other words, if the Bible is right, then the Israelite religion as such came into existence at the time of the Exodus. But when exactly was this supposed to have been?

The Bible says that at the time the Exodus occurred, the Israelite slaves were being forced to work on the building of two cities, one of which was called Ramesses.[3] The Egyptian king who is historically known to have built this city was the man after whom it was named: the pharaoh Ramesses II, also known as Ramesses the Great, who ruled from about 1292 to 1225 BC. For many years, modern biblical scholars accordingly assumed that it was during Ramesses' reign that the Exodus story was set. Recent archaeological evidence, however, now suggests that the account concerned a period in the middle part of the previous century.

The Bible asserts that directly after the Exodus, the Israelites spent forty years in the Sinai wilderness before moving north into Canaan and conquering the city of Jericho. In the 1950s, the ruins of ancient Jericho were unearthed some twelve miles northeast of Jerusalem, and since that time archaeology has revealed that the citadel was conquered by the Israelites in much the way the Bible relates. According to the Hebrew Scriptures' Book of Joshua, the Israelites were able to conquer the invincible city when God made its walls collapse. Excavations have shown that Jericho's walls did indeed collapse, due to what archaeologists believe to have been an earthquake; it would seem that the attacking Israelites took advantage of a natural disaster. As Jericho is said to have fallen forty years after the Israelites left Egypt, if the destruction of this city could be dated, so could the Exodus.

For many years, there was no way to date the fall of Jericho, until in 1996 ancient cereal grains were found under a section of the city's collapsed walls. As organic matter that had remained under the walls since the time of their collapse, the grains could be radiocarbon dated to determine when the city had fallen. Scientists from the Center for Isotope Research at Groningen University, in Holland, dated the event to 1315 BC, with a remarkably narrow margin of error for carbon dating of just thirteen years either way. This meant that if the Bible is right, and the Israelites left Egypt forty years earlier, the Exodus must have taken place somewhere between 1368 and 1342 BC, at least half a century before the reign of Ramesses the Great.[4]

Three pharaohs are known to have ruled during the period indicated by the dating of the fall of Jericho: Amenhotep III (c. 1389–1364 BC), Akhenaten (c. 1364–1347 BC), and the famous boy-king Tutankhamun (c. 1347–1338 BC). As we have seen, the height of Atenist influence in Egypt falls exactly at this time, during Akhenaten's reign. But as the biblical account specifically states that the Israelite slaves were forced to work at the city of Ramesses—a city known to have been named after Ramesses the Great—a date for the Exodus decades before this pharaoh's birth would appear to contradict the Bible.

Fortunately, this does not necessarily follow. Both archaeology and ancient Egyptian texts reveal that the city of Ramesses already existed well before the time of Ramesses the Great. It was previously called Avaris: Ramesses merely rebuilt and renamed it. Much of the Old Testament was not committed to writing until many centuries after the events it describes, sometime around the seventh century BC. Accordingly, the scribe who wrote of the events may simply have been referring to the city by the name it was known during his time. It would be similar to a modern historian referring to European colonists founding the city of New York when, in fact, it was originally called New Amsterdam. Indeed, the Old Testament refers to the same city, calling it Ramesses, concerning a period many generations before the time of the Exodus.[5]

It is certain, then, that the Old Testament scribes did indeed refer to the city by the name Ramesses during a time when we know for a fact it was still called Avaris. That the city where the Israelites toiled is referred to as Ramesses does not necessarily mean that the events occurred during the rebuilding of the city under Ramesses II. Indeed, there was another time that a large-scale rebuilding project is recorded at Avaris. This was during the last years of the reign of Amenhotep III and the first years of Akhenaten's reign, exactly during the time frame the dating of the fall of Jericho suggests the Exodus occurred.[6] If the Bible is right, therefore, the Israelite religion did indeed originate at the very time when Atenism was at its height.

The history of ancient Egypt spanned more than three thousand years. The kingdom of Egypt had existed for over five hundred years when the great pyramids were built around 2500 BC, and the pharaohs continued to rule Egypt until the last of them, Queen Cleopatra, died in 30 BC. That the monotheistic Israelite religion came into existence during the only period (and a short one at that—only about fourteen years) when Egypt had a monotheistic state religion, Atenism, is way beyond coincidence. The two surely had to have been related, or, if Aper-El is any indication, originally one and the same. In Egypt, monotheism died with the death of Akhenaten, but it appears to have continued with the Israelites, evolved into Judaism, and ultimately given rise to Christianity, which in turn played a central role in fashioning modern Western civilization.

The only problem with all this, however, at least from the perspective of modern historians and archaeologists, is that the story of Moses and the Exodus hardly seems credible. The Bible relates that when Moses returned to Egypt to demand the freedom of the Israelite slaves, the pharaoh initially refused; consequently, God inflicted on Egypt a series of what are referred to as plagues: darkness over the land, the Nile becoming poisonous and turning to blood, fiery hailstorms, cattle deaths, a plague of boils, and infestations of frogs, lice, flies, and locusts. Eventually, these dreadful plagues forced the pharaoh to free the Israelites, and Moses led them out of captivity.

Before long, the pharaoh had a change of heart and sent his army to pursue them. Trapped with their backs against the Red Sea, with the Egyptian army getting ever closer, it seemed that all was lost, until God again intervened and miraculously parted the sea so the Israelites could escape. When the Egyptians tried to follow, the waters returned and drowned them all. Surely such fantastic events are nothing but mythology, or at best religious allegory. But if the story is suspect, what reason is there to believe the biblical account of the inception of the Israelite religion at all? As unlikely as it may at first sound, the Old Testament account of the so-called plagues and the parting of the Red Sea now appears to have been inspired by real historical events.

Although I have discussed the historicity of the Exodus account at length in previous books[7], it is important here to provide a brief recap for those who are not familiar with them, for three important reasons. The third will become apparent in the next and final chapter, but the first two are these: First, it is essential to appreciate that, in regard to the historical events it describes, the biblical story of the Exodus is anything but a mythical account; and second, it offers further evidence that the Exodus events—and hence the inception of the Israelite religion—occurred at the very time Atenism was at its height in Egypt.

It is not only because the Exodus story sounds so incredible that many historians question its validity as a historical account, but also because there appears to be no evidence for it from Egypt itself. Surely, the historians argue, if the country was devastated by such ruinous events as the biblical plagues, there would be some record of them. Jewish and Christian scholars, however, counter this argument by pointing out that day-to-day records in ancient Egypt were kept on perishable papyrus that has not survived. The records that do remain are mainly in the form of tomb, temple, and palace inscriptions on stone, and they concern Egyptian religious issues, or the military achievements and domestic accomplishments of Egypt's ruling elite.

Nevertheless, there should still be some archaeological evidence that Egypt was afflicted by such catastrophes. On the contrary, at the time the Exodus story was originally thought to have been set—during the reign of Ramesses the Great—ancient Egypt was enjoying one of the most prosperous periods in its entire history. Since the dating of the fall of Jericho, however, it now seems that the Exodus events were set when Avaris was being rebuilt at the end of the reign of Amenhotep III or the beginning of Akhenaten's reign.

The plagues the Bible says God inflicted on Egypt when the pharaoh refused to free the Israelites comprised darkness over the land, fiery hailstorms, cattle and fish deaths, a plague of boils, the Nile turning to blood, and infestations of frogs, lice, flies, and locusts. There may be no evidence that Egypt had suffered anything remotely catastrophic during the reign of Ramesses the Great, but there is during the reign of Amenhotep III.

Direct evidence that Egypt suffered some kind of cataclysmic event or series of events at this time was first recognized in the 1980s by the Egyptologist Cyril Aldred, of the Royal Museum of Scotland. In his book *Akhenaten: King of Egypt,* he drew attention to the unprecedented number of statues of the goddess Sekhmet that were erected by Amenhotep III at the end of his reign. (Amenhotep, incidentally, did not, like his successor, embrace the popular Aten religion.) The pharaoh had literally thousands of images of the goddess installed in palaces and temples all over Egypt. In fact, no other deity of ancient Egypt had ever been represented by so many large-scale statues. This had to mean, Aldred suggested, that Egypt had suffered some kind of calamity. Sekhmet was the goddess of devastation!

In Egyptian mythology, the lion-headed goddess Sekhmet was the daughter of the sun god Re, who had once almost annihilated humankind in some remote period of the past. Natural disasters in Egypt were attributed to her wrath, and when things went wrong, her cult thrived. It was believed that by venerating the goddess she would leave the country in peace. The fact that Amenhotep had erected so many statues of Sekhmet at the end of his reign implied that his kingdom had suffered some kind of cataclysm.[8] Could this have been the biblical plagues?

During the twentieth century, some Jewish and Christian scholars suggested that the Exodus plagues were natural disasters that divine intervention had invoked to punish the Egyptians. The darkness could have been due to a particularly violent sandstorm; the hail could have been the result of freak weather conditions; the boils could have been caused by an epidemic; the bloodied Nile may have been the result of some seismic activity staining the river red; and swarms of locusts and flies and infestations of lice would not have been that uncommon. Scientists were unconvinced: the likelihood of them all happening at the same was just too remote.

In 1996, however, some scientists did begin to think seriously about one of the Exodus plagues. In July 1996, two of the scientists involved in the dating of the fall of Jericho drew attention to something they regarded as significant. Just three weeks earlier, other scientists had dated a volcanic eruption that might have affected Egypt to around forty-five years before the central radiocarbon date determined for the collapse of Jericho's walls (1360 BC and 1315 BC, respectively). During a press conference, Hendrik J. Bruins, of the Ben-Gurion University in Israel, and Johannes Van-der-Plicht, of the University of Groningen in Holland, told reporters: "This time difference is rather striking, as it could fit the desert period of 40 years separating the Exodus from the destruction of Jericho."[9] The volcano might, they suggested, account for one of the biblical plagues: the plague of darkness. According to the Bible, Egypt was covered by darkness for three days. Volcanoes can eject massive clouds of dust into the atmosphere, darkening the skies for miles downwind of the eruption. The scientists were referring to the ancient eruption of Mount Thera that occurred on the Mediterranean island of Santorini.

There are various types of volcanic eruption: some spew forth rivers of molten lava, others produce searing mud slides, but by far the most devastating is when the pressure of the magma causes the volcano to literally blow its top. This is what geologists determined had happened to the Mount Thera volcano around thirty-five hundred years ago. When a similar type of eruption occurred in the United States, at Mount St. Helens in Washington state, in 1980, fallout from the eruption darkened the daytime skies for hours on end over the state of Montana, more than six hundred miles downwind of the volcano. The Egyptian coast is less than five hundred miles from Mount Thera, and pumice samples taken from the Mediterranean seabed have determined that the wind carried Thera's volcanic cloud in a southeasterly direction—in the direction of Egypt. It is almost certain, then, that Egypt would have been affected similarly to the state of Montana after the Mount St. Helens eruption—and probably far worse. Today, Santorini is a crescent-shaped island forming a bay over six miles across; the bay itself is actually a crater formed by the ancient eruption that all but destroyed the island. Going by the size of the crater—over thirty square miles—the Thera eruption is estimated to have been vastly bigger than that at Mount St. Helens.

Bruins and Van-der-Plicht were not the first to propose that the Thera eruption had caused the biblical plague of darkness; a number of Jewish and Christian scholars had already done so. The problem was that the Thera eruption had been previously dated to around 1675 BC, far too early to have had anything to do with the Exodus. The new radiocarbon dating of the Thera eruption that Bruins and Van-der-Plicht referred to appeared to change all this.

The scientists who had originally dated the Thera eruption had, it turned out, been working with contaminated samples. They had used pieces of charred wood and cereal grains that had been covered by volcanic material during the eruption, and it was only later realized that these samples were useless for dating purposes. Volcanic carbon dioxide emanating from fissures in the ground had been assimilated into the plants before the eruption, significantly altering the natural amount of carbon 14 in the samples.

The new dating was made possible by other organic samples taken from beneath volcanic debris found on the nearby island of Crete. These new samples revealed that the eruption had taken place around 1360 BC, with a couple of decades' margin of error either way.[10] This meant that the Thera volcano could well have darkened the skies over Egypt, in just the way the Bible describes, during either the reign of Amenhotep III or that of Akhenaten, exactly when the Exodus story appears to be set. The Thera eruption could well have accounted for the Exodus plague of darkness, as Bruins and Van-der-Plicht suggested.

What the scientists involved in the Jericho excavation did not seem to have realized, however, is that the eruption of Thera could have accounted for all the Exodus plagues. To appreciate this, let's take Mount St. Helens as a modern comparison.[11]

Within a few hours of the Mount St. Helens eruption on the morning of May 18, 1980, a cloud of ash over five miles high, containing millions of tons of volcanic material, had rolled hundreds of miles east. In three states—Washington, Idaho, and Montana—the massive volcanic cloud covered the sky, and day was turned to night. Similar volcanic fallout from Mount Thera could well have been responsible for the biblical plague of darkness, as we have seen. Interesting enough! But there are astonishing similarities between the effects of the Mount St. Helens eruption and the Bible's description of the other Exodus plagues. After the Mount St. Helens eruption, throughout Washington, Idaho, and Montana, ash fell like rain, clogging engines, halting trains, and blocking roads. Over 17 million acres of lush farmland now looked like a gray desert, and millions of dollars' worth of crops were flattened and destroyed. For weeks afterward, fish in thousands of miles of rivers were found floating on the surface, killed by chemical pollutants in the water. The pungent odor of pumice permeated everything, and water supplies had to be cut off until the impurities could be filtered from reservoirs. According to the Old Testament, something very similar happened to the Egyptians during the Exodus plagues:

And the fish that was in the river died: and the river stank, and the Egyptians could not drink of the river.[12]

Along withs the gray pumice ash Mount St. Helens blasted skyward, there was iron oxide (the same red material that covers the surface of Mars). Thousands of tons of it were discharged into rivers, not only poisoning the water, but also staining it bloodred. According to the biblical account:

And all the waters that were in the river turned to blood.[13]

After the Mount St. Helens eruption, an acrid fallout of ash rained down for hours over five hundred miles from the volcano, suffocating wildlife; cattle perished or had to be destroyed due to prolonged inhalation of the volcanic dust. According to the Bible:

All the cattle of Egypt died.[14]

In the days following the Mount St. Helens eruption—as far away as the Montana town of Billings, six hundred miles from the volcano—hundreds of people were hospitalized with boils and skin rashes due to exposure to the acidic fallout dust. This sounds exactly like the Old Testament description of another of the Exodus plagues.

And it shall become small dust in all the land of Egypt, and shall be a boil breaking forth with blains upon man.[15]

One of the Exodus plagues, however, although sounding very much like something a volcano might have caused, does not at first seem attributable to the eruption of Mount Thera. According to the Bible:

And the Lord rained hail upon the land of Egypt. So there was hail, and fire mingled with the hail.[16]

It is understandable that the ancient Israelites might have likened a fall of volcanic debris to hail. Hail and fire, though, are a different matter. Although after the Mount St. Helens eruption the land in the immediate vicinity of the volcano was incinerated, ash that fell more than ten miles away was no longer hot enough to cause such damage. It would seem that ash from Thera would have cooled by the time it blew over the coast of Egypt, almost five hundred miles away. A massive eruption that occurred in the late nineteenth century, however, rained down fire much farther from the volcano.

In August 1883, the Krakatau volcano, near Java, exploded with a force a staggering twenty times larger than that of Mount St. Helens. The eruption was heard over three thousand miles away in Australia, and a volcanic cloud rose more than twenty miles into the air. On islands along the Sumatran coast—as much as a hundred miles away—flaming cinders that fell from the sky set fire to buildings and trees. Krakatau was one of the largest volcanic eruptions in recent history, yet even this did not deposit burning ash as far away as five hundred miles.[17]

It is difficult to imagine that hot pumice from Thera could have reached Egypt until it is appreciated just how large the Thera eruption is estimated to have been. The last nuclear weapon humans used in warfare was the atom bomb that destroyed half the Japanese city of Nagasaki in 1945. It was a twenty-kiloton explosion (the equivalent of twenty thousand tons of conventional explosives). Mount St. Helens exploded with a far greater force of fifty thousand kilotons and Krakatau reached an incredible 1 million kilotons; yet Thera dwarfs them all with a staggering 6 million kilotons. It would take six thousand of the most destructive modern nuclear warheads—each with the power to wipe out an entire city—to equal the explosive magnitude of Thera. It is very possible, then, that parts of Egypt did suffer from what witnesses might describe as fire mingled with hail, just like Sumatra after the eruption of Krakatau.

The plagues of insects the Bible records do not immediately sound as if they would have anything to do with a volcanic eruption:

All of the dust of the land became lice throughout all the land of Egypt. . . . [18] And there came a grievous swarm of flies. . . . [19] And the locusts went up over all the land of Egypt.[20]

Those who have not suffered the dreadful effects of an active volcano might imagine that once the eruption has subsided, the dead have been buried, the injured tended, and the immediate damage repaired, the survivors can begin the task of putting their lives back together, free from further volcanic horrors. This is very often far from true, as the entire ecosystem has been affected. Most forms of life suffer from volcanic devastation but, remarkably, some actually thrive. When volcanoes blanket the countryside with fallout ash, crawling invertebrates and insects in their larval, chrysalis, or egg stage can remain safe underground. Insects have a short life cycle, and accordingly reproduce at a frightening rate. After such a cataclysm, they have plenty of opportunity to establish a head start on larger predators and competitors. Moreover, compared to larger animals, they reproduce in vast numbers. Swarming insects are therefore commonly associated with the aftermath of volcanic eruptions.[21] Having survived the calamity, the insects are forced by the ash fall to seek out new habitations and food supplies—and heaven help anyone who gets in the way!

An excellent example is the flesh-crawling aftermath of the Mount Pelée eruption on the Caribbean island of Martinique in 1902. Volcanic debris covered the nearby port of St. Pierre, killing over thirty thousand people, but the horrors did not end there. The survivors endured a terrifying episode when huge swarms of flying ants descended on the sugar plantations and attacked the workers. As people fled for their lives, the vicious creatures seared their flesh with dreadful acid stings. It was no fluke that the insect assaults had followed the eruption; the creatures had attacked before when Mount Pelée had erupted in 1851. On this occasion they not only drove away workers and devoured entire plantations, but they were even reported to have attacked and killed defenseless babies while they were still in their cribs.[22]

Frogs are perhaps the best prepared of all the vertebrates for such cataclysms. Like insects, they produce vast numbers of offspring. Under normal conditions, this is a biological necessity, as the tiny tadpoles emerge from their eggs almost completely defenseless. After the Mount St. Helens eruption, however, the predatory fish were decimated. By the time the tadpoles hatched, the hazardous chemicals had washed away downriver but the fish had not yet returned. The result was a plague of frogs throughout much of Washington state. They clogged waterways, covered gardens, and infested houses. According to the Bible, this is exactly what happened to the ancient Egyptians:

And the frogs came up, and covered the land of Egypt.[23]

It now seems beyond a reasonable doubt that the Exodus plagues were real events caused by the Thera eruption. The Bible story of the Israelites fleeing captivity could be essentially true: they managed to escape in the confusion, panic, and disruption caused by the cataclysm. This, however, was not all. There was yet another event that the Bible asserts helped the Israelites flee Egypt, which could also have been a result of the Thera eruption. It was something that at first sounds even more unlikely than the Exodus plagues—the parting of the Red Sea.

According to the Book of Exodus, the Israelites began their trek out of Egypt once the plagues had persuaded the pharaoh to set them free. Before long, however, the pharaoh had a change of heart and ordered his army to pursue them. With their backs to the Red Sea, all seemed lost until God again interceded and caused the waters to part. The Israelites were accordingly able to walk across the seabed, but when the Egyptian army tried to follow, the waters returned and they were washed away. It is possible that this was another Exodus event caused by the Thera eruption. Geological surveys indicate that in the weeks following the eruption, large parts of the island collapsed into the sea. This would have created a series of tsunamis, or gigantic tidal waves, that would have thrashed the Mediterranean coast. Could this explain the Old Testament account?

First, it must be appreciated that the original biblical account set the event at the Red Sea not to the east of Egypt, but at another stretch of water in the northeast Nile Delta. It is now recognized that the name Red Sea is actually a mistranslation. The original Hebrew Bible describes the place where the Israelites crossed out of Egypt as Yam Suph—"The Reed Sea."[24] This may have been the old name for Lake Manzala on the Mediterranean coast at the extreme northeast of Egypt: a shallow lake that was covered by reeds. Its modern name is somewhat misleading, as it is actually open to the sea in places, now crossed by bridges. This was not always the case, however. In ancient times, when sea levels were lower, it was divided from the Mediterranean by a narrow ridge of dry land some thirty miles long, broken by a short stretch of water at high tide. At low tide, this became a causeway that could be crossed on foot. This is a route that makes geographical sense. If the Israelites were enslaved in Avaris, the best way to escape Egypt, avoiding the patrolled border, would have been to head north and then cross the Manzala causeway at low tide. If a tsunami had hit the coast when the Egyptians were following, the result would have been very much as the Bible describes.

Preceding the arrival of a tsunami, the coastal sea level often drops. (It is basically the same phenomenon that causes the sea to withdraw before the breaking of a normal wave, only over a longer duration). Such a phenomenon may have worked to the Israelites' advantage. If a section of the Manzala causeway usually under water had been exposed by the pre-tsunami conditions, the Israelites could have crossed in the way the Bible relates: "and the waters were divided."[25] This is an excellent description of what could have happened at the Manzala causeway, with the waters of the Mediterranean having divided from the waters of Lake Manzala. The Israelites could have made it safely across and, if the timing was right, the pursuing soldiers might have been attempting to follow when the tsunami hit.

And the waters returned and covered the chariots, and the horsemen and all the host of Pharaoh that came into the sea after them; there remained not so much as one of them.[26]

The dreadful tragedy in South Asia on December 26, 2004, when an earthquake off the coast of Sumatra caused waves as high as twenty feet to crash into coastal areas of Sri Lanka and India, over six hundred miles away, shows how devastating and far-reaching the destructive power of a tsunami can be. Geologists have estimated the magnitude of a similar tsunami following the eruption of Mount Thera: huge waves, well over twenty feet high, would easily have reached the Egyptian coast, which was less than five hundred miles from Santorini.[27]

It now seems fairly certain, then, that the story of the Israelites' flight from Egypt as it is portrayed in the Bible was set against a backdrop of real, historical events that occurred somewhere toward the end of the reign of Amenhotep III or the beginning of Akhenaten's reign, in about 1364 BC. According to the Bible, the Hebrew religion actually originated at the time of the Exodus. If the Exodus did occur around the time all the evidence suggests, then the religion of the Israelites came into existence at the very time Atenism was at its height in Egypt. When this is coupled with the similarities between the two religions, it seems that Freud may well have been right when he suggested that Atenism and the Hebrew religion were originally one and the same. If this is so, the monotheism that subsequently shaped Western civilization began with the comet of 1486 BC. I will discuss the potential implications of all this shortly, but next we should examine the all-important question: How could the comet have caused an epidemic of global violence?

14
Armageddon

WHEN A FAST-MOVING interplanetary body enters Earth's atmosphere, what is known as ram pressure, the rapid compression of air, causes it to heat up to searing temperatures. Luckily for us, this results in most meteoroids (the collective name for any relatively small interplanetary object) burning up on entry into the upper atmosphere. There is no specific boundary between the atmosphere and outer space; it just becomes thinner until it fades away. Although there is still actually a minuscule amount of atmosphere even as high as the space shuttle orbits, in a region known as the thermosphere, between fifty and four hundred miles high, for most practical purposes the atmosphere can be regarded as stretching to about fifty miles above Earth. Indeed, the NASA definition of an astronaut is anyone who has traveled more than fifty miles high.

The outermost part of the inner atmosphere, above approximately thirty miles, is called the mesosphere, and it is within this area that most meteoroids burn up to become visible from the ground as meteors, or shooting stars, as they are commonly called. Most meteors, ranging from tiny grains to the size of pebbles, safely incinerate in the mesosphere, but occasionally tennis ball–sized or even basketball-sized objects make it to the ground. Those that do reach Earth's surface are called meteorites, and it is reckoned that there are around five hundred of these each year. Most, though, land in the sea or in unpopulated areas, and only about five are ever discovered. Few of these kinds of objects are large enough to do more than local damage. It would be a very different matter if something much larger hit Earth.[1]

If a massive body such as a comet or asteroid hit Earth, it would blast millions of tons of matter so high that dust particles would remain suspended in the stratosphere, the region above around ten miles high, immediately below the mesosphere. The stratosphere is essentially cloud-free, meaning that most of the world's precipitation takes place in the lower atmosphere, known as the troposphere. This is where water vapor condenses into clouds ultimately to fall as rain, hail, or snow. Any atmospheric contaminants that make it into the stratosphere can remain suspended there for months, or even years, before dropping down into the troposphere to be rained out.

During this time, convection and stratospheric winds would distribute the fallout of an asteroid or comet impact around the world—irrespective of latitude—which would cause a period of diminished sunlight and hence colder conditions, often referred to as a nuclear winter (as it is thought that a nuclear war would result in much the same effect). Consequently, evidence of such impacts would be preserved in polar ice, which, we have already seen, holds a year-by-year record of Earth's air as it was in the past.[2] The ancient Egyptian account preserved in the Tulli Papyrus suggests that the comet of 1486 BC broke apart. If even a fragment of such a comet, say the size of the one that caused the Tunguska event of 1908, had hit Earth, there would almost certainly be evidence in ice-core samples relating to this period. But there is no evidence of any such impact around that time. On the other hand, as with the Tunguska event, it is possible that a fragment or fragments of the comet exploded in the air before hitting the ground.

The cometary fragment that is thought to have caused the Tunguska event is estimated to have been very much larger than any usual meteoroid, around two hundred feet in diameter, and it was also traveling considerably faster. If it had come in at a steep angle and survived the trip through the atmosphere to hit Earth, the results would have been devastating. It would have left a crater almost a mile across and blasted vast amounts of terrestrial debris into the air. As it happened, it came in at a shallow angle, allowing it to travel through more of the atmosphere and for a longer period, heating it up to temperatures that caused it to explode between three and six miles high. Not only was the explosion itself well below the stratosphere, but as there was no surface impact, no terrestrial debris was blasted into the air: there was no crater, no nuclear winter, and no discernible evidence of the event preserved in polar ice. It is possible that the same happened to a fragment, or fragments, of the comet of 1486 BC.[3]

But even if there was a cometary explosion in the atmosphere in 1486 BC, could it in any way have caused the global epidemic of violence that seems to have immediately followed? Surely some common cause has to have been responsible for the simultaneous and synchronous period of mass aggression that occurred around the world, yet, as we have seen, it was not climate change, nor could it reasonably be accounted for by mass hysteria.[4] Unless one of the most spectacular comets in human history appearing at this exact time was just an amazing coincidence—which seems most unlikely—it is logical to conclude that it was somehow related. How, though, could a comet possibly have caused such chaotic human behavior?

Through a process known as spectroscopy, astronomers can determine what a comet is made from without actually having to obtain a physical sample. By analyzing the properties of the light reflected from the comas of comets, we know they are composed mainly of water ice and frozen carbon dioxide (commonly known as dry ice), holding identifiable gases, chemicals, and other materials. If a fragment of a comet exploded in the air, these substances would vaporize—but they would not cease to exist. The water, for instance, would re-cool to ultimately fall as rain and snow. In fact, some scientists believe that much of the world's water actually arrived here with comets, at a time millions of years ago, shortly after the formation of the solar system, when there were vastly more comets orbiting close to Earth.

Comets are also rich in chemicals called amino acids, and some scientists think that the types of amino acids that form the essential building blocks of life were also brought to Earth by comets. But not all cometary material is so biofriendly. Chemicals and gases frozen in cometary ice can vary from comet to comet, and some comets contain toxic substances such as ammonia, carbon monoxide, and methane. When Halley's Comet appeared in 1910, astronomers announced that its tail contained the poisonous gas cyanogen. When it was also predicted that Earth would pass though the comet's tail, there was panic until it was explained that the tail stretched for millions of miles, meaning that the substance was extremely diffuse and tenuous; it was spread too thin to be a danger to life. It may have been a very different matter if a fragment of the comet had exploded in the atmosphere, however. Combined with elements in the air, cyanogen could form lethal hydrogen cyanide gas.[5] In fact, cyanogen was one of the chemical-warfare agents Saddam Hussein was accused of illegally manufacturing before the second Gulf War. But poisonous gas did not kill people following the comet of 1486 BC; people killed each other. Could there have been a gas or chemical in the comet that could have caused such violent behavior?

At the International Conference on Catastrophic Events and Mass Extinctions held at Vienna in July 2000, scientists gathered to discuss their findings regarding the possible threats to life on Earth posed by such potential catastrophes as asteroid and cometary impacts. Until this time, the general public had been relatively familiar with the notion that nuclear winters, mega-tsunamis, and global earthquakes could follow such events, but what the conference brought to the world's attention was the extent of the role that toxins released during ancient cometary collisions appear to have played in mass biological extinctions. In fact, the conference discussed at considerable length the various hazardous chemicals comets contain. As we have seen, comets contain amino acids, and one such amino acid is a substance called vasopressin, which is deadly in high doses. In the lesser quantities that might be released into the atmosphere during a cometary collision, there could be nonfatal but nevertheless detrimental effects on human beings. It would make them decidedly more aggressive.[6]

In the body, small amounts of vasopressin are produced naturally to act as hormones to facilitate preparedness for fight or flight when an individual faces a threat. Usually, natural vasopressin produces a heightened state of readiness, but in abnormally high measures, the same substance causes belligerent, even violent behavior. Experimental studies have even suggested the disturbing possibility that mass homicidal behavior would result if a city's water supply was ever contaminated with sufficient quantities of the chemical.[7]

Could a substance like vasopressin have caused the global epidemic of violence following the comet of 1486 BC? Unfortunately, at present, there is no way to determine this scientifically one way or the other; any soil contamination would have been washed away into rivers and seas long ago. And although there is no evidence in ice-core samples suggesting vasopressin in the atmosphere during the period in question, this does not negate the possibility. If a cometary fragment exploded in the air, the blast would probably occur, as it did at Tunguska, between three and six miles high, well below the stratosphere. As there would have been no terrestrial impact, the amount of vaporized cometary material would probably remain primarily within the troposphere and not circulate globally by stratospheric conditions.

Accordingly, unless the event occurred near the Arctic or Antarctic, the chances are that no evidence of it would be preserved in polar ice. Prevailing winds in the lower atmosphere, however, would disperse cometary material around the world in a shorter-term band of lateral contamination. This is precisely what happened after the Tunguska event. Although scientists at the time had no way to measure such contamination, we know it occurred because of the unusual atmospheric phenomena recorded at the time.

The epicenter of the explosion occurred at a latitude of 60 degrees north. Around the world in a band approximately 10 degrees to either side of this, strange sunsets and weird-colored skies were reported. Not only in Russia, but also in Poland, Germany, Scandinavia, the Netherlands, Britain and Ireland, and much of southern Canada, newspapers were full of reports of vivid pink sunsets and intense red twilight, and by moonlight the night sky took on an uncanny shade of blue. Areas outside this zone, such as in southern Europe, the Middle East, and southern Asia, witnessed nothing unusual. Unlike a terrestrial impact that would have blasted dust into the stratosphere to remain there for months or years, after the Tunguska airburst the contaminants causing the unusual atmospheric effects were rained out after just a few weeks. The phenomena began on the evening of the explosion, on June 30, and lasted for only around thirty days before dying away.

Fortunately, the fallout following the Tunguska event was apparently harmless. But what would have happened if the 1486 BC cometary fragment had contained large quantities of vasopressin? The chances are that the inhabitants of central Siberia, outside the area affected by the direct blast, would have been subjected to large doses of the toxin almost immediately. Throughout the rest of the world, people living between approximately 50 and 70 degrees north would have been increasingly affected over the next few weeks as the vasopressin gradually fell to Earth. But it would not end there. The substance would have contaminated water supplies and, in turn, plants and animals. It might be many years before it was fully washed away by rainfall and completely flushed from the food chain. There might well have been unaccountable and extreme violence witnessed throughout the contaminated regions for a decade or even two—which is exactly what appears to have happened around the world after the comet of 1486 BC.

The cultures and civilizations that succumbed to acute aggressive behavior after the appearance of the comet in 1486 BC were spread over a wider latitude than the area affected by fallout from the Tunguska event. The farthest north we know of was the megalithic civilization in Scotland at latitude 60 degrees north, and the farthest south was the pre-Olmec culture in Honduras and El Salvador at only 13 degrees north. This is a band of at least 47 degrees of latitude, much wider than the 20 degrees affected after the Tunguska event.[8] More than one cometary fragment, however, might have exploded in the atmosphere, and as the comet of 1486 BC seems to have broken apart, this may well have been what occurred.

The inhabitants of the area closest to any airburst would be most affected by the vasopressin release; indeed, in two regions we know of, the violent behavior following 1486 BC was initially more intense and frantic. The Aryans from Afghanistan swept southeast into the Indus

Valley, savagely massacring the Harappans and needlessly destroying their cities, while twenty-five hundred miles away in China, although a previously lenient society became abruptly cruel, oppressive, and tyrannical, and ultimately disintegrated in warfare and chaos, there is no evidence of the same kind of homicidal insanity. In the region of the northeast Mediterranean, we find the Mitannians of northern Syria initially fighting with mindless suicidal frenzy, while the Egyptians from northern Africa, although just as aggressive, wage more calculated warfare. One vivid account concerning the northeast Mediterranean demonstrates just how insane the violent behavior in that region appears to have been. The account is found among contemporary Hittite texts discovered at Hattusas. Part of the Hittite empire had included Cappadocia, in southern Turkey, and here the members of a peaceful community took to butchering one another in their own homes.

For a thousand years the ancient Cappadocians had enjoyed a tranquil existence in communal settlements cut into the wind-sculpted rocks of the Korma Mountains. From contemporary Hittite records, we learn that the inhabitants of these rock dwellings were astonishingly similar to the Buddhists of later Tibet: they abhorred violence and believed that all life was sacred. Then suddenly, sometime in the mid-1480s BC, these gentle people were seized by some kind of mass psychosis. The Hittites describe the Cappadocians fighting among themselves with unbridled savagery: brother slew brother, and men threw their women and children from cliffs. One account speaks of a visitor to one community in the area finding not a single person left alive. Archaeology supports such accounts, revealing that the hundreds of rock dwellings were suddenly abandoned in the early fifteenth century BC and remained uninhabited for generations.[9]

At present, and without further scientific study, there is no way of knowing if a cometary explosion or explosions really did cause the sudden outbreak of global hostility that occurred around 1486 BC. Such a scenario, however, certainly fits the facts. Indeed, it is difficult to envision what else could have caused it. Nonetheless, regardless of whatever actually triggered the worldwide epidemic of aggression, the comet itself

certainly appears to have changed civilization in another, more profound way. Indirectly, it seems to have brought about the concept of
monotheism.

As we saw in chapter 12, the appearance of what may have been the
most spectacular comet in the history of civilization led to the foundation
of various sects that believed the event was a manifestation of an excep-
tionally powerful god, and in some cases the only god. One religion that
embraced monotheism at the time was Atenism in Egypt, which seems
to have shared origins with the religion of the early Israelites. In chapter
13, we described how Atenism died out in Egypt during the reign of
Tutankhamun around 1340 BC, but the Hebrew religion survived—the
reason being that the Israelites seem to have escaped Egypt during the
calamitous effects of the Thera eruption. Their religion might well have
died with them in the Sinai wilderness had the Israelites not been able
to reconquer Canaan after the fall of Jericho, due to yet another natural
catastrophe, an earthquake that fortuitously brought down its walls.
With at least three spectacular natural events working in favor of their
religion, it is understandable that the Judaism which subsequently developed in Canaan endured with absolute faith in its God. Whether or not
these events were the result of divine intervention are theological issues
and still a matter of faith. It could certainly be argued that the likelihood
of all these spectacular natural events happening to further a particular
religious concept by chance alone is remote.

Strangely, the Bible itself predicts that something sounding very
much like an impact event will instigate the Armageddon—humankind's
last and most devastating conflict. According to the Book of Revelation,
chapter 8, verses 10–12:

> And there fell a great star from heaven, burning as it were a lamp,
> and it fell upon the third part of the rivers, and upon the fountains
> of waters. And the name of the star is called Wormwood: and the
> third part of the waters became wormwood; and many men died of
> the waters, because they were made bitter. . . . And the third part of
> the sun was smitten, and the third part of the moon, and the third

part of the stars; so as the third part of them was darkened, and the day shone not for a third part of it, and the night likewise.

Many modern biblical commentators have speculated that this passage refers to a comet or asteroid. The use of the name Wormwood is particularly interesting in this context. It was the common name for the toxic plant *Artemisia absinthium*. Because of the plant's use for poisoning enemy wells in an ancient form of chemical warfare, the term is used in the Bible to refer to what we today would describe as pollution. If a comet released vasopressin into the water supply, it would certainly pollute it. That the passage also describes the skies darkening is also interesting in relation to a cometary impact. The Bible maintains that this passage concerns a vision by an early Christian scribe. Regardless of whether it is a genuine prediction or just a religious allegory, as some biblical scholars believe, if a comet containing sufficient quantities of vasopressin did explode in the atmosphere today and caused an epidemic of mass aggression as evidenced around 1486 BC, with our modern weapons, it might very well bring about the end of the world. So could such a terrifying scenario really occur?

What happened to the comet of 1486 BC? It may have broken up completely, never to be seen again, or it may, like Comet Encke, which was responsible for the Tunguska event, have only partially disintegrated. If it survives, it may have such a long orbit that it hasn't been seen since. From the list of known periodic comets, however, there is a surviving comet that is calculated to have passed within the inner solar system around 1486 BC—and that is Comet 12P/Pons-Brooks. This might possibly have been the comet in question.

Comet 12P/Pons-Brooks was first recorded in 1812 by the French astronomer Jean-Louis Pons, and was observed again and recognized as the same comet by American astronomer William Robert Brooks in 1883. It was accordingly named after both of them. It is now known to have a relatively short orbit of between seventy and seventy-one years, which takes it to within 72 million miles of the sun and across the orbit of Earth. Disturbingly, not only has it been observed to move closer to us on each successive orbit since 1812, but it is also starting to behave erratically. In 1812 Jean-Louis Pons described it as an ill-defined nebulosity, without a tail, and visible only through a telescope. When it returned in 1883, it was visible to the naked eye as a bright starlike object with a small tail. When it reappeared in 1954, it was far more spectacular, coming within 59 million miles of Earth, less than half the distance of Comet Hale-Bopp in 1997. In 1954, the comet also underwent several unexplained outbursts of brightness between July and September that year.

At present, astronomers have insufficient data to know what is happening to Comet 12P/Pons-Brooks, but it has been speculated that it is becoming unstable, and that the next time it enters the inner solar system, it might break up. Whether it contains large amounts of vasopressin is also unknown, as the spectroscopy analysis of 1954 was able to determine only its surface content. At the moment, it is uncertain how close to us its orbit will bring it next. We will have to wait and see. It returns in 2024.

The comet may have been responsible for only the initial two decades of violence throughout the world, but civilizations were so irrevocably altered during this period of unbridled savagery that in most cases cultures thereafter remained permanently more aggressive. The establishment of warrior ruling classes shifted the emphasis of societies from peaceful to warring preoccupations, while distrust, paranoia, and even the desire for revenge enduringly tainted humanity.

For the first two millennia of its existence, the kingdom of Egypt never once attempted to build an empire, but following 1486 BC, persistent endeavors by the Egyptians to establish their influence throughout the eastern Mediterranean ultimately led to the kingdom's downfall. In Mesopotamia, wars had been limited to localized battles in which remarkably few people actively took part, but from the early fifteenth century BC, its kingdoms of Babylonia and Assyria maintained huge standing armies that engaged in ferocious conflicts again and again.

In Turkey and Syria, the Hittites and Mitannians had coexisted so peacefully that Mitanni had never considered it necessary to form an army, but from the mid-fifteenth century BC, the Hittites established a militaristic empire that completely absorbed the region of Syria. Before Aryans of Afghanistan invaded the Indus Valley, they had never once banded together as a single fighting unit, let alone forcibly invaded a foreign land; nor had the Yaz culture from Armenia before moving into Iran. Yet from these two peoples there arose two mighty empires: from Iran, the Persian empire eventually spread throughout half the Middle East, while the Aryans conquered virtually all of what is now India.

In China, the passive Erlitou culture had survived harmoniously for fifteen hundred years, while the Erligang culture that followed became a civilization renowned for feuding warlords and warrior-kings. Before 1486 in Central America, there is no evidence whatsoever of the kind of empire building, rigid social divisions, and the practice of human sacrifice that were trademarks of civilization in that region for centuries to come. And in northwest Europe, the megalithic civilization that had never created weapons of war or built a single known defensive structure was transformed into a society characterized by its hillforts and warrior graves.

Today we accept warfare and violence as a normal part of the human condition. Both the historical and archaeological evidence, however, shows categorically that this was far from true until the early fifteenth century BC. But then, and for no reason fathomable to the people of the time, everything changed. Once the global fury calmed down, populations throughout the world would surely have been left bewildered, wondering why they had suddenly and inexplicably behaved so diabolically. To rationalize their own incomprehensible behavior, some societies, such as the Olmec, may well have attributed the phenomenon to angry gods that thereafter demanded continual appeasement. Monotheism, on the other hand, with only one God, may have come up with another notion entirely—the concept of Satan. One of the main precepts of monotheism that evolved from the religion of the ancient Israelites is the notion of the fall from grace, as portrayed in the biblical story of the Garden of Eden. According to the Book of Genesis, humanity, symbolized by Adam and Eve, once lived in a harmonious state, free from warfare and violence, until Satan, in the form of a serpent, brought corruption into the world. Although it may not exactly have been paradise, humanity does indeed seem to have been far less belligerent, brutal, and hostile before 1486 BC. Could the events of this time explain the origin of the Garden of Eden story?

Most historians agree that the Genesis account was written around 550 BC, and that the Garden of Eden story was borrowed from the ancient Babylonians. From both the biblical account and Babylon's own records, we know that in the year 587 BC the Babylonian king Nebuchadnezzar sacked Jerusalem and returned home with many thousands of Jews in chains. For the next half century, the Jews endured slavery in Babylon—a period referred to as the Babylonian Exile. Nevertheless, the Jews in captivity continued to practice their religion, under the guidance of such prophets as Ezekiel. It was during this period that Babylonian mythology appears to have influenced the Jews to incorporate it into their own account of the world's beginnings.

Much of what is known of Babylonian mythology comes from discoveries made during archaeological excavations of the Assyrian city of Nimrud, some twenty miles south of Mosul in northern Iraq. In 1845, the British archaeologist Sir Austen Henry Layard excavated the ruins of the royal palace built for the Assyrian king Ashurnasirpal II around 880 BC. Among the treasures discovered were artifacts accumulated from all over the Middle East, including tablets originating from Babylon. Now in the British Museum, these texts contain the tale of Dilmun, the mythical Garden of Delight. Said to be somewhere along the river Euphrates, the Garden of Dilmun was where the Babylonians believed that humankind was created. The similarities between this myth and the Garden of Eden story found in the book of Genesis are too similar to be ignored.

In the Genesis account, after God has created the world in seven days, he plants the Garden of Eden and there puts the first man, Adam, and from one of Adam's ribs he creates the first woman, Eve. In the middle of the garden there are two forbidden trees: the Tree of Life, the fruit of which can bestow eternal life, and the Tree of Knowledge, the fruit of which can impart the knowledge of good and evil. God, who appears personally to Adam and Eve, tells them that they can eat any fruit in the garden except from these two trees. Before long, however, Satan tempts Adam and Eve to eat the fruit from the Tree of Knowledge, and God expels them into the harsh, wide world. We are not told where the Garden of Eden was but, judging by the fact that one of its rivers is called the Euphrates, it seems to have been somewhere in Mesopotamia. In the Babylonian Dilmun story, the first man is also created in a garden paradise beside the river Euphrates and, like Eve, the first woman is created from one of his ribs. Both are likewise eventually expelled from the garden by the supreme Babylonian god after they have disobeyed him.

In both stories, humankind is thereafter plagued by bloodshed and chaos of its own making. Unlike the Jews, the Babylonians had kept written records since the fifteenth century BC, and so it is very possible that the myth of humanity's fall from grace originated with their accounts of the terrible events following the comet of 1486 BC.

Our investigation began with an examination of the megalithic civilization and an attempt to solve the enigma of its mysterious demise. We can now see that its tragic end was merely a part of a global scenario. The culture that existed in northwest Europe until 1486 BC is a perfect example of just how harmonious societies had once been. Here there was no army to maintain law and order, or to enforce the beliefs of absent leaders.

There was no infrastructure to connect settlement spread throughout hundreds of miles, and there were no cities from which a select few could forcibly control the majority. Yet for two millennia, despite the fact that the civilization absorbed two mass waves of foreign migrants, the culture endured without ever having to resort to any form of warfare or violence. Time and again, people spread far and wide came together to work on communal projects that were vast in relation to their technology and available population. Megalithic monuments such as Stonehenge no doubt reflect the religious beliefs that inspired these people, but what these may have been will probably never be known. We do know, however, that whatever ideology they embraced, it was intrinsically nonviolent and was willingly maintained by an entire civilization for centuries. Once they succumbed to warfare and violence, however, there appears to have been no going back. It was, to use the perfect analogy, the End of Eden.

Chronology of Key Events

7000 BC   Start of the Mehrgarh culture in the Indus Valley and the
Uruk culture in Mesopotamia.

5500 BC   Building of the first towns in both the Indus Valley and
Mesopotamia.
The first permanent settlements are established in Egypt.

3500 BC   The first long barrows are erected in Britain.
Start of the Harappan city-building civilization in the
Indus Valley.
First city-building civilization in Egypt.

3300 BC   In Britain the causewayed enclosure at Windmill Hill is
constructed to the northeast of what would later be the
Avebury stone circle.

3100 BC   The Cursus earthwork is built to the north of what
would later be Stonehenge.
Unification of Upper and Lower Egypt into a single
kingdom.

3000 BC   The Stonehenge outer ditch and embankment are
constructed.
Settled village life begins in China.

2800 BC   In England, the Avebury north and south inner stone
circles are erected.

2750 BC   In England, Silbury Hill is built to the south of
Avebury.

2600 BC   In England, the bluestones are erected at Stonehenge,
and a huge circular ditch and embankment are

constructed at Durrington Walls to the northeast of the site. The main outer stone circle is erected at Avebury, and the surrounding ditch and embankment are constructed.

2580 BC   Building of the Pyramid of Cheops in Egypt.

2400 BC   In England, the West Kennett and Beckhampton Avenues are erected at Avebury.

2350 BC   Rise of Akkadian Empire in Mesopotamia.

2300 BC   At Stonehenge the Station Stones, Heel Stone, and portal stones are erected, and the Avenue is constructed.

2150 BC   Sumerian Renaissance.

2100 BC   In England, at Stonehenge the Sarsen Circle and the Trilithon Horseshoe are erected, while the Sanctuary stone circle is erected at the end of the West Kennett Avenue at Avebury.
Birth of the Erlitou culture, the first city-building civilization in China.

2000 BC   The Woodhenge monument is constructed near Stonehenge.
First pre-Olmec settlements in Central America.

1950 BC   Sumerian influence declines, and Babylon becomes the principal city of Mesopotamia.

1900 BC   First Assyrian kingdom is founded in northern Mesopotamia.

1750 BC   The Hittite kingdom is founded in Turkey.

1600 BC   Kingdom of Mitanni is founded in northern Syria.

1550 BC   The last phase of building at Stonehenge.

1486 BC   Tulli Papyrus records "disk of fire" in Egypt. Tuthmosis III seizes power from his mother in a palace coup and invades Canaan.

c. 1486 BC   The Mawangdui Silk Almanac records that an exceptional comet is seen in China.
Olmec culture emerges in Central America.
Aryans invade Indus Valley.

Start of the Erligang culture and the Shang dynasty in China.

Hittites invade northern Assyria.

Mitannians invade western Assyria and attack the Egyptians in Canaan.

Large-scale burning of Jomon settlements in Japan.

Yaz people from Armenia invade Iran.

Zoroastrianism, which employed a winged disk to represent Ahura Mazda, is founded in Iran.

The cult of Antum, which represented its deity by a winged disk, is first referenced in Assyria.

The Kumarbis winged disk is first employed by the Hittites.

Atenism, which represented its god by a rayed disk, is first recorded in Egypt.

The earliest evidence for the cult of Ir and the use of the winged disk symbol to represent him is found in the Mitanni kingdom.

c. 1360 BC	Akhenaten is king of Egypt. Height of the Aten cult in Egypt. The eruption of Thera and the biblical Exodus.
1347 BC	Tutankhamun is king of Egypt.
1315 BC	The fall of Jericho.
1292 BC	Ramesses the Great is king of Egypt.
700 BC	Celts first arrive in Britain.
400 BC	First evidence of the Mayan culture in Central America.

NOTES

CHAPTER 1

1. B. Cunliffe and C. Renfrew (eds.), *Science and Stonehenge* (Oxford, U.K.: Oxford University Press, 1997), 15–37.
2. For a concise guide to Stonehenge, see: J. Richards, *English Heritage Book of Stonehenge* (London: Batsford, 1991).
3. R. Castleden, *The Stonehenge People* (London: Routledge, 1992).
4. Cunliffe and Renfrew, *Science and Stonehenge*, 231–56.
5. Ibid., 16–19.
6. Sean McGrail, *Ancient Boats and Ships* (Princes Risborough, U.K.: Shire Publications, 2006).
7. Cunliffe and Renfrew, *Science and Stonehenge*, 172–80.
8. G. J. Wainwright and I. H. Longworth, "Durrington Walls Excavations 1966–1968." *American Anthropologist*, n.s., 75 (no. 6, 1973).
9. Mick Aston, professor of landscape archaeology at the University of Bristol, speaking on the British television series *Time Team* during the summer excavations at Durrington Walls in 2005.
10. M. Parker-Pearson, "The Stonehenge Riverside Project and New Discoveries." *Journal of Material Culture* 11 (2006): 227–61.
11. Guy Underwood, *The Pattern of the Past* (London: Sphere Books, 1972), 137–39.
12. Frances Lynch, *Megalithic Tombs and Long Barrows in Britain* (Princes Risborough, U.K.: Shire Publications, 1997).

CHAPTER 2

1. John Aubrey, *Wiltshire: The Topographical Collections* (Devizes, U.K.: Henry Bull, 1862).

2. For a concise guide to Avebury, see: Aubrey Burl, *Prehistoric Avebury* (New Haven: Yale University Press, 2002).

3. Julian Cope, *The Modern Antiquarian* (London: Thorsons, 1998), 203.

4. Michael Dames, *The Silbury Treasure* (London: Thames & Hudson, 1976).

5. Cope, *Modern Antiquarian*, 204.

6. Michael Baillie, *A Slice Through Time: Dendrochronology and Precision Dating* (London: Routledge, 1995).

7. M. J. Aitken, *Thermoluminescence Dating* (London: Academic Press, 1985).

8. Sheridan Bowman, *Radiocarbon Dating* (Berkeley: University of California Press, 1990).

9. For a concise guide to the Ridgeway, see: Anthony Burton, *The Ridgeway* (London: Aurum Press, 2005).

10. *Western Mail*, Cardiff, U.K., 24 June 2005.

11. Cunliffe and C. Renfrew (eds.), *Science and Stonehenge* (Oxford, U.K.: Oxford University Press, 1997).

12. F. Lynch, J. Davies, and S. Aldhouse-Green, *Prehistoric Wales* (Stroud, U.K.: Sutton Publishing, 2000).

13. *The Guardian*, London, 21 June 2004.

14. The scientific examination of the teeth was conducted by the British Geological Survey based at Keyworth in the English county of Nottinghamshire.

15. P. A. Jewel, *The Experimental Earthwork on Overton Down, Wiltshire, 1960* (London: British Association for the Advancement of Science, 1963).

16. For scientific estimation of man-hours needed for these and other megalithic projects, see: D. Startin, "Prehistoric Earthmoving," in *Settlement Patterns in the Oxford Region*, ed. by H. Case and A. Whittle (London: Council for British Archaeology, 1982), 153–56.

CHAPTER 3

1. G. Brown, D. Field, and D. McOmish (eds.), *The Avebury Landscape: Aspects of the Field Archaeology of the Marlborough Downs* (Oxford, U.K.: Oxbow Books, 2005), 103–14.

2. For a concise guide to megalithic Cornwall, see: Cope, *Modern Antiquarian*, 155–90.

3. Rodney Legg, *Stanton Drew: Great Western Temple* (Wincanton, U.K.: Dorset Publishing, 1998).

4. For a concise guide to megalithic north Wales, see: Cope, *Modern Antiquarian*, 303–330.

5. T. G. E. Powell, "The Gold Ornament from Mold, Flintshire, North Wales." *Proceedings of the Prehistoric Society* 19 (1953), 161–79.
6. Cope, *Modern Antiquarian*, 269–72.
7. Anne Ritchie, *Prehistoric Orkney* (London: Batsford, 1995).
8. Kenneth McNally, *Ireland's Ancient Stones: Megalithic Ireland Explored* (Belfast: Appletree Press, 2006).
9. Michael J. O'Kelly, *Newgrange: Archaeology, Art and Legend* (London: Thames & Hudson, 1988).
10. For a concise guide to megalithic Brittany, see: Aubrey Burl, *From Carnac to Callanish: Prehistoric Stone Rows of Britain, Ireland and Brittany* (New Haven: Yale University Press, 1993).

CHAPTER 4

1. Robert Gurney, *Celtic Heritage* (London: Chatto & Windus, 1969).
2. John Aubrey, *Wiltshire: The Topographical Collections* (Devizes, U.K.: Henry Bull, 1862).
3. William Stukeley, *Stonehenge: A Temple Restored to the British Druids* (Abingdon, U.K.: Taylor & Francis, 1984).
4. M. Dillon and N. Chadwick, *The Celtic Realms* (New York: New American Library, 1967).
5. For a concise guide to proposed astronomical theories concerning stone circles, see: Aubrey Burl, *A Guide to the Stone Circles of Britain, Ireland and Brittany* (New Haven: Yale University Press, 1995).
6. Erich Von Daniken, *Chariots of the Gods* (London: Souvenir Press, 1990).
7. G. W. Trompf, *Cargo Cults and Millenarian Movements: Transoceanic Comparisons of New Religious Movements* (Berlin: Mouton De Gruyter, 1990).
8. John Michell, *The Flying Saucer Vision* (London: Sidgwick & Jackson, 1967), 152–54.
9. Alfred Watkins, *The Old Straight Track* (London: Abacus, 1989).
10. John Michell, *The View over Atlantis* (London: Sidgwick & Jackson, 1969).
11. Tom Graves, *Needles of Stone* (London: HarperCollins, 1983).
12. For an examination of pagan elements in Christianity, see: Ramsay MacMullen, *Christianity and Paganism in the Fourth to Eighth Centuries* (New Haven: Yale University Press, 1999).
13. C. F. C. Hawkes, "The Rillaton Gold Cup." *Antiquity* 57 (1983): 124–25.
14. T. G. E. Powell, "The Gold Ornament from Mold, Flintshire, North Wales." *Proceedings of the Prehistoric Society* 19 (1953): 161–79.

15. For more on folktales associated with megalithic sites, see: Kevin Crossley-Holland, *British Folk Tales* (London: Orchard Books, 1987).

CHAPTER 5

1. M. S. Midgley, "The Origin and Function of the Earthen Long Barrows of Northern Europe." *British Archaeological Reports* 20 (1985).

2. See: Michael Dames, *The Avebury Cycle* (London: Thames & Hudson, 1977).

3. Richard Wainwright, *A Guide to Prehistoric Remains in Britain* (London: Constable, 1978).

4. Olivier Dunrea, *Skara Brae: The Story of a Prehistoric Village* (New York: Holiday House, 1986).

5. For a concise guide to the prehistoric peoples of the British Isles, see: T. C. Darvill, *Prehistoric Britain* (London: Routledge, 1995).

6. F. Lynch, *Megalithic Tombs and Long Barrows in Britain* (Princes Risborough, U.K.: Shire Publications, 1997).

7. Robert Wernick, *The Monument Builders* (New York: Time-Life Books, 1973).

8. James Dyer, *Hillforts of England and Wales* (Princes Risborough, U.K.: Shire Publications, 1992).

9. I. M. Allen, D. Britton, and H. Coghlan, *British and Irish Bronze Age Implements and Weapons* (Oxford, U.K.: Oxford University Press, 1970).

10. C. Evans and M. Knight, *Bronze Age Landscapes: Tradition and Transformation* (Oxford, U.K.: Oxbow Books, 2001), 83–98.

11. R. Sernander, *On the Evidence of Post-Glacial Changes of Climate Furnished by the Peat Mosses of Northern Europe* (Stockholm: Förhaldlinger, 1908).

12. Lennart Von Post, "The Prospect for Pollen Analysis in the Study of the Earth's Climatic History." *New Phytologist* 45 (1946).

13. Harry Godwin, *Archives of Peat Bogs* (Cambridge, U.K.: Cambridge University Press, 1981).

14. T. Simkin and R. S. Fiske, *Krakatau 1883: The Volcanic Eruption and Its Effects* (Washington, DC: Smithsonian, 1984).

15. R. J. Delmas, *Ice Core Studies of Global Biochemical Cycles* (Berlin: Springer-Verlag, 1995).

CHAPTER 6

1. David C. Grove and Rosemary A. Joyce (eds.), *Social Patterns in Pre-Classical Mesoamerica* (Washington, DC: Dumbarton Oaks, 1999).
2. M. Coe and D. Grove, *The Olmec and Their People* (Washington, DC: Dumbarton Oaks, 1981).
3. Richard A. Diehl, *The Olmec: America's First Civilization* (London: Thames & Hudson, 2005.)
4. R. Jurmain, H. Nelson, L. Kilgore, and W. Trevathan, *Essentials of Physical Anthropology* (Belmont, CA: Wadsworth, 1998), 108.
5. G. Haslip-Viera, O. De Montellano, and W. Barbour, "Robbing Native American Cultures." *Current Anthropology* 38 (1997): 423.
6. L. M. Raab, M. A. Boxt, K. Bradford, B. Stokes, and R. Gonzalez-Lauck, "Current Research on the Gulf Coast of Mexico." *Journal of Field Archaeology* 27 (no. 3, 2000): 257–70.
7. Ibid.
8. John S. Henderson, *The World of the Ancient Maya* (Ithaca, NY: Cornell University Press, 1997).
9. Philip J. Arnold, "Early Formative Pottery from the Tuxtla Mountains and Implications for Gulf Olmec Origins." *Latin American Antiquity* 14 (2003).
10. David C. Grove and Rosemary A. Joyce (eds.) *Social Patterns in Pre-Classic Mesoamerica* (Washington, DC: Dumbarton Oaks, 1999), 155–81.
11. Michael D. Lemonick, "Mystery of the Olmec." *Time,* July 1996.

CHAPTER 7

1. Walter A. Fairservis, *The Roots of Ancient India: The Archaeology of Early Indian Civilization* (New York: Macmillan, 1971).
2. Mortimer Wheeler, *The Indus Civilization* (Cambridge, U.K.: Cambridge University Press, 1968).
3. G. Singh, R. D. Joshi, and A. B. Singh, "Stratigraphic and Radiocarbon Evidence for the Age and Development of Three Salt-Lake Deposits in Rajasthan, India." *Quaternary Research* 2 (1972): 494–505.
4. Stuart Piggott, *Prehistoric India to 1000 BC* (London: Cassell, 1962), 138–57.
5. Ibid., 228–37.
6. For a concise account of the fall of the Harappan civilization, see: J. McIntosh, *A Peaceful Realm: The Rise and Fall of the Indus Civilization* (Boulder, CO: Westview, 2001).

7. Michael Loewe and Edward Shaughnessy, *The Cambridge History of Ancient China: From the Origins of Civilization to 221 BC* (Cambridge, U.K.: Cambridge University Press, 1999), 462–599.

8. Yun Kuen Lee, "Building the Chronology of Early Chinese History." *Journal of Archaeology for Asia and the Pacific* 41 (2002): 15–42.

9. David N. Keightley, *Sources of Shang History: The Oracle-Bone Inscriptions of Bronze Age China* (Berkeley: University of California Press, 1978).

10. Xiong Chuanxin, *The Number 2 and Number 3 Han Tombs at Mawang-dui, Changsha,* vol. 2 (Beijing: Cultural Relics Publishing House, 2004), 538–42.

CHAPTER 8

1. Mitchell S. Rothman (ed.), *Uruk Mesopotamia and Its Neighbors: Cross-Cultural Interactions in the Era of State Formation* (Santa Fe, NM: SAM Press, 2001).

2. Harriet Crawford, *Sumer and the Sumerians* (Cambridge, U.K.: Cambridge University Press, 1991).

3. Gwendolyn Leick, *Mesopotamia: The Invention of the City* (London: Penguin, 2002).

4. J. G. MacQueen, *The Hittites and Their Contemporaries in Asia Minor* (London: Thames & Hudson, 1996).

5. Donald Redford, *Egypt, Canaan and Israel in Ancient Times* (Princeton, NJ: Princeton University Press, 1993).

6. Henri Frankfort, *Kingship and the Gods: A Study of Ancient Near Eastern Religion as the Integration of Society and Nature* (Oxford, U.K.: Oxford University Press, 1978).

7. Erik Hornung and John Baines, *Conceptions of God in Ancient Egypt* (Ithaca, NY: Cornell University Press, 1996).

8. For a concise guide to the early New Kingdom, see: Donald Redford, *History and Chronology of the Eighteenth Dynasty of Egypt* (Toronto: Toronto University Press, 1967).

9. Lionel Casson, *Everyday Life in Ancient Egypt* (Baltimore, MD: Johns Hopkins University Press, 2001).

10. George Steindorff and Keith Seele, *When Egypt Ruled the East* (Chicago: University of Chicago Press, 1942), 47–71.

11. Redford, *Egypt, Canaan and Israel,* 156.

12. Steindorff and Seele, *When Egypt Ruled the East,* 105–20.

13. H. Tadmor and M. Weinfeld (eds.), *History, Historiography and Interpretation: Studies in Biblical and Cuneiform Literatures* (Jerusalem: Magnes Press, 1983), 21–43.

14. P. Thieme, "Mitanni Treaties." *Journal of the American Oriental Society* 80 (1960): 301–17.

15. S. Maul, *The Ancient Middle Eastern Capital* (Frankfurt: Saarbrücker, 1997), 109–24.

CHAPTER 9

1. Alan Gardiner, *Egypt of the Pharaohs* (Oxford, U.K.: Oxford University Press, 1964), 193–201.

2. D. Wiseman, *The Hittites and Hurrians* (Oxford, U.K.: Clarendon Press, 1973), 78–80.

3. Albert Kirk Grayson, *Assyrian and Babylonian Chronicles: Texts from the Cuneiform Sources,* vol. 5 (Winona Lake, IN: Eisenbrauns, 2000), 104–10.

4. Enrico Ascalone, *Mesopotamia: Assyrians, Sumerians, Babylonians* (Berkeley: University of California Press, 2007).

5. For a concise outline of Tuthmosis III's campaigns in Syria, see: Donald Redford, *The Wars in Syria and Palestine of Thutmose III* (Boston: Koninklijke Brill, 2003).

6. Wiseman, *Hittites and Hurrians,* 217–21.

7. Ascalone, *Mesopotamia.*

8. David N. Keightley, *Sources of Shang History: The Oracle-Bone Inscriptions of Bronze Age China* (Berkeley: University of California Press, 1978).

9. Ibid.

10. Stuart Piggott, *Prehistoric India to 1000 BC* (London: Cassell, 1962), 53–131.

11. K. Jones-Bley and D. G. Zdanovich (eds.), *Complex Societies of Central Eurasia from the 3rd to the 1st Millennium BC* (Washington, DC: J.I.E.S. Publishing, 2002) 224–31.

12. J. Habu, *Ancient Jomon of Japan* (Cambridge, U.K.: Cambridge University Press, 2004).

CHAPTER 10

1. Richard A. Parker, *The Calendars of Ancient Egypt* (Chicago: University of Chicago Press, 1950).

2. Ibid.

3. Donald Redford, *History and Chronology of the Eighteenth Dynasty of Egypt* (Toronto: Toronto University Press, 1967), 183–215.

4. B. Ebbell (English trans.), *The Papyrus Ebers* (Copenhagen: Levin & Munksgaard, 1937).

5. James Henry Breasted, *Ancient Records of Egypt,* vol. 2, ed. by Peter A. Piccione (Chicago: University of Chicago Press, 2001), 407–15.

6. Erik Hornung and John Baines, *Conceptions of God in Ancient Egypt* (Ithaca, NY: Cornell University Press, 1996).

7. Cyril Aldred, *Akhenaten: King of Egypt* (London: Thames & Hudson, 1988).

8. K. Sethe, *Documents of the Eighteenth Dynasty,* vol. 1 (Leipzig: Hinrichs, 1906), 64–71.

9. Aldred, *Akhenaten,* 291–302.

10. Ibid., 16–21.

11. Ibid.

12. Tom Simkin and Richard S. Fiske, *Krakatau 1883: The Volcanic Eruption and Its Effects* (London: HarperCollins, 1984).

13. Manfred Lurker, *The Gods and Symbols of Ancient Egypt* (London: Thames & Hudson, 1999), 130.

14. Stephane Rossini, *Egyptian Hieroglyphics* (Mineola, NY: Dover Publications, 1989).

15. Donald Redford, *Akhenaten: The Heretic King* (Princeton: Princeton University Press, 1987), 170.

16. Rossini, *Egyptian Hieroglyphics.*

CHAPTER 11

1. B. DeRachewiltz, *An Introduction to Egyptian Art* (London: Spring Books, 1960), 56–59.

2. R. F. S. Starr, *Nuzi* (Cambridge, MA: Harvard University Press, 1937).

3. E. Porada, "The Seal of Shaushtatar." *American Journal of Archaeology* 60 (no. 3, 1956): 289–90.

4. M. E. L. Mallowan, *Nimrud and Its Remains* (London: Collins, 1966).

5. J. Meuszynski, S. Paley, and R. Sobolewski, *The Reconstruction of the Relief Representations and Their Arrangement in the Northwest Palace of Kalhu* (Mainz, Germany: Zabern Publishers, 1987).

6. H. Winckler, "Provisional Messages over the Excavations in Boghazkoei in the Summer 1907." *Communications of the German East Society* no. 35 (Berlin: Deutsche Orient-Gesellschaft, 1907), 25.

7. J. W. Crowfoot, "Mission en Cappadoce 1893–1894." *Journal of the Anthropological Institute of Great Britain and Ireland* 29 (no. 3, 1899): 320–24.

8. K. Jones-Bley and D. G. Zdanovich (eds.), *Complex Societies of Central Eurasia from the 3rd to the 1st Millennium* BC (Washington, DC: J.I.E.S. Publishing, 2002), 224–31.

9. N. Sims-Williams (ed.), *Indo-Iranian Languages and Peoples* (London: British Academy, 2003).

10. J. A. Hammerton (ed.), *Wonders of the Past,* vol. 2 (New York: Wise, 1937), 760–67.

11. David N. Keightley, *Sources of Shang History: The Oracle-Bone Inscriptions of Bronze Age China* (Berkeley: University of California Press, 1978).

12. R. McCray and Z. Wang, *Supernovae and Supernova Remnants* (Cambridge, U.K.: Cambridge University Press, 1996).

13. Xiong Chuanxin, *The Number 2 and Number 3 Han Tombs at Mawangdui, Changsha,* vol. 1 (Beijing: Cultural Relics Publishing House, 2004).

CHAPTER 12

1. J. S. Lewis, *Comet and Asteroid Impact Hazards on a Populated Earth* (Gainesville, FL.: Academic Press, 1999).

2. Carl Sagan, *Comet* (London: Michael Joseph, 1985), 129–43.

3. Ibid., 3–12.

4. Xiong Chuanxin, *The Number 2 and Number 3 Han Tombs at Mawangdui, Changsha,* vol. 1 (Beijing: Cultural Relics Publishing House, 2004), 106–23.

5. Sagan, *Comet,* 13–38.

6. David N. Keightley, *Sources of Shang History: The Oracle-Bone Inscriptions of Bronze Age China* (Berkeley: University of California Press, 1978).

7. Roberta Olson, *Fire and Ice: A History of Comets in Art* (New York: Walker, 1985).

8. B. DeRachewiltz, *An Introduction to Egyptian Art* (London: Spring Books, 1960), 56–59.

9. Xiong Chuanxin, *The Number 2 and Number 3 Han Tombs at Mawangdui, Changsha,* vol. 1.

10. Ibid.

11. *The Rig Veda,* trans. by Wendy Doniger (London: Penguin, 2005), Book 1:44.

12. Ibid., 1:69.

13. Ibid., 1:59.
14. Ibid., 1:45.
15. Ibid., 1:27.
16. Sagan, *Comet*.
17. J. S. Lewis, *Comet and Asteroid Impact Hazards on a Populated Earth*.
18. Ibid.
19. B. DeRachewiltz, *An Introduction to Egyptian Art*.
20. Peter Jenniskens, *Meteor Showers and Their Parent Comets* (Cambridge: Univesity Press, 2006).
21. B. DeRachewiltz, *An Introduction to Egyptian Art*.
22. Roberta Olson, *Fire and Ice: A History of Comets in Art*.
23. R. Turco, C. Park, R. Whitten, J. Pollack and P. Noerdlinger, "An Analysis of the Physical, Chemical, Optical and Historical Impacts of the 1908 Tunguska Meteor Fall." *Icarus* 50 (1982), 1–52.

CHAPTER 13

1. Sigmund Freud, *Moses and Monotheism* (London: Vintage, 1955).
2. Alain Zivie, "The Treasury of Aper-El." *Egyptian Archaeology* (Summer 1991): 26–29.
3. Exodus 1:11. This and all other biblical citations refer to the King James I English Bible.
4. *The Guardian,* London, 18 July 1996.
5. Genesis 47:11.
6. Manfred Bietak, *Avaris: Capital of the Hyksos* (London: British Museum Press, 1995).
7. Graham Phillips, *The Moses Legacy* (London: Pan, 2002) and *Atlantis and the Ten Plagues of Egypt* (Rochester, VT: Bear & Co, 2003).
8. Cyril Aldred, *Akhenaten: King of Egypt* (London: Thames & Hudson, 1988), 148–49.
9. *Guardian,* London, 18 July 1996.
10. Phillips, *Atlantis,* 315–17.
11. For a full account of the Mount St. Helens eruption and its similarities to the Thera eruption, see: Phillips, *Atlantis,* 207–35.
12. Exodus 7:21.
13. Exodus 7:20.
14. Exodus 9:6.
15. Exodus 9:9.
16. Exodus 9:23–24.

17. T. Simkin and R. S. Fiske, *Krakatau 1883: The Volcanic Eruption and Its Effects* (Washington, DC: Smithsonian, 1983).

18. Exodus 8:17.

19. Exodus 8:24.

20. Exodus 10:14.

21. D. P. Sheets and D. K. Grayson (eds.), *Volcanic Activity and Human Ecology* (New York: Academic Press, 1990).

22. George Kennan, *The Tragedy of Pelée* (Westport, CT: Greenwood Press, 1970).

23. Exodus 8:6.

24. M. Magnusson, *B.C. The Archaeology of the Bible Lands* (London: Bodley Head, 1977), 64–65.

25. Exodus 14:21.

26. Exodus 14:29.

27. A. G. Galanopoulos, "Tsunamis Observed on the Coasts of Greece from Antiquity to Present Time." *Annali de Geofisica* 23 (1960): 371–86.

CHAPTER 14

1. Peter Jenniskens, *Meteor Showers and Their Parent Comets* (Cambridge, U.K.: Cambridge University Press, 2006).

2. R. J. Delmas, *Ice Core Studies of Global Biochemical Cycles* (Berlin: Springer-Verlag, 1995).

3. R. Turco, O. Toon, C. Park, R. Whitten, J. Pollack, and P. Noerdlinger, "An Analysis of the Physical, Chemical, Optical and Historical Impacts of the 1908 Tunguska Meteor Fall." *Icarus* 50 (1982), 1–52.

4. Roberta Olson, *Fire and Ice: A History of Comets in Art* (New York: Walker, 1985).

5. Carl Sagan, *Comet* (London: Michael Joseph, 1985), 148–50.

6. M. V. Gerasimov, "The Production of Toxins During an Impact and Their Possible Role in a Biotic Mass Extinction," International Conference on Catastrophic Events and Mass Extinctions, Vienna, 9–12 July 2000, abstract no. 3051.

7. H. K. Caldwell and W. S. Young, "Oxytocin and Vasopressin: Genetics and Behavioral Implications," in *Handbook of Neurochemistry and Molecular Neurobiology* (New York: Springer, 2006), 573–607.

8. Turco et al., "Tunguska Meteor Fall," 1–52.

9. H. Tadmor and M. Weinfeld (eds.) *History, Historiography and Interpretation: Studies in Biblical and Cuneiform Literatures* (Jerusalem: Magnes Press, 1983), 38.

Bibliography

Aitken, M. J. *Thermoluminescence Dating*. London: Academic Press, 1985.

Aldred, Cyril. *Akhenaten: King of Egypt*. London: Thames & Hudson, 1988.

Allen, I. M., D. Britton, and H. Coghlan. *British and Irish Bronze Age Implements and Weapons*. Oxford, U.K.: Oxford University Press, 1970.

Arnold, Philip, J. "Early Formative Pottery from the Tuxtla Mountains and Implications for Gulf Olmec Origins." *Latin American Antiquity* 14 (2003).

Ascalone, Enrico. *Mesopotamia: Assyrians, Sumerians, Babylonians*. Berkeley: University of California Press, 2007.

Aubrey, John. *Wiltshire: The Topographical Collections*. Devizes, U.K.: Henry Bull, 1862.

Baillie, Michael. *A Slice Through Time: Dendrochronology and Precision Dating*. London: Routledge, 1995.

Bietak, Manfred. *Avaris: Capital of the Hyksos*. London: British Museum Press, 1995.

Bowman, Sheridan. *Radiocarbon Dating*. Berkeley: University of California Press, 1990.

Breasted, James Henry. *Ancient Records of Egypt*, vol. 2. Peter A. Piccione, ed. Chicago: University of Chicago Press, 2001.

Brown, G., D. Field, and D. McOmish (eds.). *The Avebury Landscape: Aspects of the Field Archaeology of the Marlborough Downs*. Oxford, U.K.: Oxbow Books, 2005.

Burl, Aubrey. *From Carnac to Callanish: Prehistoric Stone Rows of Britain, Ireland and Brittany*. New Haven: Yale University Press, 2000.

———. *Prehistoric Avebury*. New Haven: Yale University Press, 2002.

Burton, Anthony. *The Ridgeway*. London: Aurum Press, 2005.

Casson, Lionel. *Everyday Life in Ancient Egypt*. Baltimore, MD: Johns Hopkins University Press, 2001.

Castleden, R. *The Stonehenge People*. London: Routledge, 1992.

Chuanxin, Xiong. *The Number 2 and Number 3 Han Tombs at Mawangdui, Changsha,* vol. 2. Beijing: Cultural Relics Publishing House, 2004.

Coe, M., and D. Grove. *The Olmec and Their People*. Washington, DC: Dumbarton Oaks, 1981.

Cope, Julian. *The Modern Antiquarian*. London: Thorsons, 1998.

Crawford, Harriet. *Sumer and the Sumerians*. Cambridge, U.K.: Cambridge University Press, 1991.

Crossley-Holland, Kevin. *British Folk Tales*. London: Orchard Books, 1987.

Crowfoot, J. W. "Mission en Cappadoce 1893–1894." *Journal of the Anthropological Institute of Great Britain and Ireland* 29 (no. 3, 1899).

Cunliffe, B., and C. Renfrew (eds.). *Science and Stonehenge*. Oxford, U.K.: Oxford University Press, 1997.

Dames, Michael. *The Silbury Treasure*. London: Thames & Hudson, 1976.

———. *The Avebury Cycle*. London: Thames & Hudson, 1977.

Daniken, Erich Von. *Chariots of the Gods*. London: Souvenir Press, 1990.

Darvill, T. C. *Prehistoric Britain*. London: Routledge, 1995.

Delmas, R. J. *Ice Core Studies of Global Biochemical Cycles*. Berlin: Springer-Verlag, 1995.

DeRachewiltz, B. *An Introduction to Egyptian Art*. London: Spring Books, 1960.

Diehl, Richard A. *The Olmec: America's First Civilization*. London: Thames & Hudson, 2005.

Dillon, M., and N. Chadwick. *The Celtic Realms*. New York: New American Library, 1967.

Dunrea, Olivier. *Skara Brae: The Story of a Prehistoric Village*. New York: Holiday House, 1986.

Dyer, James. *Hillforts of England and Wales*. Princes Risborough, U.K.: Shire Publications, 1992.

Ebbell, B. (English trans.). *The Papyrus Ebers*. Copenhagen: Levin & Munksgaard, 1937.

Evans, C., and M. Knight. *Bronze Age Landscapes: Tradition and Transformation*. Oxford, U.K.: Oxbow Books, 2001.

Fairservis, Walter, A. *The Roots of Ancient India: The Archaeology of Early Indian Civilization*. New York: Macmillan, 1971.

Frankfort, Henri. *Kingship and the Gods: A Study of Ancient Near Eastern Religion as the Integration of Society and Nature*. Oxford, U.K.: Oxford University Press, 1978.

Freud, Sigmund. *Moses and Monotheism*. London: Vintage, 1955.

Galanopoulos, A. G. "Tsunamis Observed on the Coasts of Greece from Antiquity to Present Time." *Annali de Geofisica* 23 (1960).

Gardiner, Alan. *Egypt of the Pharaohs.* Oxford, U.K.: Oxford University Press, 1964.

Godwin, H. *Archives of Peat Bogs.* Cambridge, U.K.: Cambridge University Press, 1981.

Graves, Tom *Needles of Stone.* London: Harper-Collins, 1983.

Grayson, Albert. *Assyrian and Babylonian Chronicles: Texts from the Cuneiform Sources,* vol. 5. Winona Lake, IN: Eisenbrauns, 2000.

Grove, David C., and Rosemary A. Joyce (eds.). *Social Patterns in Pre-Classic Mesoamerica.* Washington, DC: Dumbarton Oaks, 1999.

Gurney, Robert. *Celtic Heritage.* London: Chatto & Windus, 1969.

Habu, J. *Ancient Jomon of Japan.* Cambridge, U.K.: Cambridge University Press, 2004.

Hammerton, J. A. (ed). *Wonders of the Past,* vol. 2. New York: Wise and Co., 1937.

Haslip-Viera, G., O. De Montellano, and W. Barbour. "Robbing Native American Cultures." *Current Anthropology* 38 (1997).

Hawkes, C. F. C. "The Rillaton Gold Cup." *Antiquity* 57 (1983).

Henderson, John S. *The World of the Ancient Maya.* Ithaca, NY: Cornell University Press, 1997.

Hornung, Erik, and John Baines. *Conceptions of God in Ancient Egypt.* Ithaca, NY: Cornell University Press, 1996.

Jenniskens, Peter. *Meteor Showers and Their Parent Comets.* Cambridge, U.K.: Cambridge University Press, 2006.

Jewel, P. A. *The Experimental Earthwork on Overton Down, Wiltshire, 1960.* London: British Association for the Advancement of Science, 1963.

Jones-Bley, K., and D. G. Zdanovich (eds.). *Complex Societies of Central Eurasia from the 3rd to the 1st Millennium* BC. Washington, DC: J.I.E.S. Publishing, 2002.

Jurmain, R., H. Nelson, L. Kilgore, and W. Trevathan. *Essentials of Physical Anthropology.* Belmont, CA: Wadsworth, 1998.

Keightley, David N. *Sources of Shang History: The Oracle-Bone Inscriptions of Bronze Age China.* Berkeley: University of California Press, 1978.

Kennan, George. *The Tragedy of Pelée.* Westport, CT: Greenwood Press, 1970.

Lee, Yun Kuen. "Building the Chronology of Early Chinese History." *Journal of Archaeology for Asia and the Pacific* 41 (2002).

Legg, Rodney. *Stanton Drew: Great Western Temple.* Wincanton, U.K.: Dorset Publishing, 1998.

Leick, Gwendolyn. *Mesopotamia: The Invention of the City.* London: Penguin, 2002.

Lemonick, Michael D. "Mystery of the Olmec." *Time,* July 1996.

Lewis, J. S. *Comet and Asteroid Impact Hazards on a Populated Earth.* Gainesville, FL: Academic Press, 1999.

Loewe, Michael, and Edward Shaughnessy. *The Cambridge History of Ancient China: From the Origins of Civilization to 221 BC.* Cambridge, U.K.: Cambridge University Press, 1999.

Lurker, Manfred. *The Gods and Symbols of Ancient Egypt.* London: Thames & Hudson, 1999.

Lynch, F., J. Davies, and S. Aldhouse-Green. *Prehistoric Wales.* Stroud, U.K.: Sutton Publishing, 2000.

Lynch, Frances. *Megalithic Tombs and Long Barrows in Britain.* Princes Risborough, U.K.: Shire Publications, 1997.

MacQueen, J. G. *The Hittites and Their Contemporaries in Asia Minor.* London: Thames & Hudson, 1996.

Magnusson, M. BC: *The Archaeology of the Bible Lands.* London: Bodley Head, 1977.

Mallowan, M. E. L. *Nimrud and Its Remains.* London: Collins, 1966.

Maul, S. *The Ancient Middle Eastern Capital.* Frankfurt: Saarbrücker, 1997.

McCray, R., and Z. Wang. *Supernovae and Supernova Remnants.* Cambridge, U.K.: Cambridge University Press, 1996.

McGrail, Sean. *Ancient Boats and Ships.* Princes Risborough, U.K.: Shire Publications, 2006.

McIntosh, J. *A Peaceful Realm: The Rise and Fall of the Indus Civilization.* Boulder, CO: Westview, 2001.

McNally, Kenneth. *Ireland's Ancient Stones: Megalithic Ireland Explored.* Belfast: Appletree Press, 2006.

Meuszynski, J., S. Paley, and R. Sobolewski. *The Reconstruction of the Relief Representations and Their Arrangement in the Northwest Palace of Kalhu.* Mainz, Germany: Zabern Publishers, 1987.

Michell, John. *The Flying Saucer Vision.* London: Sidgwick & Jackson, 1967.

———. *The View over Atlantis.* London: Sidgwick & Jackson, 1969.

MacMullen, Ramsay. *Christianity and Paganism in the Fourth to Eighth Centuries.* New Haven: Yale University Press,1999.

Midgley, M. S. "The Origin and Function of the Earthen Long Barrows of Northern Europe." *British Archaeological Reports* 20 (1985).

O'Kelly, Michael J. *Newgrange: Archaeology, Art and Legend.* London: Thames & Hudson, 1988.

Olson, Roberta. *Fire and Ice: A History of Comets in Art.* New York: Walker, 1985.

Parker, Richard A. *The Calendars of Ancient Egypt.* Chicago: University of Chicago Press, 1950.

Parker-Pearson, M. "The Stonehenge Riverside Project and New Discoveries." *Journal of Material Culture* 11 (2006).

Phillips, Graham. *The Moses Legacy.* London: Pan, 2002.

———. *Atlantis and the Ten Plagues of Egypt.* Rochester, VT: Bear & Co, 2003.

Piggott, Stuart. *Prehistoric India to 1000 BC.* London: Cassell, 1962.

Porada, E. "The Seal of Shaushatar." *American Journal of Archaeology* 60 (no. 3, 1956): 289–90.

Post, Lennart Von. "The Prospect for Pollen Analysis in the Study of the Earth's Climatic History." *New Phytologist* 45 (1946).

Powell, T. G. E. "The Gold Ornament from Mold, Flintshire, North Wales." *Proceedings of the Prehistoric Society* 19 (1953).

Raab, L. M., M. A. Boxt, K. Bradford, B. Stokes, and R. Gonzalez-Lauck. *Journal of Field Archaeology* 27 (no. 3, 2000).

Redford, Donald. *History and Chronology of the Eighteenth Dynasty of Egypt.* Toronto: Toronto University Press, 1967.

———. *Akhenaten: The Heretic King.* Princeton: Princeton University Press, 1987.

———. *Egypt, Canaan and Israel in Ancient Times.* Princeton, NJ: Princeton University Press, 1993.

———. *The Wars in Syria and Palestine of Thutmose III.* Boston: Koninklijke Brill, 2003.

Richards, J. *English Heritage Book of Stonehenge.* London: Batsford, 1991.

The Rig Veda. Wendy Doniger (trans.). London: Penguin, 2005.

Ritchie, Anne. *Prehistoric Orkney.* London: Batsford, 1995.

Rossini, Stephane. *Egyptian Hieroglyphics.* Mineola, NY: Dover Publications, 1989.

Rothman, Mitchell S. (ed.). *Uruk Mesopotamia and Its Neighbors: Cross-Cultural Interactions in the Era of State Formation.* Santa Fe, NM: SAM Press, 2001.

Sagan, Carl. *Comet.* London: Michael Joseph, 1985.

Sernander, R. *On the Evidence of Post-Glacial Changes of Climate Furnished by the Peat Mosses of Northern Europe.* Stockholm: Förhaldlinger, 1908.

Sethe, K. *Documents of the Eighteenth Dynasty,* vol. 1. Leipzig: Hinrichs, 1906.

Sheets, D. P., and D. K. Grayson (eds.). *Volcanic Activity and Human Ecology.* New York: Academic Press, 1990.

Simkin, Tom, and Richard S. Fiske. *Krakatau 1883: The Volcanic Eruption and Its Effects.* Washington, DC: Smithsonain, 1984.

Sims-Williams, N. (ed.). *Indo-Iranian Languages and Peoples*. London: British Academy, 2003.

Singh, G., R. D. Joshi, and A. B. Singh. "Stratigraphic and Radiocarbon Evidence for the Age and Development of Three Salt-Lake Deposits in Rajasthan, India." *Quaternary Research* 2 (1972).

Starr, R. F. S. *Nuzi*. Cambridge, MA: Harvard University Press, 1937.

Startin, D. "Prehistoric Earthmoving." In Case, H., and Whittle, A. (eds.), *Settlement Patterns in the Oxford Region*. London: Council for British Archaeology, 1982.

Steindorff, George, and Keith Seele. *When Egypt Ruled the East*. Chicago: University of Chicago Press, 1942.

Stukeley, William. *Stonehenge: A Temple Restored to the British Druids*. Abingdon, U.K.: Taylor & Francis, 1984.

Tadmor, H., and M. Weinfeld (eds.). *History, Historiography and Interpretation: Studies in Biblical and Cuneiform Literatures*. Jerusalem: Magnes Press, 1983.

Thieme, P. "Mitanni Treaties." *Journal of the American Oriental Society* 80 (1960).

Trompf, G. W. *Cargo Cults and Millenarian Movements: Transoceanic Comparisons of New Religious Movements*. Berlin: Mouton De Gruyter, 1990.

Turco R., O. Toon, C. Park, R. Whitten, J. Pollack, and P. Noerdlinger. "An Analysis of the Physical, Chemical, Optical and Historical Impacts of the 1908 Tunguska Meteor Fall." *Icarus* 50 (1982).

Underwood, Guy. *The Pattern of the Past*. London: Sphere Books, 1972.

Wainwright, G. J., and I. H. Longworth. "Durrington Walls Excavations 1966–1968." *American Anthropologist*, n.s., 75 (no. 6, 1973).

Wainwright, Richard. *A Guide to Prehistoric Remains in Britain*. London: Constable, 1978.

Watkins, Alfred. *The Old Straight Track*. London: Abacus, 1989.

Robert Wernick, *The Monument Builders* (New York: Time-Life Books, 1973).

Wheeler, Mortimer. *The Indus Civilization*. Cambridge, U.K.: Cambridge University Press, 1968.

Winckler, H. "Provisional Messages over the Excavations in Boghaz Koei in the Summer 1907." *Communications of the German East Society* (no. 35, 1907).

Wiseman, D. *The Hittites and Hurrians*. Oxford, U.K.: Clarendon Press, 1973.

Index

BOOKS OF RELATED INTEREST

Atlantis and the Ten Plagues of Egypt
The Secret History Hidden in the Valley of the Kings
by Graham Phillips

Cataclysm!
Compelling Evidence of a Cosmic Catastrophe in 9500 B.C.
by D. S. Allan and J. B. Delair

The Cycle of Cosmic Catastrophes
Flood, Fire, and Famine in the History of Civilization
by Richard Firestone, Allen West, and Simon Warwick-Smith

The Lost Civilization of Lemuria
The Rise and Fall of the World's Oldest Culture
by Frank Joseph

From the Ashes of Angels
The Forbidden Legacy of a Fallen Race
by Andrew Collins

The Triumph of the Sea Gods
The War Against the Goddess Hidden in Homer's Tales
by Steven Sora

The Baltic Origins of Homer's Epic Tales
The Iliad, the Odyssey, and the Migration of Myth
by Felice Vinci

Forbidden History
Prehistoric Technologies, Extraterrestrial Intervention,
and the Suppressed Origins of Civilization
Edited by J. Douglas Kenyon

INNER TRADITIONS • BEAR & COMPANY
P.O. Box 388
Rochester, VT 05767
1-800-246-8648
www.InnerTraditions.com

Or contact your local bookseller